Organizational Climates and Careers

The Work Lives of Priests

QUANTITATIVE STUDIES IN SOCIAL RELATIONS

Consulting Editor: Peter H. Rossi

THE JOHNS HOPKINS UNIVERSITY
BALTIMORE, MARYLAND

Peter H. Rossi and Walter Williams (Eds.), **EVALUATING SOCIAL PROGRAMS:** *Theory, Practice, and Politics*

Roger N. Shepard, A. Kimball Romney, and Sara Beth Nerlove (Eds.), **MULTIDIMENSIONAL SCALING:** *Theory and Applications in the Behavioral Sciences,* Volume I – Theory; Volume II – Applications

Robert L. Crain and Carol S. Weisman, **DISCRIMINATION, PERSONALITY, AND ACHIEVEMENT:** *A Survey of Northern Blacks*

Douglas T. Hall and Benjamin Schneider, **ORGANIZATIONAL CLIMATES AND CAREERS:** *The Work Lives of Priests*

Kent S. Miller and Ralph Mason Dreger (Eds.), **COMPARATIVE STUDIES OF BLACKS AND WHITES IN THE UNITED STATES**

Robert B. Tapp, **RELIGION AMONG THE UNITARIAN UNIVERSALISTS:** *Converts in the Stepfathers' House*

In Preparation

Arthur S. Goldberger and Otis Dudley Duncan, **STRUCTURAL EQUATION MODELS IN THE SOCIAL SCIENCES**

Organizational Climates and Careers

The Work Lives of Priests

DOUGLAS T. HALL

Faculty of Administrative Studies
York University
Toronto, Canada

BENJAMIN SCHNEIDER

Department of Psychology
University of Maryland
College Park, Maryland

731331

SEMINAR PRESS   1973   New York and London

SEMINAR PRESS, INC.
111 Fifth Avenue, New York, New York 10003

United Kingdom Edition published by
SEMINAR PRESS LIMITED
24/28 Oval Road, London NW1

LIBRARY OF CONGRESS CATALOG CARD NUMBER: 78-187261

PRINTED IN THE UNITED STATES OF AMERICA

To our parents

Contents

viii   Contents

Chapter Three. Background and Procedure of the Research

Chapter Four. Personal Styles and Values of the Diocesan Priest

Chapter Five. The Nature and Climate of the Priest's Work

Chapter Six. Outcomes of Psychological Success and Failure

Chapter Seven. The Changing Roles of the Priest

Preface

The scene could be described as incongruous at best. In the cold, gray interaction laboratory in the basement of Yale University's Administrative Sciences Building, one of the authors entered the room and was lost in a full circle of white collars and black suits. This was our initial contact with the Personnel Board of the Roman Catholic Archdiocese of Hartford, who had approached our department to help them deal with the growing discontent among parish priests. They weren't quite sure about what an organizational behavior approach to their problems might be, thinking perhaps they might be better off hiring personnel consultants. At the same time, after becoming accustomed to dealing with business and government leaders, we were not sure how an Episcopalian and a Jew would go about working with "all those collars."

Happily, as we will report later, our mutual doubts were soon resolved, and a unique partnership began. The study reported in this book was undertaken at the initiative of the Archdiocese—the first and only study we know of to date in which a Roman Catholic diocese invited and sponsored independent university researchers to conduct a behavioral science diagnosis of their diocese. Furthermore, no restrictions were placed on our work and subsequent publications; we had complete access to information and autonomy throughout the study. In view of the reluctance of some parts of the Church to reveal information, we felt that our study represented a significant act of strength and trust on the part of Archbishop Henry O'Brien and his Senate of Priests. Recently the Catholic Church has shown more openness to social science research, which is clearly needed, and the Archdiocese of Hartford should be commended for its pioneer efforts.

We are grateful to Archbishop O'Brien, the Temporary Personnel Board who hired us and with whom we worked closely for two years, and Archbishop John Whealon who later implemented key recommendations proposed by the Personnel Board which grew out of the study we will report. Among the Personnel Board members, particular thanks go to Father Robert McGrath, Chairman, and to Father Douglas Morrison, who conducted one third of the individual interviews.

Another critical factor in the execution of this study was the collaboration and guidance provided by our colleague at Yale, Chris Argyris. He encouraged us to conceive of our project not simply as research but more broadly as organizational intervention, and he was an important model for us as we learned the processes of organizational diagnosis and intervention. Professor Argyris also was largely responsible for assembling an outstanding faculty of organizational behavior and a high-quality, supportive research climate in Yale's Department of Administrative Sciences in the late 1960's and early 1970's. Those who know of his work will note that the climate he helped create has left an imprint upon our own thinking and research, indeed in our careers.

Later stages of the research, specifically the funds to help support the writing of this book, were provided by a Ford Foundation grant to the Administrative Sciences Department. We were fortunate in having highly competent and committed research and secretarial help, initially at Yale and more recently at Maryland and York. Dale Nichols stayed with the project throughout its duration, first as our secretary and later as a research assistant. Lois Lehman and Sue Bender provided key research inputs in the initial stages of the study. Other secretaries who made our work much easier and more pleasant were Martha Harris, Frances Walker, Leona Burns, and Sharon Dorfman.

Several colleagues at Yale read and commented on drafts of the manuscript, and we express our gratitude to them: Chris Argyris, Edward Lawler, Andrew Pettigrew, and Gerrit Wolf.

Many copyright holders graciously consented to our reprinting material: Academic Pres, Inc., Administrative Science Quarterly, Chandler Publishing Co., Dr. Patricia Cain Smith, Harper and Row Publishers, Inc., Holt Rinehart and Winston, Inc., Industrial Management Review,

McGraw-Hill Book Co., Inc., Pilgrim Press, Prentice-Hall, Inc., The Catholic Transcript, The Free Press, and University of Notre Dame Press.

A crucial and easily overlooked feature of this study has been the opportunity for the two of us to work together. Our work was a collaborative effort in the best sense, with each of us learning from the other's strengths and each assuming equal responsibility for the management of the project. More importantly, the study has helped build a valued relationship, a key intrinsic fringe benefit.

Our parents and our wives contributed strongly to this book, in different ways. The contributions of our parents come from that early family climate which soon becomes internalized and affects everything we do later in life. Our wives and the climates they create have been deeply involved with and affected by this book. We hope that our wives and parents feel the sense of psychological success they deserve for the influence they have had upon our work.

Introduction

There are three major purposes for writing this book. The first is to present a theory of career development in organizations which draws on a number of social and behavioral science disciplines in specifying the personal and situational characteristics likely to lead to experiences of psychological success. The second is to devise measures to test the theory on a sample of working men who have distinctive personal characteristics and who work under clearly and uniquely defined organizational conditions—Roman Catholic diocesan priests. The third is to study intensively the careers of priests as a distinctive group of working men.

It seems clear that the role of work in a priest's life is strong relative to other professionals. This high degree of personal involvement in his career work may be the result of several factors. First, the person entering the priesthood is choosing not just a type of life but a total style of life. He enters the priesthood knowing that he must sacrifice other potential aspects of his life—i.e., being a husband and father—so that he may invest himself in the role of priest. Years of minor (high school) and major (college) seminary training provide a series of ordeals and initiations the seminarian must pass through before he is ordained a priest. As a result of these personal sacrifices and institutional socialization experiences, the priest may emerge with the priesthood thoroughly imbedded in his total being.

Several sociologists (see Becker and Strauss, 1956) and psychologists (see, e.g., Super 1957; Tiedeman and O'Hara, 1963) have stressed this connection between a person's work career and his total identity. Research studies make the point in different but dramatic ways. When Abraham Maslow (1969) asked a sample of self-actualizing professionals what they would be if they were not in their respective professions, many hesitated and had difficulty in answering. Others responded with comments such as, "I can't say. If I weren't a [doctor, scientist, etc.], I just wouldn't be me. I would be someone else." Similarly, people often have fantasies that death is imminent when they are about to retire (Friedman and Havinghurst, 1954). In fact, it appears that one of the major factors in the successful adjustment of a person to retirement is involvement in some form of meaningful work activity (Smith *et al.*, 1969). This need for work was also demonstrated in a survey by Morse and Weiss (1955) in which they asked people what they would do if they had enough money so that they would never be required to work again. Most respondents said that after a few months of free time they would want to resume working. Thus, these respondents, and most other employees, we would argue, during their careers become "compulsive workers" because so much of their personal identity, their satisfaction, and sense of self-worth is attained through their work.

The apparent strong commitment of the priest to his work role and the relatively great proportion of his life invested in his career are reasons why we would expect the personal dimensions of career development to stand out in studying priest's careers. Probably, the personal changes priests experience in their careers give clues to similar changes among people in other types of careers. Thus, one reason why we are interested in studying priests is to learn more about the changing role of personal factors in career experiences.

A second unique feature of the priesthood is the nature of the organization in which the priest's career unfolds—the Roman Catholic Church. The Catholic Church is the world's oldest bureaucracy and as such illustrates well many of the defining features of bureaucratic administration: a well-defined hierarchy of offices, responsibilities, and authority; employment in the organization seen as a career commitment; behavior governed by a clear code of impartially administered rules (Weber, 1947).

Perhaps the most critical aspect of the Church administration is the permanent commitment of its members. Although this policy is coming increasingly into question as more priests leave the priesthood, it does mean that those who accept this life commitment are voluntarily submitting themselves to an extremely high degree of loyalty to and control by the organization. The priest also commits himself to a life of celibacy, which reduces the chances that he will experience social commitments that will rival his commitment to the Church. Also, the parish priest works, eats, and lives in the church-rectory building complex of his parish, which represents a physical environmental factor forcing him into a high degree of involvement in the Church system. For these reasons, the priest may experience the Church as what Goffman (1961) calls a *total institution*, described as follows:

> A basic social arrangement in modern society is that the individual tends to sleep, play, and work in different places, with different co-participants, under different authorities, and without an overall rational plan. The central feature of total institutions can be described as a breakdown of the barriers ordinarily separating these three spheres of life (pp. 5–6).

The Roman Catholic parish does not represent a completely total institution for the priest; it is more open than the examples of religious total institutions Goffman provides: abbeys, monasteries, convents, and other cloisters. However, the parish system does come closer to meeting Goffman's criteria than do most other organizations in which professional workers are found. The separation of the barriers between sleep, play, and work is probably less evident for priests than for most other professionals.[1]

Along with the near-total involvement of the priest in his work and organization goes a correspondingly high amount of organizational influence over the priest. Priests are greatly *changed* as they operate within the framework of the Church. Since one of the pressing needs of career research is to understand better the impact of different kinds and levels of organization characteristics upon the career experiences of its members, there is no place where these effects would be more marked and powerful than in a relatively total system. The impacts of the organization observed in this system should in turn provide clues for finding more subtle changes in open systems. Goffman (1961), who uses the same reasoning in his analysis of mental institutions as a guide to identifying general institutional influence processes, states that

---

[1]Examples of professionals whose total involvement might approach that of the priest could be medical interns, prep-school teachers, and staff members in residential medical or psychiatric treatment centers.

> The total institution is a social hybrid, part residential community, part formal organization; therein lies its special sociological interest. There are other reasons for being interested in these establishments, too. In our society, they are forcing houses for changing persons; each is a natural experiment on what can be done to the self (p. 12).

The preceding two reasons—learning more about the role of personal and organizational factors, respectively, in organizational career development—involve (generalizing from priests to people in other types of careers) studying priests to learn more about general career processes. The third reason for conducting this research is to shed more light on the career of the priest per se. In light of present concern over the fate of the Catholic Church and the "crisis of authority" in the Church, little has been said about the work experiences of the individual parish priest and how his experiences relate to the effectiveness of the Church as a system. There has been considerable philosophical analysis of the spiritual and theological dimensions of the priesthood; there has not been an equal concentration on sociopsychological analysis.

One of the arguments against conducting social science research on the priesthood is the belief that the term career, with its connotations of achievement, upward striving, and success, detracts from the spiritual uniqueness of the priestly vocation. Another argument against such research is that the priest simply cannot be studied as a working man because of the importance of spiritual factors in his vocation. Both of these points are disputed by Joseph Fichter (1961), a Jesuit sociologist who speaks strongly of the lack of and need for social science research in the priesthood.

> The vocation in the Church, or the "ecclesiastical occupation," is another and specialized career. . . . The social scientist adds a different kind of knowledge, and also provides a different dimension, or perspective to the knowledge already obtained about these people [in the priesthood, brotherhood, and sisterhood] . . . . . In spite of the "other-worldliness" of these dedicated individuals, there is a worldly plane upon which their vocation can be discussed as an occupation or profession. It is indeed like no other way of "making a living," even though each of these persons is, in a true sense, a life-long "employee" of the Church. . . . Yet, these people are "occupied"; they are "professionals." Much of what they do in the service of the Church is paralleled by the patterns of human relations that are common to the society in which they live and work. In fact, it is difficult to imagine that they could be successful in their vocation if they were culturally alienated from the society which they serve. These ways of behaving, of relating themselves to one another, to the laity, and to those outside the Church, are obviously open to scientific study and analysis (pp. XIII–XIV).

Hopefully, the present volume will be a contribution to this underdeveloped area of investigation.

Before looking too deeply into the priestly profession, however, it will first be necessary to review some of the literature on careers and organizational climate and to present the model of career psychological success (Chapter 1) which will form the framework of this book. In Chapter 2 we will introduce the reader to some of the literature on priests, and Chapter 3 will be an introduction to the methods of our study and to the diocese in which it was conducted.

It will be hypothesized that three sets of factors influence the career development of priests as well as all other people: (1) personal factors (i.e., values and skills), (2) organizational and work assignment conditions (i.e., job challenge, supervision, peer relationship), and (3) time. Chapters 4 and 5, respectively, will be devoted to exploring the nature of the personal and organizational factors; time (i.e., age) seems to need no such introduction. In Chapter 6 we will introduce the criteria for career psychological success. In Chapter 7 we will examine the relationship between time and other sets of factors—personal, organizational, and career criterion variables. In Chapter 8 we will explore how priests adapt to their organizational careers. In Chapter 9 we will discuss how one group of priests in the diocese (the Personnel Board which was our liaison with the diocese) worked together as a problem-solving group. Chapter 10 examines in detail the relationships between personal, organizational, and career outcome variables. Chapter 11 presents a revised model of careers in organizations and the conclusions drawn from the research. Finally, in Chapter 12 we report some of the changes which had occurred in the diocese by the time we completed this manuscript.

ONE
A Theoretical Model
of Organizational Career Development

In this chapter we present a model of career development based on cycles of work success. The model will then be utilized to suggest organizational conditions and personal characteristics which are necessary ingredients for the individual to experience an enhanced self-image and psychological success. The model is a general one, not restricted to priestly careers, although in this book we will apply it specifically to Roman Catholic diocesan priests.

A Model of Psychological Success and Failure

Psychological Success

The basic assumption of the present model is that individuals strive to increase their sense of self-esteem through experiencing psychological success. Self-esteem and psychological success are seen as two key indicators of the quality of a person's life. One important means of achieving a high level of self-esteem is through performing competently in some personally valued task (White, 1959).[1] As one comes increasingly to see himself as a person who can successfully act upon his environment, he values himself more as a total person; he experiences increased self-esteem or a more positive self-image.[2]

The conditions under which personal effectiveness in a task situation can lead to increased self-esteem have been discussed by Lewin (1936) and Argyris (1964). If (1) the individual sets a challenging goal for himself (i.e., a goal representing a high level of aspiration), and (2) he determines his own means of attaining that goal, and (3) the goal is relevant to his self-concept, then he will experience *psychological success* upon attainment of that goal. This sense of personal success will lead in turn to an increase in self-esteem, which in turn will lead to increased future levels of expectation.

The basic personality process of developing a competent identity through psychological success may be illustrated as in Figure 1.1.

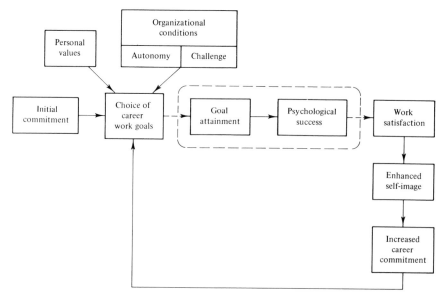

Fig. 1.1. Hypothesized model of career development in organizations.

The need for competence leads the individual to seek situations where he thinks his self-esteem will be enhanced and to avoid situations

[1]References are arranged alphabetically at the end of the book.

[2]In the present discussion, the terms self-image and self-esteem will be used interchangeably since we are concerned more with the evaluative components of self-image than with its descriptive elements.

where he thinks it will be reduced. He "reaches" for or "stretches" toward success. When he experiences success, the resultant increase in self-image serves as reinforcement and will feed back to make him more committed to setting and striving for future goals (Lewin, Dembo, Festinger, & Sears, 1944; Porter & Lawler, 1968). Simply put, this theory suggests that "success breeds success." This cycle of events can be self-reinforcing and continuing and is applicable to the study of people's careers. Should the cycle occur, the person shows great enthusiasm for the career and may describe himself as "really finding himself" or being "really turned on" by his work. This choice-initiated cycle of career development is summarized in the following proposition:

Proposition I. Increases in career self-image, career commitment, and self-esteem will result from success in attaining a career-relevant goal which satisfies the following criteria:
1. The goal was set by the person.
2. The path to the goal was defined by the person.
3. The goal was perceived as challenging or difficult but attainable.
4. The goal was central to his self-image.
5. The goal was attained.

The increased commitment and self-esteem resulting from the success will feed back to increase the person's probability of setting further challenging career goals.

Operationally, the particular job characteristics most likely to provide these five conditions for psychological success are the amount of *challenge* in the job and the amount of *autonomy* it provides. Challenge is important to permit the setting of difficult goals. Autonomy is important to permit the individual to set his own goals and means of achieving them; autonomy might also provide enough leeway so that the person could select goals central to his self-image.

Results of Psychological Failure in the Career

The effects of self-perceived failure in one's work appear to be more complex than simply the opposite of the success cycle. Argyris (1957) and Merton (1957) have discussed at length the effects of pro-longed psychological failure in work settings. According to Argyris (pp. 78–79), the individual faced with a situation structured for failure may attempt to minimize his feelings of failure in the following ways:
1. Withdrawing emotionally from the work situation by lowering his work standards and becoming apathetic and uninterested.

2. Placing increased value on material rewards and depreciating the value of human or nonmaterial rewards (as a result of his apathy and disinterest).

3. Defending his self-concept through the use of defense mechanisms.

4. Fighting the organization.

5. Attempting to gain promotion to a position with greater prospects of success.

6. Leaving the organization.

Argyris argues (1957, Chapter 4) that experiencing psychological failure tends to decrease the psychological maturity of the individual. Under the experience of failure the person tends to regress along several dimensions in the following ways:

1. Person becomes more dependent.

2. Person becomes more passive.

3. Person develops a short-range rather than a long-range time perspective.

4. Person experiences decreased self-esteem and self-confidence.

5. Person tends to fear new tasks, give up quickly, and expect more failure.

6. Person loses interest in his work.

7. Person develops a tendency to blame others.

Because the experience of failure may have these negative outcomes, most people will adopt some coping strategies to avoid or minimize the experience when placed in a failure-prone situation. Athough strategies such as the six mentioned by Argyris might be defined as deviant behavior from an organization's perspective, to the individual they are quite logical means of maintaining mental health. This point is emphasized by Merton (1957, p. 132) as follows:

> Our primary aim is to discover how *some social structures exert a definite pressure upon certain persons in the society to engage in nonconforming rather than conforming conduct.* If we can locate groups peculiarly subject to such pressures, we should expect to find fairly high rates of deviant behavior in these groups, not because the human beings comprising them are compounded of distinctive biological tendencies but because they are reponding normally to the social situation in which they find themselves. Our perspective is sociological. . . . Should our quest be at all successful, some forms of deviant behavior will be found to be as psychologically normal as conformist behavior, and the equation of deviation and psychological abnormality will be put in question. [Emphasis in original.]

Merton goes on to describe five forms of adaptation to social systems which do not meet the expectations of its members, all of which are based on the person's acceptance or rejection of system goals and procedures. *Conformity* results from an acceptance of both the goals and the institutionalized means or procedures of the organization. *Innovation* entails acceptance of the basic goals but nonacceptance of the formal procedures. *Ritualism*, the opposite of innovation, results from rejection of the basic goals and acceptance of the formal means. Rejection of both the procedures and the goals is termed *retreatism*. A more complicated response, *rebellion*, involves rejection of present means and goals along with attempts to institutionalize new goals and procedures; it thus refers to the change of the system rather than the accommodation of the individual to the system.

In response to certain failure–avoidance strategies and to the failure symptoms, the higher management of the organization may increase the formal controls over the individual (i.e., defines proportionally more of his goals and work methods for him) in the hope of increasing his effort and performance. These responses may produce short-term benefits but they do eventually tend to increase rather than decrease the employee's failure-oriented coping behavior, to which management responds again with further increased controls, and a downward cycle is created. Just as challenging and autonomous work conditions can lead to one's personal growth through career success, so too can the lack of conditions lead to personal pathology through career failure. A paper by Abraham Maslow (1968) with the descriptive title "Neurosis as a Failure of Personal Growth" argues this point convincingly.

Like success, the effects of failure also are compounded over time. The past experiences of the individual can be as important as his present working conditions in determining the likelihood of success. If a person has grown accustomed to experiencing psychological failure, he will not be able to immediately perform well under the conditions for success; indeed, seeing that he is unable to perform well under favorable conditions may only heighten his sense of failure and lead to further low self-esteem. A useful analogy here would be a deep-sea diver who might develop the bends if he ascends from the high pressure ocean depths to the lower pressure surface too quickly. If he changes environments too quickly, his own internal body state, which had altered itself to help *defend* him against high pressure conditions, could turn against him and actually *threaten* his safety at normal atmospheric pressure. Thus a person may suffer the "psychological bends" following the transition from a failure-oriented to a success-oriented work assignment. In a later section we will discuss the developmental process of becoming ready to utilize the conditions for psychological success.

Because of the complexities of the individual's responses to psychological failure, we will not attempt to state a general proposition regarding the process of failure. However, it appears that under failure there is generally an attempt to minimize the impact of the work upon the person's self-image in some way, perhaps by increasing the psychological distance between his self-image and his feelings about his work.

The Critical First Year

In view of the apparent compounding nature of the career growth process, the very beginning of a man's career becomes critical. When the individual first enters an organization, that portion of his life space associated with the organization is essentially blank; i.e., his *subidentity* as a member of the organization is virtually nonexistent. He begins with certain (perhaps unrealistic) expectations but little reality in which to ground his perceptions and attitudes. For this reason the career subidentity grows at a faster rate in the first year than in subsequent years. As in the development of a young child, the early career years undoubtedly represent a critical period for learning (Bowlby, 1951) and leave a lasting imprint on the person's attitudes and aspirations.

Because the process of psychological success involves learning—developing confidence in the environment and, indeed, coming to expect or anticipate success following goal setting, effort, and performance—the opportunities present in the person's first assignment probably have a continuing impact upon his career in subsequent years. This idea of a "critical period" in career development is similar to the same concept as used by behavioral biologists (Hess, 1962) and suggests:

Proposition II. The extent to which a person's initial job assignment provides the conditions for psychological success (challenge and autonomy) will continue to be positively related to his career commitment, performance, and success in subsequent years. An initial job experience of psychological failure may, conversely, be related to decreased commitment, performance, and success in later years.

This proposition receives partial support from a longitudinal study by Berlew & Hall (1966), who found that the amount of job challenge in the first assignments of young managers was positively related to success and performance 6 and 7 years later. Livingston (1969) also presents evidence for the relationship between initial challenge and later success. Schneider (1970) has shown how initial experiences in organizations are deterministic of even short-term success.

This is not to suggest that initial experiences are more important than more current experiences. The underlying theory of the impact of time is that there exist two countervailing career forces. The first force is the primacy effect, indicating the relatively greater or enduring impact of early over later experience. The second would be a recency effect, suggesting greater salience or awareness of more recent over earlier experiences. The overall influence of any one year would be a resultant of these two forces (see Hovland, 1964).

Transitions in Career Roles

As the person progresses in his career and moves from one position or status to another, his career identity, satisfactions, and attitudes frequently change. Contained in this change is the perception of more role-related characteristics as being relevant to his own subidentity and often a greater sense of competence along these dimensions. For example, as the medical student progresses through medical school, at some point it occurs to him that he possesses expert authority (a characteristic of the doctor role) in dealing with patients, and he begins to feel comfortable with that authority as a legitimate aspect of himself. Presumably, over time he also perceives himself as possessing increasingly more of this expertise. Evidence of career-identity growth was found by Hall (1968) in a group of aspiring academics; following their qualifying examinations, successful Ph.D. candidates used more professorial adjectives to describe themselves, and they rated their self-perceived intellectual competence and personal potency higher than they had prior to the exams. Identity growth among professional students is also reported by Becker, Geer, Hughes, & Strauss (1961), Huntington (1957), and Fox (1957). The relationship between identity—an attitude toward oneself—and role is also supported by studies of role playing and opinion change (Janis & King, 1954) and of transitions of union men into management and then back from management to the union ranks (Lieberman, 1956). Studies of satisfaction show clearly and consistently that the positive relationship between this variable and organizational status undoubtedly relates strongly to individual career outcomes.

Proposition III. The transition from one organizational status to another is often accompanied by significant changes in the person's self-image, satisfaction, and attitudes toward his work.

It is important to digress at this point and examine the manner in which reseach on careers has been accomplished by psychologists and sociologists, because transition in careers has not always been a focus of interest. Indeed, the next section of the chapter, dealing with the work and work environment of the person's career, has been of even less interest to career researchers.

Categories of Career Research

Table 1.1 presents in summary form the five different ways in which careers have been researched. These five approaches are described in Hall (1971) and will be briefly considered here. These types, to be described subsequently, are: (1) occupational choice; (2) career development; (3) career transitions; (4) intracareer-role analysis; and (5) intercareer-role analysis. Organizational behaviorists, while not explicitly utilizing the concept of career, have suggested two areas of research that cut across the five others but which we feel logically belong in the study of careers: (a) the career work itself and (b) the climate in which the work is accomplished.

Concerning *occupational choice*, if one views career development as a process of synthesizing some aspect of the individual's self-identity[3] with the demands of his career role, then it follows that a person would tend to choose a career area which will be congruent with his self-concept. If the researcher can measure the self-concept qualities required for a certain career role and measure the strength of these qualities in a given individual, then he can predict the potential fit or match between that person and that role area. Inquiry into career choice has been pursued both by researchers interested in predicting or explaining career choice and by practitioners (mainly guidance counselors) concerned with facilitating these choices for their clients (cf, Holland, 1966; Osipow, 1968; Super, 1957).

As with career or occupational choice, inquiry into *career development* is concerned with the match between characteristics of the person (self-concept, values, skills, etc.) and career role. The assumption here, however, is that over time the person's self-conception and role conception are undergoing changes resulting from both his own unique experiences and those experiences common to others in the same role and at the same stage in the life cycle (cf Hall & Nougaim, 1968; Super, 1957; Tiedeman & O'Hara, 1963).

---

[3]For the purpose of this discussion, the terms self-identity, identity, self-concept, and self-image will be used interchangeably.

TABLE 1.1
A Framework of Career Inquiry[a]

Career approach	Concept of time	Identity-role issue investigated	Location of individual occupation	Assumed identity state	Assumed role state	Consideration of individual differences?	Level of process
1. Occupational choice	Static	Identity-role *matching* (choosing identity and role)	Preentry	Fixed	Fixed	Yes	Individual
2. Career development	Dynamic	Identity-role matching (changes in identity *and* role)	Pre- and postentry	Changing	Changing	Yes	Individual
3. Career transitions	Dynamic	Identity-role matching (changes in identity to match role)	Pre- and postentry	Changing	Quasi-fixed	No	Social
4. Intracareer role	Usually static	Identity-role *description*	Postentry	Usually fixed	Fixed	No	Social
5. Intercareer role	Usually static	Intercareer identity and role *comparison*	Postentry	Usually fixed	Fixed	No	Social

[a] From Hall (1971).

The third branch of career investigation, *career transitions*, has focused upon regularized, common changes in career status or role and the impact of these role transitions upon the incumbent's identity. Examples of such normally ocurring status changes would be medical student to intern, intern to resident, and resident to specialist for a doctor, or graduate student to management trainee, trainee to first-line supervisor, and first-line supervisor to middle management for a businessman. The emphasis in this approach is upon *common elements* in career histories rather than the individual differences in experience studied in the career development area (cf, Becker, Geer, Hughes & Strauss, 1961; Strauss, 1968).

The fourth area of career research, *intracareer role analyses*, contains studies pertaining to one particular career role or line, such as a profession. In these studies a wide range of issues related to that role are explored, such as relationships with colleagues, clients, career norms, "tricks of the trade," activities, role conflicts, and characteristic coping responses (cf, Becker, 1963; Davis, 1959; Menzies, 1960).

Inquiry into the fifth area is similar to that preceding except that here the emphasis is upon comparing two or more career areas, such as science vs. management, called *intercareer comparisons*. Intercareer analysis is conducted either by psychologists interested in individual differences characterizing people in the two areas or by sociologists concerned with the differing social structures (cf, Miner, 1962; Roe, 1953; Taguiri, 1965).

As the preceding discussion indicates, the main differences between the approaches lie in the career issues investigated. In occupational choice, the emphasis is upon *matching* initial interests and self-image and eventual role through role choice. In career development research the focus is upon continual *matching of altering identity and perceived role*. The career-transitions approach examines matching altering self-perception in response to shifting roles (which, between shifts, can be considered fixed). Intracareer-role analyses focus on describing *identity and role per se within a career area* or role, while intercareer role analyses compare *across-career roles*. The approaches also differ with regard to the time span of the material covered, the assumed state (fixed or changing) of the identity and role in the data examined, and the level, individual or social, of the analysis.

In the analyses in this book we will concentrate mainly on the career development, career transition, and intracareer role analyses. In addition, however, major stress will be placed on the conditions established for the occupant of the role and how these conditions are related to his experience of psychological success.

This necessitates a detailed examination of two aspects of careers which career researchers have not previously emphasized: the career work and the career environment. These two aspects of careers cut across the five types of analyses detailed previously. We will consider the career work and then detail the kinds of work environments necessary for development and transition to result in the role occupants' experiencing psychological success.

The Career Work

Organizational behaviorists, predominantly industrial psychologists, have described the different component tasks of various jobs. Much of this analysis has been made on lower-level manufacturing employees, attempting to characterize jobs by a common set of behavioral descriptions. At this level the research of Primhoff (1957) for the Civil Service Commission, McCormick and his co-workers (McCormick, 1965; Mecham & McCormick, 1969), and Flanagan (1954) have contributed to an understanding of common skill or job elements. Jobs are thus viewed as profiles of common elements, where differences in jobs are reflected in high or low scores on a number of dimensions.

Because of the more complex, less overtly physical characteristics of more professional (managerial) positions, the common-element approach to job description has not been effective (Campbell, Dunnette, Lawler & Weick, 1970). While the more skill-oriented jobs have been described along common-behavior dimensions, managerial and professional jobs have been described by unique-behavior descriptions. In both cases the task actually performed is the focus of interest. The unique-behavior–description approach makes intercareer comparisons difficult at the specific task level, but clusters of tasks may be utilized to make comparisons at another level or order of abstraction. Intracareer comparisons and role-transition correlates of career activities may also be investigated. Such research is exceedingly rare in the literature on careers. More typically, information has been collected about how people feel about what they do at different points in their career rather than on what tasks they actually do at different stages.

The Career Environment

Like career work, the career environment has not generally been examined by career researchers. Theory and research describing the impact of the organizational environment on the individual (e.g., Argyris, 1964; McGregor, 1967) generally do not consider the person's long-term job experience, i.e., his career. Conversely, in studying careers there is a tendency to overlook the influence of the work and social environment.

The concept of a climate for work has not been examined in the career literature, yet it seems obvious that it plays a major role in the development of individual careers in organizations (Litwin & Stringer, 1968; Schneider & Bartlett, 1968, 1969, 1970; Steiner, 1965).

Organizational Climates for Psychological Success

We are using climate here as an "umbrella" concept, encompassing the array of situational demands and opportunities present in a work assignment; we use climate as a concept incorporating the psychological aspects of the work environment which the person finds most salient. Under the concept of meteorological climate one would think of variables such as precipitation, temperature, humidity, and air pressure as perhaps the most salient features. Under the concept of organizational climate, research studies have tended to identify four basic features: (1) leadership or supervisory style, (2) interpersonal relationships, (3) intrinsic meaning in work, and (4) extrinsic reward characteristics (Campbell, 1968; Thornton, 1969).

The work of Steiner (1965) and Pelz & Andrews (1966) has shown how organizational climates are related to the creativity of professional employees.Undoubtedly, climate affects a number of other aspects of performance among other groups of employees as well. Litwin & Stringer (1968) have recently published a summary of some of their research suggesting that organizational climates may have differential affects on individuals, depending upon the motives of the individual. Specifically, they have shown, both in the laboratory and in the work world, that the McClelland (1961) and Atkinson (1958) conception of motivation is most applicable when one also understands the organizational conditions under which the motives will operate. In brief they have demonstrated that people with a given motive work best in climates conducive to that motive.

Schneider & Bartlett (1968, 1969, 1970) have conceptualized organizational climate in a similar manner, suggesting that an individual's readiness for particular organizations is a function of his previous *general* experiences and experiences specific to organizations.

Missing from most of these studies on climate are three factors. The first is the question of how climate relates to actual work behavior: How does climate affect the way people spend their time? A second shortcoming is the failure to consider the work world of professionals in nonindustrial settings (except for the work of Pace (1968) and Stern (1970) on educational environments. Most of the research has been carried out in industrial environments; hospitals, churches, governmental, and other kinds of organizational environments have not been investigated from the point of view of the worker, although Moos and his co-workers (see Moos, 1967; Moos & Houts, 1968) have researched work atmosphere in hospitals from the point of view of staff *and* patients. A third problem is that in this research the way in which the career work and the career environment affect career development has been neglected. Either production or satisfaction at one point in time has tended to be the criterion of interest. The present research will attempt to provide all three of these presently missing elements.

Specifically, then, how can the climate of an organization provide opportunities favoring psychological success? Let us consider the relevant climate characteristics for each of the five success conditions in turn.

1. Independent Setting of Work Goals. In order for an individual to be able to participate in the setting of his work goals, his work climate must provide a high degree of autonomy. It is not unusual for a lower level employee to be given autonomy in determining how to best reach a goal or task that was set for him by a superior, but being free to choose the goals constitutes a higher and more unusual degree of autonomy.

What sort of personal characteristics are required in order for a person to participate in setting his work goals? Schneider (1968) has suggested a difference among individuals in their readiness to be autonomous; i.e., some people are better able to perform effectively and experience satisfaction under autonomous conditions than other people.

Vroom (1960) has shown that a personality characteristic, authoritarianism, is one important factor in the effects of participation on decision making. People low in authoritarianism are better suited to autonomous and participative work conditions than are people high in this characteristic.

McGregor (1960, 1967), however, has suggested that this readiness to set work goals autonomously can be learned or developed. In a set of assumptions which he calls Theory Y he outlines the potential for autonomous performance and intrinsic work satisfaction which he sees in most people (1960, pp. 47–48):

1. The expenditure of physical and mental effort in work is as natural as play or rest.

2. External control and the threat of punishment are not the only means for bringing about effort toward organizational objectives. Man

will exercise self-direction and self-control in the service of objectives to which he is committed.

3. Commitment to objectives is a function of the rewards associated with their achievement.

4. The average human being learns, under proper conditions, not only to accept but to seek responsibility.

5. The capacity to exercise a relatively high degree of imagination, ingenuity, and creativity in the solution of organizational problems is widely, not narrowly, distributed in the population.

6. Under the conditions of modern industrial life, the intellectual potentialities of the average human being are only partially utilized.

This view of human potential stands opposed to the more traditional models of man implicit in the organization theories of Weber (1947) (bureaucratic theory), Taylor (1911) (scientific management and economic man), and Mayo (1945) (human relations). These models generally rest on the assumption that man's primary motivation for work stems from factors extrinsic to the work itself—factors such as pay, future career prospects, pleasant social relationships on the job, etc. McGregor (1960, pp. 33–34) summarizes the assumptions of these models under the heading Theory X:

1. The average human being has an *inherent dislike of work* and will avoid it if he can.

2. Because of this human characteristic of dislike of work, most people must be coerced, controlled, directed, threatened with punishment to get them to put forth adequate effort toward the achievement of organizational objectives.

3. The average human being prefers to be directed, wishes to avoid responsibility, has relatively little ambition, wants security above all.

A critically important feature of Theory X and Theory Y is that neither one is necessarily right or wrong, not even for a particular person. Theory Y is a statement of *potential* in the work setting: Given the proper conditions, most people can *learn* to experience intrinsic satisfaction and psychological success through their work. However, given the failure-oriented working conditions of most lower level employees, Theory X may be a better assessment of the present state of their motivation. As Argyris (1957, 1964) has shown, most lower level jobs are structured to provide psychological failure, the consequences of which are boredom, withdrawal, apathy, short time perspective, and dependency.

However, both Theory X and Theory Y may be equally valid descriptions of a given person at two different points in time. If a lower level employee or ghetto school child has become accustomed to failure over a 15- or 40-year period, he will probably not jump at the opportunity for autonomy; or if he does jump, he will probably misuse the opportunity and attempt to sabotage the organization or avoid work. But if that person is given autonomy *and* stimulating work *and* support in performing effectively, after a few cycles of the psychological success process, and perhaps a few failures, he may learn to anticipate success rather than failure, or at least a high enough probability of success to make the attempt exciting.

Thus Theory Y (and the psychological success model for that matter) gives a view of human *potential* and the level of intrinsic commitment and motivation that *can be developed* in the work setting. This level can also be lost if conditions change.

McGregor's discussion of self-control and personal target setting in *The Human Side of Enterprise* is perhaps one of the most neglected portions of that book; perhaps the material on Theory X and Theory Y overshadows the subsequent chapters. However, the discussion of target setting is critical because it presents a view of how conditions of Theory Y might be established. In this target-setting meeting the employee and his supervisor set goals and discuss how the subordinate will achieve these objectives. This is a mutual problem-solving session to provide *ideas* for the subordinate but not *control*; it will be up to him to decide ultimately how he is going to attack his objectives. Then during the 6 months following the target setting, the superior is available to help the person solve problems which may arise in working toward his goals, but this coaching is under the control of the subordinate. Here the superior must avoid the extremes of being overcontrolling (even overhelping), on the one hand, and of abdicating all responsibility by making the subordinate "sink or swim" on his own, on the other hand.

It is clear from this discussion that an important condition for psychological success is an open and trusting relationship between superior and subordinate. If the subordinate does not trust the superior and does not see his efforts in the target-setting process as attempts to be helpful, the process may create more problems than it will solve.

It is also clear that people have to learn to assume this degree of autonomy and responsibility for their own careers. The readiness for autonomy and self-control must be developed over many cycles of psychological success, with occasional failures to be expected as well.

2. Determining One's Own Means of Attaining Work Goals. Much of the preceding considerations about autonomy regarding setting objectives also applies here to the actual effort toward attaining them. As was mentioned earlier, it may not be as unusual for an employee to have goal-attainment independence as it is for him to have goal-setting freedom; yet even the former is probably missing as often as it is present in most work settings.

As with goal setting, an important organizational factor in finding effective means for goal attainment is the support and coaching provided by the superior. If the individual can receive consultation from his superior without feeling bound or controlled by the superior's ideas, he then has available a wider source of possible solutions to his work problems. Like an athletic coach, the boss needs to stay on the sidelines and let the subordinate do the actual deciding and performing.

The technical competence of the superior and subordinate are also important factors in this phase of the psychological success process. A certain level of intelligence or competence is required to solve work problems, and the required level can vary with the problem. The more competent the subordinate is, the more likely he will be to figure out effective means of attaining his work goals; the more competent the superior, the more effective a coach he will be.

The competence or effectiveness of the superior is also important in determining his value as an identification model for the subordinate. Much of what the subordinate—especially the young subordinate—learns comes from simply observing his boss in action, working on his own tasks. The more effective the boss is, the more the subordinate learns by simply working with him.

This kind of learning through identification is especially important in the career development of professionals, where work tasks are difficult to pin down and define, and where many of one's actual work skills are acquired on the job, over a number of years, as opposed to during the period of one's formal education.

3. Challenging Work Goals. In order for a person to be able to set challenging work objectives, he needs to be in an assignment which is either inherently difficult (and thus demands the setting of challenging goals) or capable of being made difficult by the individual. An example of the latter situation might be the assignment of a priest to an urban ghetto parish with declining membership. The formal, programmed demands, such as Masses, weddings, home visits, etc., might be minimal, while the social problems would be numerous. The priest can essentially define the job challenge level for himself, depending on whether he tends to accept the job as formally defined or tends to seek out problems and personally take on additional challenges.

Thus, there are two important factors involved in determining the challenge level of a person's work objectives. The first, an organizational condition, is the *objective level of challenge* either demanded or available. The second, a personal factor, is the *individual's willingness to actively search his environment and set risky, challenging goals for himself.*

Atkinson (1958) has suggested that personal risk taking is a function of one's need for achievement (nAch) and fear of failure (ff). The high nAch person tends to set task goals with an expectancy of success near .50, an intermediate point at which success is possible but far from guaranteed. The high fear-failure person would tend to avoid such a task, choosing instead a task with either an extremely easy or nearly impossible task to minimize either the likelihood or the pain of failing. Self-esteem seems to operate here in the same manner as nAch, with high self-esteem people more likely to favor challenging but attainable goals (Korman, 1967) than people with low self-esteem.

Another important personal factor here is the competence of the individual. People obviously have different types and levels of skills, and what may be extremely difficult for one person is often boring and routine for another. Also, a task that is challenging for a person at one stage in his career may be unchallenging at a later stage after he has performed it numerous times. Thus, although we will here speak of certain types of work as being inherently challenging or not, the important variable is the challenge perceived by the individual, and these perceptions may deviate from the objective measures because of individual differences in ability. These individual differences can occur both over a number of different people and over a number of years for a given person.

4. Personally Valued Work Goals. In addition to being challenging, one's work goals must be personally valued or central to one's identity in order for psychological success to occur; they must require skills and abilities that are important to the person. If, for example, a person is playing a ring-toss game, he may set a challenging goal for himself, figure out how to achieve it, and, in fact, shoot the aspired score. Yet, if he does not see throwing rings accurately as central to his self-concept, no amount of task success will produce psychological success. Indeed, it is for this reason that research on nAch usually includes some attempt to make an essentially irrelevant task appear to be more central to the person's self-identity. For example, to make the ring-toss game more personally meaningful, the person's achievement motivation is aroused with instructions such as "Go ahead and shoot and *see how good you are* at this!" (Litwin, 1966; emphasis added). Other nAch arousal conditions involve providing contrived norms from competing groups (e.g., fake mean scores from Harvard for subjects at Yale). The general idea is that the more the task is defined so that success or failure will enhance or threaten the person's self-concept, the more potent the task might be in facilitating psychological success.

In a work setting, centrality can be assessed in terms of the value the individual attaches to the activities in his assignment. Generally, the more meaningful the person says his work is and the more he values that work, the more central we might assume that that work is to his self-identity.

An important personal factor related to a person's values is the length of time he has been in a career—i.e., simple chronological age in most cases. Age is obviously an important variable in developmental psychology (which is usually defined as child development psychology), and it is of no less importance in the development of careers. There is a growing body of literature which suggests that there are rather clearly defined stages in career processes. These stages are characterized by typically different types of concerns or values during particular age periods.[4]

The existence of career stages means that the definition or content of success may vary from one stage to another. In an early stage a valued activity might be gaining recognition and status in an organization, while at a later stage such a goal may have little incentive value and thus contribute little to perceived success. Perhaps developing a sense of the ultimate meaning in one's work contributes to psychological success during the mid-career years (H. Levinson, 1969; E. Mills, 1970; D. Levinson, 1968), a goal may be less salient to a man in his twenties (Hall & Nougaim, 1968).

5. *Actual Attainment of Goals.* Most of what was said regarding condition 3 (identifying means of attaining goals) also applies to the eventual attainment of the goals. Individual autonomy and competence, superior support, coaching, and competence are all important to help the person perform well. Perhaps the most important additional factors at this stage are *feedback* and *recognition*. Feedback is important to let the person know that he has, in fact, attained the goal. Recognition from superiors, colleagues, subordinates, and clients helps provide additional rewards (in addition to intrinsic rewards) for success and helps confirm the new level of personal competence demonstrated by that success.

Career Variables To be Used in the Present Research

Now that the theoretical concepts guiding our research have been presented, we are in a position to summarize the career variables to

[4]See, e.g., the work of Cain (1964), Erikson (1963), and Piaget (Flavell, 1963).

be used in this study. We will present these career variables in terms of the four basic factors of organizational career variables to be used in this research: career criteria, organizational factors, personal factors, and role transition.

Career Criteria

Since the model of career development (shown in Fig. 1.1) presented here is essentially a model of career identity development, the central criterion variable to be employed will be the priest's self-image—his general image of himself as he relates to his environment. We will also examine a number of career-relevant facets of his identity, or sub-identities—his subidentity vis-à-vis his superior, his subidentity when relating to close friends, and his subidentity in his relations with parishioners. This concept of identity will be operationalized (measured) by asking the priest how he sees himself in general and when in relation-ships with these salient others. General self-image will also be seen as a feedback variable, leading back to influence the priest's choice of work activities.

Related to the concept of identity is the extent to which the priest feels his important skills and abilities are being used and developed in his work. This use of important skills will be used as an important input to self-image growth; the more the priest is developing his impor-tant abilities, the more he is extending the boundaries and competence of his self-image.

Related to use of skills is the priest's satisfactions in his work. Satisfac-tion will be measured in five specific areas: supervision, work itself, pay, promotion opportunities, and co-workers.

Perhaps from the organization's point of view, the most important career outcome is the priest's commitment to the organization and, there-fore, to his priestly career.

Organizational Factors

As Fig. 1.1 indicates, the important organizational factors in the present model are those affecting the priest's choices or decisions in task situations. This means, then, that the most relevant organizational factors will be those relating to work assignments. In particular, we will examine the psychological climate in which the priest works. Included in the work climate will be variables related to the conditions necessary for psychological success: challenge and meaning of work tasks, the amount of support and autonomy provided by the superior, and the extent to which the priest feels accepted by others. A related factor, discussed earlier in the chapter but not shown in Fig. 1.1, is the effectiveness of the superior. This is an important consideration since an effective superior can provide both competent coaching to the priest and a good identification model of psychological success.

In addition to climate, the psychological nature of the work assignment will also be assessed by examining the actual work activities of the priest. Climate will tell us how he feels about the conditions under which he works; the work activities will tell us what he does on the job.

One of the propositions presented earlier hypothesized the importance of a person's first assignment in the later unfolding of his career. Therefore, we will also examine these four climate variables as the priest recalled the extent to which they existed in his initial permanent assignment following ordination.

A third group of organizational variables—in addition to climate and activities—covers the physical environment in the present assignment. These variables measure what Herzberg (1966) calls the context of the assignment rather than its intrinsic content. The psychological success model deals with the intrinsic content rather than the context. Thus this model, as well as Herzberg's theory, would lead us to expect environmental characteristics to be less strongly related to positive career outcomes than factors such as work climate and work activities. However, as determinants of negative career outcomes (e.g., dissatisfaction), Herzberg's theory would predict that contextual factors would be more important than intrinsic assignment characteristics. Therefore, to help understand negative as well as positive career outcomes, it is important to include measures of environmental factors in the assignment.

Personal Factors

Since the psychological success cycle is initiated by the process of personal choice or decision making, an important personal characteristic affecting a priest's career development is his readiness to make mature career decisions. This variable has been stressed elsewhere as a key—if not *the* key—personal factor in career development (Hall, 1971; Schneider, 1968, Tiedeman, 1970).

One of the conditions necessary for psychological success is the relevance of a task activity to the priest's self-image. To measure this condition, we measured the activities performed by the priest and the degree of importance to him of those activities. Comparison of these two sets of variables was used as an operational measure of the personal relevance of the priests work activities; the separate variables were examined individually as well.

Related to the issue of what constitutes a personally relevant work goal to the individual are his more general values. One aspect of personal values was described in the preceding section—the value (or importance) the priest attaches to various work activities. The more he values the work he is doing, the more likely he is to experience psychological success.

The second aspect of personal values is the value the individual attaches to various organizational goals. The more the priest values the present goals of the institutional Catholic Church the more likely he is to experience satisfaction as he works toward those goals. Therefore, both types of values were employed—value for particular work activities and value for various organizational goals.

If, as was suggested in the earlier theory, priests at various points in their career cycles have systematically different concerns, then our data must be examined in the perspective of the particular *career stages* of the individual priests. The relationships between particular assignment characteristics and career outcomes may differ from one stage to another.

Role Transitions

The important role transitions for priests are the change from seminarian to priest, curate to pastor, and pastor to retiree. To identify the effects of these role transitions, we will look at the three categories—personal and organization factors and career criteria—for priests in different stages of their careers.

Summary

To summarize the theory presented earlier, let us restate the main elements in the form of general hypotheses to be examined in this research. First, we presented a model of psychological success and argued that to the extent that the conditions are met, we would expect priests to experience high satisfaction, feelings of self-utilization, and self-esteem. If the conditions are generally not met, we would expect to find little evidence of positive career experiences on these criterion dimensions.

Hypothesis I. The priest's career development will be positively related to the extent to which the following conditions for psychological success are present in his work: (1) work challenge, (2) autonomy, (3) valued work activities, and (4) support in achieving his work goals.

Using the reasoning presented earlier, we would also expect the nature of the priest's first assignment to have a lasting impact upon his career development.

Hypothesis II. The extent to which the priest's initial assignment provided the conditions for psychological success or failure will be related to later career development.

If the conditions for psychological success were lacking for a significant or major proportion of the priests in the diocese, we would expect failure to be a fairly universal organizational phenomenon and not merely a problem for the individual priests experiencing failure. This general prediction is stated in the following hypothesis:

Hypothesis III. If the conditions for psychological success are generally lacking in the work world of most priests, not only the priestly career but also aspects of the organization itself would tend to be characterized by some symptom(s) of psychological failure or some strategy (or strategies) to minimize failure.

From the theory of role transitions we would expect that each of the major role transitions in the career of the priest would be stressful periods characterized by altered self-image, satisfaction, and perceived utilization of skills. The major role transitions are those from seminarian to first parish assignment (i.e., ordination), from curate to pastor, and from pastor to retiree.

Hypothesis IV. The transitions from seminarian to priest, from curate to pastor, and from pastor to retiree will be characterized by altered self-identity, satisfaction, and utilization of skills as well as a general experience of personal stress.

The psychological success model of career development will form the conceptual framework for analyzing the career development of our sample of diocesan priests. Simply put, we will be looking at the extent to which work opportunities and personal capabilities exist for personal choice making and challenging activity in the assignments of priests and at the impact of these factors upon priests' career development. Prior to moving on to these analyses, it is important for the reader to understand the context in which our research was accomplished.[5] Thus in Chapter Two we explore previous literature specifically related to the priesthood as a career.

---

[5] The results of a national survey of priests were reported at the same time that this book was completed. Those data were not available to us in our research.

TWO
Clergy As Career

This chapter has two goals: (1) to discuss the kinds of empirical-quantitative research that has been accomplished on clergymen, including priests, and (2) to paint a portrait of what is known about the working, professional parish priest.

The Lack of Research on the Priest's Work World

When one examines the empirical, theoretical, and theological writings about clergymen at work, particularly priests, it is obvious that the concentration has been on the individual and how his personal characteristics are related to his adjustment in the work world rather than on his assignment, relationships, or the Church as an organization. If we take the three most comprehensive sources of research on clergymen and examine the titles of the studies cited or reviewed, the overwhelming evidence supports this conclusion. For example, in their now-classic annotated bibliography Menges & Dittes (1965) present some 700 references to psychological research on clergymen. In this review neither the word career nor the word work appear in the subject index. In addition, there is no category for authority. The research reported is overwhelmingly oriented toward the personal or individual aspects of success. Even in studies examining the correlates of success, more often than not the independent variable of interest is personality or career choice style. Koval (1970) has suggested that whenever there has been a problem of any kind concerning Catholic religious, the first research attempt has always been to study the personality of the priest; the organization structure, including the bishop, has not come under scrutiny.

A second source of research reports, this one specifically directed to Roman Catholic priests, has been assembled by D'Arcy (1968). This review included 527 entries of which 215 also appeared in Menges and Dittes. Whereas the Menges & Dittes (1965) review concentrated on psychological research and reported research summaries, the D'Arcy contribution simply reported references; it is more general in that citations are reported for sociological studies as well.

D'Arcy identified nine major categories of research on priests: (1) statistical studies of candidates, dropouts, and deployment; (2) environmental factors in the background of religious vocations (one-sixth of all cited studies); (3) studies of religious vocations in the light of vocational development theory; (4) psychological characteristics as measured by personality, interest, aptitude, and achievement tests; (5) studies of illness, both physical and mental, and length of life; (6) attitudes of laity toward religious personnel; (7) role studies, especially those regarding teaching and counseling (one-eighth of all studies); (8) sociological studies of the structure of religious communities; and, (9) bibliographies. Not one of the major categories concerns the role of external influences on current individual behavior except for those studies dealing with the parental and other influences prior to selection or ordination (category 2). Although these studies are conducted under the assumption that there is some relationship between these factors and later individual behavior, they only describe these environmental factors rather than relating them to later career experiences.

It should be noted that the D'Arcy category 2, concerning the preordination experiences of priests, constitutes the largest percentage of studies that have been conducted. It seems paradoxical that so much emphasis has been placed on the early experiences of men who become priests to the virtual exclusion of the experiences they encounter after their careers as priests begin. In the area of vocational development theory (D'Arcy category 3) the fact that there are a considerable number of studies might at first glance hold some prospects for the kind of research we are emphasizing, but this would deny the reality which we have presented in Chapter One: Career development has been typically defined by psychologists as the study of career selection, as if it only occurred at one period in a man's life.

The third source of information regarding research on clergymen is a book by Joseph Fichter (1961). For an area of research interest that is some 50 years old (D'Arcy, 1968) it is surprising to find that Fichter's book was one of the first to consider in depth the question of whether or not what clergymen do can be considered work, a profession, and a career, and to argue in the affirmative.

Clergy as Career

Of course, once the question of the work-world influence is raised, then one must consider whether the clergyman's life is of the natural or supernatural order. If the answer is that the priesthood is of the supernatural order, then the problem of career definition is unimportant since careers imply the extraspiritual domains of work, human relationships, and human organizations. If the minister, priest, or rabbi is "called," and his ministrations to man consist solely of spiritual and mystical elements, then consideration of his occupation or profession is not warranted. If priests and ministers are also at least part mortal men, however, then their day-to-day activities are involved with the lives of other mortal men, and the standards for the evaluation of what is or is not a career or profession apply equally well to the priest's role.

The social scientist conducting research on clergy-as-man has a long history of debating the issue of whether to regard the priesthood as vocation or career. The early work in screening applicants (career selection) for the priesthood (Bier, 1954, 1960) concerned itself with the question: "Are we not interfering with the work of Grace by introducing psychological methods into evaluation?" (Bier, 1960, p. 8). The problem has always been consideration of the element of "mystery" in the religious life. Bier (1960) and others (Coville, D'Arcy, McCarthy, & Rooney, 1968) have resolved the issue by speaking to the other elements in religious life—mystery, they have assumed, is only *one* of the elements.

There is no doubt that the clergyman is a professional. He is an *educated* man who has been sanctioned by peers and superiors to be *expert* in rendering services through the *institutional* Church. He professes competence in his various professonal roles, and he is dedicated to the performance of his role in the service of others. (Carr-Saunders & Wilson, 1933; Fichter, 1961; Glasse, 1968.) Glasse (1968, pp. 57–76; after Blizzard, 1956) defines five professional roles for the minister: professional preacher—the giver of sermons; professional priest—the leader of worship services; professional pastor—counseling through biblical and psychological knowledge of man; professional teacher—sharing knowledge as well as using his knowledge; and professional organizer and administrator. Regarding the latter roles of organizer and administrator, Glasse says, "It seems to me that most ministers are least professional in these roles" (p. 71). This issue is one which we will discuss in detail in later chapters. Suffice it to say at this point that priests who have careers and are thus susceptible to the benefits and liabilities of other humans working in organizational settings will be considered professionals.

For example, the reader should note the concentration on relationships with others in all the roles identified by Glasse; whether the priest is delivering a sermon, counseling, or teaching, his profession is one in which relationships play an important part. This involvement with others suggests the necessity of examining the patterns of these relationships with others for correlates of pastoral success; researchers should study relationships among clergy as well as the individual clergyman. If there is work involved in what the priest accomplishes in his ministrations to his parishioners, then we should examine the way he views his work. Indeed, Glasse (1968, pp. 20–21), in speaking about the crises that Protestant ministers have experienced, suggests that "what is at stake here is not the minister's calling or his dignity or his office, but his *work.* The critical issue is not his ecclesiastical identity in the church, but his occupational identity in the world of work."

Fichter (1961, 1968) has shown that the world of work of clergymen is indeed a potent source of individual meaning; that, based on the literature generated in other settings, full consideration must be given to the current environment, the postordination environment, as a source of individual satisfactions and feeling of worthfulness. Jud, Mills, & Burch (1970) show the importance of environmental support systems, especially family support, in the decisions of Protestant pastors to stay in or leave the parish ministry. In his later volume, Fichter (1968) demonstrates the crucial role of this environment for the assistant pastor. Similarly, Mitchell (1966) has shown the importance of relationships in the context of the multiple staff ministry, a relationship similar to the pastor–curate relationship in the Roman Catholic parish. The interesting aspect of Mitchell's study is that he approached his research from a view somewhat similar to ours; he assumed that persons continue to develop through their adult lives and that the environment in which they find themselves has much to do with the choices and, therefore, success of the developmental possibilities they have as individuals. He based these ideas on the developmental theory of Erik Erikson (1963) and the field theory of Kurt Lewin (1951). Obviously, this idea is similar to our presentation. Indeed, Mitchell makes the following prediction: "If the relationships, the opportunities and the tasks available in the multiple staff situation contribute toward a positive resolution of critical, personal, developmental concerns, then, I believe, the situation itself may be expected to be more stable and therefore more productive of meaningful work" (p. 33). This is similar to predictions we would make regarding the necessary organizational conditions for psychological success. It is interesting to note that while much of the research we have cited has concentrated solely on the personal aspects of the successful ministerial work, Mitchell concentrates almost exclusively on the organizational conditions.

Another important organizational analysis is a study of the career experiences of United Church of Christ pastors and expastors conducted by Jud *et al.* (1970). They found that the median age of decision to enter the ministry was between 20 and 21 years, and the age at ordination averaged between 27 and 28 years. About one-fourth of the ministers had worked full time in other occupations before entering the ministry.

Expastors reported a wide variety of reasons for leaving the parish ministry, although they appear to the present writers to fall into three general categories: (1) the nature of parish work and the resulting sense of personal nonfulfillment or inadequacy, (2) family stress, especially the wife's dissatisfaction and marital difficulties, and (3) the structure and goals of the institutional church (i.e., its relevance to current problems). Despite the fact that ministers' salaries are extremely low compared to other professionals (median salary of $8037 for Episcopal ministers in 1968) (Rodenmayer, 1970), and that this led to financial strain for many ministers, it did not seem to be of primary importance in the decision to leave. (However, money problems may have been an important indirect factor, through their effect on general marital and family problems.)

The husband–wife relationship was found to be pivotal for both pastors and expastors. Respondents were asked, "During your pastorate, please indicate how much you would have valued the praise of each of the persons or groups listed below." The list included fellow pastors in the same denomination, denominational executives, lay leaders, wife or husband, fellow pastors of other local churches, others on the church staff, and other close friends. Both pastors and expastors rated their wives as their most important reference person—the one whose praise they valued most. More than three-fourths of the people responding to the question said they desired their wives' praise "extremely much" (the highest response point on the scale).

Jud *et al.* (1970) asked a similar question to determine how much support the minister received from each of the seven groups just listed: "Now you are asked to make a slightly different evaluation about these persons or groups: how supportive (helpful) they actually were and how much they tended to isolate or nullify your efforts as pastor." Again the wife was ranked first by both pastors and expastors. The authors concluded, "The fact that the family is a crucial support structure for the UCC minister as well as his most important reference group makes it obvious that ministers' career decisions are heavily influenced by family relationships" (p. 95).

Whereas most studies of men who leave the Roman Catholic priesthood have looked at the personality or background of the individual priest to identify the problems responsible for his leaving, it is interesting that Jud *et al.* see the Protestant church as suffering from organization problems, not a collection of individual problems.

> Among Protestant clergy the evidence points not to a drop-out crisis, but to a mobility and morale crisis, a situation in which there are too many ministers for the congregations that can adequately support them, and in which sluggish placement breeds sinking morale. We may very well, if the situation continues this way, have a sharp increase in movement out of church ministries; but it is not now a reality. Where and if it occurs, however, as our study plainly shows, it will be a *system crisis* through and through, and not simply the actions of disgruntled individuals (p. 59).

The authors go on to summarize their diagnosis of the present state of the Protestant church:

> 1. Ex-pastors are not ex-ministers, nor are pastors permanently pastors. A broad understanding of vocation, which is marked by an intense desire for the ministry, exists among both groups. If sometimes that ministry is defined over against the institution, the gradual liberalization and pragmatization of theology makes it relatively easy to redefine ministry in secular terms. Ex-pastors have done so on a large scale, and the basic rationale is shared by many pastors.
> 2. In addition to sharing recent theological trends, ex-pastors and pastors are similar in racial, parental, and community background, and in age—except for the very youngest and oldest. In general, they enjoy the same role tasks most and least, and are satisfied most and least with the same aspects of ministry. They both regard peers and denominational executives with low esteem, and invest wives and nonpeer close friends with the major support and reference functions. Ex-pastors feel they were inadequately prepared by seminaries.
> 3. Ex-pastors have a stronger pattern of early changes than pastors in denomination, in career, and in jobs; they are better educated, more interested in community activities, and less in the core pastoral roles of preaching, calling, and helping individuals to commitment, less satisfied with the rewards and opportunities of the parish (including salary) and less hopeful about making a difference there. Ex-pastors are disproportionately more from pastorates as opposed to specialized,

non-parish work, are more likely than pastors to be under 30 and less likely to be over 55, feel less support from laymen and desire it less, and have greater marital problems.

4. Ex-pastors left church employment for a variety of reasons, none of which accounts for a majority of the decisions. The reasons include personal crises, a sense of inadequacy, disillusionment and frustration with the church, inability to relocate when necessary, family problems, attractive work opportunities. Some problems are chronic, leading to low interest in returning to church ministry; other problems are acute, more often followed by a desire to return. Ex-pastors earn more, are freer and more relaxed, and report improved financial and family situations. They found their jobs most often through system contacts, although a fourth made sudden, ill-prepared decisions. Most had contemplated leaving for a long time.

5. The church as an occupational system fails to meet the needs of its professionals adequately. Weaknesses in the training, hiring, work, rewards, and support systems are evident in the experience of ex-pastors. At the same time, new careers are opening in "mission" occupations such as social service, social change, and education; and the combined effects produce intense pressures outward from pastoral ministries.

6. The family bears special importance in clergy careers. Family welfare, wife's role satisfaction, and marital harmony are crucial determinants of career decisions. Few ministers seem to realize this fact.

7. Faith changes are marked in recent years, growing out of maturity and social involvement (ex-pastors) or pastoral involvement (pastors). Deepening commitment may still accompany loosening ties to institution and the radical redefinition of ministry. Loss of faith is not a major basis for career change.

8. Career-change decisions often have roots in years of deliberation but are precipitated by "tipping point" experiences which coincide with the eroded occupational commitment. The combined effect of system conflict and accumulated dissatisfaction shift the hope/frustration balance and begin the search for other kinds of work. Evidence that ex-pastors and pastors differ by being on opposite sides of the tipping point makes it essential to develop support structures to nurture hope and manage frustration (pp. 59–60).

Fichter (1961, p. xii) indicated that "the structural or organizational aspects of the [Roman Catholic] Church calling have hardly been scrutinized from a scientific point of view, while the relations between administrators and subordinates have been treated mainly in ascetical and canonical literature." Fichter attempted to remedy this situation somewhat in his early work, but it is his later work, *America's Forgotten Priests* (Fichter, 1968), to which we turn for information related specifically to the diocesan priesthood.

The Diocesan Priest

Diocesan priests comprise about 60% of all priests in the United States, and as of 1966 this 60% numbered approximately 36,000. These 36,000 priests are members of 150 dioceses ranging in size from 1400 priests for 541 square miles in the Archdiocese of Newark to the 327 priests for 54,679 square miles in the Archdiocese of Denver (Fichter, 1968, pp. 25, 53). Each diocese has a number of deaneries which are geographical areas containing separate parishes. Each parish has 1 *pastor* and from 0 to 4 or 5 *assistant pastors (curates)*. A *bishop*, called the ordinary (archbishop for larger diocese, or archdiocese), presides over these parishes and also "a large variety of functional offices and commissions" (p. 60). In his diocese, the bishop has complete authority over his priests; in his parish the pastor has complete authority over his curates.

The other type of position a diocesan priest may hold is the *special* assignment. The special assignment may range from full-time teaching to university or hospital chaplaincy to newspaper work to liturgical commission activities. Between ordination and the advancement to pastorate, the priest in the diocese we studied spends the largest proportion of his 22 years as an assistant, responding to the way in which his pastor exercises his authority. [It should be noted that this figure may be as few as 5 years (Nebraska) and as many as 30 years (Brooklyn).] Transfers *between* dioceses (called incardination and excardination) are rare.

Assignment changes for the 600 diocesan priests in our diocese are made about every 5 to 7 years, and for the most part they affect only specials and curates. Pastors are usually offered the opportunity to refuse a reassignment, but curates and specials are not. Assignment changes were announced 3 days before they became effective at the time this research was conducted. Length of time on a given assignment in our sample ranges from 3 months to 21 years. Promotion to pastor is almost exclusively accomplished on the basis of seniority.

There are no intermediate formal hierarchical steps between curate and pastor. We say "formal" because many curates consider the special assignment to have more status than the curacy. Beyond pastor there is the bishopric or the honorary title of monsignor.

All priests, except for some specials assigned to hospitals and universities, live in a rectory which is run by the pastor of the particular parish. Thus for many priests, their work environment is undifferentiated from the rectory in which they live, eat, and sleep. This set of conditions, we were told, is particularly oppressive in some rectories.

In preparation for this career, all priests undergo at least 4 years of seminary education. In fact, probably more than 35% of all priests enter some form of seminary (high school or minor seminary) prior to their seventeenth birthday (Fichter, 1968, pp. 73). This education has tended to be oriented toward spiritual and academic training rather than toward training on how to deal with lay people or how to handle practical parish problems. (cf. Potvin & Suziedelis, 1969). Priests who enter various orders (nondiocesan priests) tend to receive more specialized training, although diocesan priests are expected "to be able to handle anything."

Diocesan Governance

The bishop of a diocese has tremendous potential autonomy and authority. He owes allegiance to no one but the pope. All of his offices and commissions, notably the chancery office (all administrative or bureaucratic functions), exist at his discretion and are merely advisory bodies. Many dioceses now have a senate of priests and a personnel committee, both suggested by the Second Vatican Council and both existing at the discretion of the bishop. The personnel committee in the archdiocese studied was the initiator of the research to be described; indeed, this committee was formed at the suggestion of the priest's senate.

The Roman Catholic Church is a bureaucracy. As such, it portrays in bold relief many Weberian characteristics of the ideal type of bureaucratic administrative structure: a rational-legal basis of authority, a clearly defined sphere of legal competence for each office, appointment (not election) of members to offices, definition of the office as the sole (or at least primary) occupation of the incumbent, membership in the organization seen as a career, and officeholder subject to strict and systematic control in the conduct of his office (Weber, 1947, pp. 333–334). In fact, Weber listed the Catholic Church as his first example of the bureaucratic organization (p. 333).

There is currently great debate regarding the effectiveness of this structure, which has undergone little change, especially in the United States, in the past two or three generations (Greeley, 1967). That there is spiritual ferment within the Church cannot be denied. There is also ferment within the priesthood, and not just over the issue of celibacy (Fichter, 1961, 1968). One of the central issues of this ferment is the bureaucratic structure, the feeling of an inability to influence higher authority which priests have suggested is at the root of their dismay with their priestly career.

Precisely because of its traditional bureaucratic nature and flavor of being a total institution (Goffman, 1961), the Roman Catholic Church allows the investigation of various issues in organizational behavior. Studying the careers of professionals in this particular type of organization should shed light on variables of interest in other less clearly defined organizational environments. Thus, as behavioral scientists, we have had the opportunity to study in bold relief the impact of bureaucratic authority on the careers of the organization's members, its priests.

The People in the Priesthood

Now that we have seen something of the work environment of the
priest and the organizational structure of the Roman Catholic diocese,
let us consider the type of peson who becomes a priest. A logical place
to begin our discussion of relevant literature on the people in the priesthood is the background of the priest, including the variables that may
be related to the initial career decision. This aspect of clergy careers
has been researched from a number of different vantage points, in
a number of different religions, and with a number of different conclusions (Menges & Dittes, 1965). Investigations have been made concerning
the *background* of the individual who enters the ministry (education,
socioeconomic status, geographical location), the *personality* of individuals
choosing these careers (active-passive, dominant-submissive, MMPI,
Rorschach), the *interests* of priests, ministers, and rabbis (Strong, Kuder),
the *influences* on the individual to choose this particular type of career
(parents, other clergy), and the *age* of the decision to become a clergyman.
The use of these particular variables has not been different from the
attempts made to understand the career decisions of people in other
fields of work. The results are examined in terms of various criteria
of interest: how priests differ from the laity in general or from those
in other careers, terminators vs. nonterminators, and so forth.

In the case of influence and background, research has been published by CARA (Center for Applied Research in the Apostolate) titled
Seminarians of the Sixties (Potvin & Suziedelis, 1969). A 20% probability
sample of 95 diocesan and religious, minor and major seminaries from
all sections of the United States was contacted, and approximately 6400
individuals (90% of the sample) responded to a mailed questionnaire.
The data generated in this study reflect previous research summarized
in works by Fichter (1961, 1968), Menges & Dittes (1965), and D'Arcy
(1968). Menges & Dittes (1965), D'Arcy (1968), and Fichter (1961) all
provide excellent summaries of psychological research on the clergy
and clergy careers. However, since the CARA study is the most recent
and complete assessment of persons preparing for the priesthood, their
findings regarding the background and influences of individuals who
entered a seminary will be summarized.

Background Data

Potvin & Suziedelis (1969) suggest that their research results agree
well with the earlier conclusons of Fichter (1961) that "the average
seminarian comes from a middle class, urban family with a little more

than four children, is neither the first born nor last born, reports his early childhood as happy, has been educated in Catholic schools and has one or more close relatives who are also following the religious life as seminarian, priest, Brother or Sister" (p. 19). To be more specific, they indicate that three-quarters of their sample come from homes with reported incomes of $5000–15,000, 80% come from suburban households, 50% come from families in which there are more than four children, and 38% are firstborns (a figure which somewhat contradicts the Fichter conclusions, but may be due to the fact that families were smaller at the time of the later study). The family is described by seminarians as generally positive though somewhat strict. Sixty-eight percent of the high school seminarians attended only Catholic schools, and 95% of the parents of seminarians attend mass weekly or more often.

Fortunately, the Potvin and Suziedelis research included some data collected on a comparable sample of Catholic boys who were not in seminaries. The most striking differences between this group and those enrolled in seminaries was that seminarians came from larger families than nonseminarians, a greater proportion of nonseminarians attended public schools, the parents of seminarians were more faithful in attending mass than the parents of nonseminarians, and nonseminarians described their parents in less positive terms. Obviously, no one of these factors is necessarily causative in determining which children entered seminaries, but, as Potvin and Suziedelis indicate, "they are certainly part of the socio-religious matrix from which vocations have arisen in the present sample" (p. 32).

Personality and Interests

There exist literally hundreds of studies assessing the personality of clergymen. There is evidence also of active selection programs employing preordination personality assessment, as well as the more typical study comparing clergymen to each other or to nonclergymen (Coville et al., 1968).

In a brief early (1960) review of literature on personality aspects of the priesthood, McCarthy saw groups of studies revolving around two main questions: (1) Are priests and religious different in personality and interest than the average person? (2) What are the reasons for the personality differences between religious and other persons? In response to the question regarding personality, McCarthy reports that the typical religious-in-training is somewhat more submissive, dependent, introspective, and self-conscious than the average American. The conclusion has been a pervasive one.

The studies McCarthy cites as attempts to explain these differences strongly suggest that personality is changed by living the religious life. Indeed, McCarthy (1960) showed that these personality changes were "associated with critical choice points and the particular behavioral demands being made on the religious at those points . . ." (p. 38). Thus a candidate who scores on a personality or interest test like the "typical" priest or religious-in-training "may not in fact be scoring as those people did when they applied" (McCarthy & Dondero, 1963, p. 76). Citations other than this could not be found which were reports of longitudinal designs.

Dunn (1965), in a review of personality patterns among religious personnel, was able to report some consistent findings from study to study.[6] He reports that Bier (1948), e.g., showed MMPI profiles of Catholic seminarians to be markedly deviant from the normal, the seminarians scoring significantly higher on each scale. Subsequent studies by Jalkenen on Lutheran seminarians yielded similar deviant responses, especially on the Hs (hypochondriasis), Hy (hysteria), Pd (psychopathic deviate), Mf (masculinity-femininity—seminarians more feminine), and Pa (paranoia) (Dunn, 1965). While these studies of seminarians seem to yield consistent results, Dunn suggests that results on priests are not as consistent, some showing the priest to be worrisome, perfectionistic, and withdrawn, while others show him to enjoy a healthy personality adjustment. J. Murray (1957) suggested that some of these differences between priest and seminarian could be accounted for by seminary life experiences. He reasoned, much as we have in Chapter One, that perhaps situations have effects on people and that these effects are reflected in personality test scores. In testing preseminarians, seminarians, and priests he was able to support previous data on seminarians (Bier, 1948), but on either side of the seminary phase the profiles were more like those of normals. J. Murray (1957) concluded that the deviant scores of seminarians was in part due to the type of people attracted to the religious life and in part to the seminary atmosphere.

Dunn (1965) reached a similar conclusion, indicating surprise in the consistency he found in data regarding situational influences on personality. He further concluded that "there are definite personality differences between individuals who are attracted to the religious life and those who are not, with the religious-prone people appearing to

---

[6]It should be noted that the Dunn (1965) article and many others (see, e.g., those in Menges & Dittes, 1965) cite the research of Moore (1936a,b) as the impetus for psychological assessment of priests. Moore had concluded in one of his papers (1936a, p. 497) that "prepsychotic" individuals were attracted to the religious life.

be more perfectionistic, withdrawn, insecure, and in some cases depressed" (p. 130).

These conclusions should not be interpreted as indicating the capability of predicting success (persistence) in the seminary or priesthood. Murray & Connolly (1966) reviewed some of the studies attempting to predict success. They found that across three follow-up studies utilizing MMPI scales as predictors and perseverance in seminary as a criterion, two scales consistently descriminated between perseverers and nonperseverers: Pd (psychopathic deviate) and Sc (schizophrenia). Indeed, in their own study Sc also was a statistically significant descriminator.[7] They interpreted the relative similarity of perseverers and nonperseverers as possibly being due to homogenization as a result of seminary life.

Wauck (1960, p. 23) stated that "on the basis of available evidence, it may be concluded that there is no religious personality, per se. The norms for adjustment in the religious life are the same as norms which are used in clinical settings throughout the country." Wauck concludes (p. 24) that to concentrate on personality testing to the exclusion of social-psychological variables such as the learnings and social interaction in religious communities would "maximize the conforming, stereotyping, and deadening effect of mass testing techniques." We do not agree with Wauck that no particular type of person becomes a priest, for we feel that the person who becomes a priest must be different from one who chooses other careers; the studies just cited are clear on this point. We would argue that appropriate assessment techniques are not yet available for indicating how these differences come about. Wauck's thesis regarding the impact of social-psychological variables agrees with our position, for we think that both the personal and social variables must be considered; this, too, seems clear from the data presented regarding the impact of seminary life.

It is interesting that in all of Fichter's (1961) book on clergy careers there exists no chapter on personality or interest kinds of issues, nor does the word personality appear in his index. One might suggest that this is due to his orientation as a sociologist, but another view would indicate that little has been gained in understanding career issues of clergy from the administration of thousands of MMPI's and Strong Vocational Interest Blanks. The data are not consistent from study to study. The variables assessed bear only marginal relations to career process issues, and the criteria against which the measures are validated have

---

[7]It should be noted that reference to the MMPI throughout this report is to the original test (Hathaway & McKinley, 1951) and to Bier's (see Wauck, 1960; Dunn, 1965) modification.

assumed that what an individual can become is not at all influenced
by the environment to which he goes.

The Priest and His Career:
A Hypothetical Case Study

In a few pages we have covered a good deal of research and information regarding the priest: his background, interests, personality, seminary
experiences, and some of the conditions surrounding his postordination
organizational situation. We would like the reader to have more of a
sense of continuity, a gestalt, of the priest as person than can be obtained
from these seemingly disjointed snapshots of various aspects of the priest
and his work world. Drawing most heavily on the work of Potvin &
Suziedelis (1969) for the background and seminary influences and the
research of Fichter (1968) for responses to the fact of being a professional
priest, we present a picture of the diocesan priest—Father Tom Smith.

Father Smith came from a family of five children, three brothers
and two sisters; he was the first born. His father worked as a carpenter
in the suburban town in which they lived, and although the family was
not rich, the $10,500 per year left sufficient money for Tom to attend
the local Catholic minor seminary. Father Smith's mother encouraged
this decision, for she was a devout person who rarely missed mass or
the receiving of communion. Father Smith still feels good about his
family life and describes his parents, especially his mother, in very positive
terms. When younger he noticed that some of his friends did not seem
to have the same kind of happy home life he had, but they went on
to public school and did not join him in the Catholic high school. He
remembers that while quite young, he entertained the idea of becoming
a priest; his uncle was already a priest, and Tom enjoyed the picture
of himself saying mass and administering the sacraments. He enjoyed
the minor seminary and found less to complain about than some other
young men; and when he finally decided to enter the major seminary,
it was with a group of fellows with whom he seemed to have a lot in
common. Indeed, he noted that he was interested in and valued things
related to helping people, certainly not the mechanistic kinds of things
like engineering or business.

The seminary he was sent to was one of the larger ones, about
350 miles from home and in a different archdiocese than the one some
of his hometown friends had gone to. Now, he recalls, these friends
were not as satisfied with their seminary as he was with his—they com-
plained of lack of facilities, poor instruction—in general they thought

their seminary was rather low in quality. Some of them never were ordained. Tom liked the seminary and felt dedicated to ideals similar to his uncle's; he would not have gotten married even if celibacy was not required, and he viewed the priest's role more in sacred than secular terms. He found the support of others in the seminary, particularly his peers, to make him feel more convinced than ever that he had made the right choice.

Although he had not been visited by the bishop from his small hometown diocese (the one to which he would be assigned), he felt closer to him than some of his classmates who came from larger archdioceses.[8] The lack of a personal interest in him, though, entered his thoughts. Finally, he was ordained and sent to his first parish assignment.

Five years have passed since Tom was ordained, and they have been eventful. For the first 4 years after Tom was ordained he was in a parish assignment, but now he is on special work, as a hospital chaplain. In retrospect he feels the seminary prepared him well for leading a holy intellectual life but not at all well for dealing with lay people and handling parish problems (p. 85). His dealings with the bishop have not been any less distant than during his seminary days, and he is in favor of having a clergy personnel committee for handling priest work issues and a senate for making his views known to the bishop. He feels strongly about these matters, and feels that this is due to the conditions he found in the work world of the priest. On his first assignment he did not call his pastor by his first name (although he now calls his superior by his first name) (p. 119). Aside from his poor relationship with his first assignment pastor, he enjoyed working with the people and, while in agreement with the idea of having different assignment experiences (p. 124), he wishes he had been consulted about his most recent move (p. 139). The element that really bothered him was whether he would get a parish assignment with a good pastor or a poor pastor (p. 143). The actual work to be accomplished was not a big issue, but the kind of superior he would have was very important.

Tom has been around now and he has ideas about how the diocese should do things. First, promotion to pastorate should be based on ability rather than seniority (p. 145); second, there should be a definite retirement age for pastors and bishops (p. 152-153) since it takes too long to get the kind of responsibility for which he feels ready; third, the bishop should emphasize his pastoral and apostolic role over his adminis-

---

[8]This section draws on the research of Fichter (1968), and page numbers refer to sections in which the interested reader may examine those data in greater detail.

trative and juridical one (p. 203); fourth, and most important, if these things were accomplished, there would not be such a huge waste of energy, zeal, and talent (p. 207).

Tom feels that the pastors he knows want to treat him more like a son than an associate (p. 207), and he likes the freedom to work as hard as he wants to extend his capacity in his special assignment (p. 132).

Tom will continue in his special or curate role for about another 15 years. He will be promoted on the basis of seniority and will consider a "good" parish to be a large one with many active parishioners and few debts (p. 118). He will give a more positive appraisal of personal relations in his rectory then than he does now (p. 116) and will feel more like he and his curate(s) plan things jointly than he felt as a curate or than his curates will feel about him (p. 117). If a curate feels close to him, then the curate will feel that the work is extending him to capacity. As a pastor, of course, there will be a good chance (36%) that the assignment he gets is one he will be asked whether or not he wants, considerably different from the chance he has as a curate to help decide his fate (3%) (p. 139). He will think that his promotion to pastor was based on a combination of ability and seniority rather than that promotion is due to seniority alone (p. 144), his current view.

The picture we have painted is an average one and leaves out many facets of the priest's career. Questions arise such as the following—what is a priest's typical day like? What do priests find makes for a good or bad day? How do they see themselves in their different roles? How do their experiences in parish assignments contribute to a sense of success or failure? How do priests change as a result of their years in the priesthood? These questions about the ongoing process of the priest's career are largely unexplored in the literature and will be the focus of the present study.

THREE
Background and Procedure
of the Research

In this chapter we will consider the research methods employed in the study. An important aspect of the method is the process by which the study was planned and executed in collaboration with the personnel board of priests from the archdiocese studied. Since the process of the study and our relationship with the archdiocese and the personnel board are so important, we will devote a separate chapter (Chapter Nine) to these issues. (We do this later in the book because of the parallels between issues in our relationship to the board and issues emerging from our interview and questionnaire analyses.) In the present chapter, then, we will confine ourselves to the more technical procedures of the research design.

The overall design of the study was announced formally in the following article in the archdiocese's newspaper, *The Catholic Transcript*, on April 5, 1968:

39

The Catholic Transcript—Friday, April 5, 1968

Priest's Commitment Subject of Study

Hartford—A proposal for research on the personal growth and commitment of priests and organizational effectiveness in the Archdiocese of Hartford—a recommendation of the preliminary personnel board established last year at the suggestion of the Senate of Priests—has been approved by Archbishop Henry J. O'Brien.

The research program, to be conducted over the next 12 months, will be undertaken by professors Douglas T. Hall and Benjamin Schneider of Yale University's Department of Administrative Sciences.

In a letter to priests of the archdiocese, Archbishop O'Brien explained that the members of the preliminary personnel board "have discussed at length issues relating to the satisfactions, dissatisfactions, interpersonal relationships, and individual growth opportunities of priests in the Hartford archdiocese."

"After extended study and consultation," the Archbishop said, "the board reached the conclusion that only through a comprehensive research program could meaningful answers be found for the problems mentioned above."

The results of the study will be "helpful to me in the assignment of priests to the greater advantage of all concerned," he added.

The study will get underway shortly.

Within a few weeks a random sample of priests to participate in interviews will be contacted, followed by the compiling of a questionnaire to which all priests of the archdiocese will be asked to respond, the Archbishop said.

Professors Hall and Schneider will work in collaboration with Chris Argyris, Beach Professor and chairman of the Department of Administrative Sciences at Yale.

According to the proposal for the study, research will center on individual priests' responses to problems such as: (1) enthusiasm for, and satisfaction with present work; (2) the extent to which the priest feels he is using and developing important skills and competencies; (3) the level of esteem which he feels he receives from his peers, superiors, parishioners and the esteem with which he regards himself; and, (4) the relationship between his own needs for utilizing his most preferred capabilities and the demands of his assignment.

These factors will be used as criteria for individual growth and organizational effectiveness, and the purpose of the research is to explore factors which may influence this growth.

The outcome of the meetings between the personnel board and the research team was a proposal designed to study the work career of the priest. It was a combination proposal, a combination of (a) the needs of the host organization for information concerning its patterns and procedures vis-a-vis its professionals and (b) the needs of the research team for a setting to test some conceptions regarding the impact of personal and organizational characteristics on individual growth and organizational commitment. Although data from the interviews was to orient some of the specific aspects of the research to answer questions not raised in the original proposal, the basic purpose of the research was to remain unchanged.

The Collection of Data

The data collection procedures employed in social science research are often overlooked by the results-oriented layman. This is unfortunate because one of the most important contributions social science research has to make to society is its methodological approach to obtaining information. The difference between the journalist and the behavioral scientist is not in what they describe but how they describe it.

In our attempt to obtain reliable information we utilized three data gathering procedures: individual interviews, questionnaires, and constant liaison with the board members.

The Individual Interviews

We conducted the interviews for three reasons. The most important immediate need that was served by the interviews was to obtain specific information on the various issues outlined in the proposal. This was required for the development of a questionnaire to assess the opinions, attitudes, and feelings of the total diocese. The second purpose of the interviews was their obvious value as data, for they would be a source of information about the work life of priests that is not obtainable through the questionnaire. Thus the expressions and feelings of the recorded interview are difficult if not impossible to capture on the questionnaire.

The third use to which the interviews were put was their use as quotes to serve as summary integrative statements of statistical analyses. Thus we have presented quotes from the interviews that exemplify what the data analyzed at a more formal level are suggesting.

The Interview Sample. Ninety-five priests were randomly selected to be interviewed. The sample was accomplished by selecting every sixth name in the diocesan directory. This procedure results in a very close approximation to the number of pastors, curates, and specials in the diocese, but since the number of specials resulting was less than 20 (a minimum we had established), the names of special assignment personnel were drawn until a sample of 20 was obtained. The final interview sample contained 35 pastors, 40 curates, and 20 specials. All priests were contacted by telephone and asked if they had received the summary of the proposal and the covering letter from the bishop. They were told that they had been randomly chosen to participate in the interview phase of the research and asked if they could come to Yale for the interview. We called a total of 103 priests to obtain the 95 interviews; there were 8 refusals; some were due to illness, and others simply refused. There was no pressure applied to any individual. The bishop had explained in his letter to the priests that participation in the project was on a voluntary basis. Each priest was informed that the interview was to be for approximately 1½ hours. In addition, since a priest from the diocese was also conducting interviews, the interviewee was asked if he had a preference for being interviewed by one of the research team members or by the priest.

The Interview Schedule. Although the basic outline of the research project was fixed in the original proposal, the design of the questions to be asked and the order in which to ask them had to be accomplished. With the consultation of the personnel board and the priest who assisted us with the interviews, the interview schedule was prepared.

In the outline of the interview which follows, one can note the first steps in a process of carefully defining the concepts to be researched. The sections of the semistructured interview were as follows:

1. General introduction to the study. This involved a restatement of the research proposal summary, how the interviewee was selected, and an emphasis on the interviewee's perceptions of himself as a member of the archdiocese. Since an attempt was made to tape-record all interviews, considerable time was spent informing the interviewee about the confidentiality of the tapes and the fact that, during the session, the tape was to be under his complete control; he could turn it off at any point in the interview session. Two people did not want their interviews taped, and four asked to have it turned off one or more times during the interview. No one who began the interview with the tape recorder on asked to have it turned off permanently once the interview had started. In one case the tape recorder failed to operate. Therefore, our final taped interview sample consisted of 92 priests—39 curates, 33 pastors, and 20 specials.

2. Present assignment. The idea of including this as the first substantive area of investigation was to allow the interviewee to review the current aspects of his role as priest. We began with descriptions of the current assignment on such variables as the size of the parish or hospital or school, geographical location, socioeconomics of the area, etc., and then asked such questions as how long he had been ordained, how many assignments he had had since ordination, and what he did on a typical day.

After these introductory questions, the priest was asked what makes a good or bad day, in what aspects of his work he feels most competent, how much of an opportunity he has on his present assignment to develop new skills and abilities, and to what extent he has control over his present work activities—to add challenge to his assignment, to add new elements to his assignment—and whether or not there is another type of assignment that would be more in keeping with his important skills and abilities.

3. Relationships with others. As indicated in Chapter Two, one of the issues which seemed of concern to studies accomplished on priests and other clergymen was the relationship between pastor and assistant. In this section of the interview we were attempting to obtain descriptions of the interviewee and the way he related to his superior (subordinate), fellow priests of different age groups, and parishioners. More specifically, questions were directed to the openness and trust felt with various salient others, what the interviewee felt these others expected of him in his role as priest, and how these expectations fit with his own expectations of himself. Another major segment was directed at ascertaining how the interviewee saw himself and his subordinate (superior) responding to conflict and the use of authority.

4. Relationships with the system. This section of the interview was differentiated from the previous portion by the focus of the relationship; concern here was with the hierarchy, the chancery, the diocese, and the bishop rather than priests and parishioners as individuals. We introduced this concept with the following: "In addition to the interpersonal relationships you have in being a priest, there are numerous other relationships that exist—one important one most probably is the way you relate to the diocese as a whole." Questions concerning the perceived amount of influence over the hierarchy of the diocese, views of the hierarchical structure of the diocese, the receptivity and openness of the diocese to change, and their opinions regarding the way assignments were made were all issues to which responses were sought.

5. Background review—self and role. The next to the last section of the questionnaire reviewed with the interviewee issues surrounding his family background, decision to become a priest, expectations of the priesthood, and a detailed exploration of the first assignment. Thus the two assignments which received the greatest attention in the interview (and later in the questionnaire) were the first and present assignment.

6. The life line. In the last portion of the interview the interviewee was presented with a sheet of paper on which appeared a horizontal line and the following directions:

We want to learn what are the significant events and stages in a priest's life history. Could you think of the line below as representing your perceptions of your past, present and future life experiences? As you think about these life experiences, please illustrate these perceptions for us by subdividing and labelling this line with what you perceive are important STAGES and TURNING POINTS. Below are some definitions of terms:

STAGE is a state of relatively stable, continuous and related events (styles of behavior) bounded by turning points.

TURNING POINTS are critical experiences (thoughts, actions of self or others, etc.) which are associated with important personal changes (i.e., in the ways one views the world and oneself).

The Questionnaire

The questionnaire was a further attempt to operationalize the concepts of the research so that the hypotheses might be tested.

The need for a questionnaire in order to define one's concepts is not always obvious, and the necessity of conducting the interview prior to the construction of the questionnaire is not always clear. It is conceivable that with the data analysis techniques now available for summarizing the content of an interview, the questionnaire was not necessary. There were, however, two reasons for deciding to use the questionnaire: (a) The personnel board and the research team both felt that the maximum number of priests should participate in the data collection so that recommendations forthcoming from the personnel board as a result of the research would be associated with information provided by the maximum number of people; and (b) the questionnaire lends itself to more rapid and reliable scoring procedures than does the interview. These two reasons, maximum coverage and economy, suggest the use of the questionnaire. It is useful to note that most survey research techniques employ a sample of respondents when utilizing a questionnaire. It was our opinion that the questionnaire should not be sent out to only a sample because of the future intended use of the research results.[9]

This philosophy, underlying our research procedures, was extended to requesting the board's participation in constructing the questionnaire. While the interview served as a source of priest career-specific items for development of data to test our hypotheses, the board provided valuable assistance in insuring use of appropriate terminology, in evaluating the content or face validity of the questionnaire, and in seeing that questions for which they desired specific answers were included in the questionnaire. In both interview schedule development and questionnaire design the liaison gave the research team a sense of "being on top of it"—able to communicate to the larger diocese our purposes, our desires, and our enthusiasm for the research.

---

[9]In later chapters we examine the extent to which content analyses of the interviews are related to the questionnaire responses for the same people. We show, in Campbell's & Fiske's (1959) terminology, both convergent and discriminant validity.

The questionnaire was mailed to each nonretired diocesan priest listed in the diocesan directory, for a total mailing of approximately 550. Of this total we actually received back 373 questionnaires which we were able to process, and this number constitutes the questionnaire sample size. In addition to these usable questionnaires, however, there were additional responses to the mailing. In this category of respondents were priests who wrote or called and explained why they were not going to complete the questionnaire (8 priests), priests who had left the priesthood and never received the questionnaire (2 priests), priests who had passed away after the printing of the directory (5 priests), and miscellaneous returns (three questionnaires). Thus of the total mailing of 550 we had some form of response from 391 priests, or 71%. The questionnaire data to be reported on in the remainder of this book are based on a maximum sample of 120 pastors, 198 curates, and 55 priests on special assignment. We say "maximum" because for some sections of the questionnaire not all priests responded.[10]

The questionnaire was accompanied by a letter from the research team and a return envelope. Each respondent was asked to put his name on the questionnaire. Of all the respondents only one failed to do this. We have no way of estimating the effect the request for names had on the response rate, but our experience with other research studies suggests it has little, if any, impact. The names were required to establish the relationships between questionnaire and interview data and in addition they allowed for future follow-up studies.

The final questionnaire (reproduced in Appendix A) was 32 pages long and contained questions ranging in content from the initial decision to enter the priesthood through rather complete descriptions of the present assignment to opinions about what the goals of the Roman Catholic Church should be. These stimuli to which the priest responded were presented in a number of different formats, ranging from the essay, open-ended question ("What do you feel the goals of the Roman Catholic Church should be?"; "In a meeting, an effective leader is one who . . .") through check lists of items ("How much of each of the following list of activities do you do?") to items responded to on a descriptive scale ("To what extent do you feel you are utilizing your important skills and abilities in your present assignment?").

5	4	3	2	1
a great deal	fairly much	to some degree	comparatively little	not at all

[10]All statistical analyses were accomplished with computer programs which account for missing data. For all analyses we present the sample size on which the results are based. For all tests of statistical significance we have adjusted for differences in sample size.

Each section of the questionnaire was designed with the purpose of obtaining many responses to specific aspects of the priest's work world: his work activities, his physical and psychological work environment, how he sees himself as a person interacting with relevant others, his work satisfactions, work and interpersonal values, and how he perceives what the goals of his organization are and should be. The details of each section of the questionnaire will be presented with the relevant data. However, prior to describing techniques utilized in summarizing the data that were collected, we want to describe our procedure for comparing priests' work experiences with work experiences of other men.

Our operational definition of work satisfaction is one component of a measure of job satisfaction, the Job Descriptive Index (JDI), developed by Smith, Kendall & Hulin (1969). The basic philosophy underlying this unique research endeavor was similar to the conception we are stating in this chapter: "Theory cannot be tested fairly, nor modified and improved, until its concepts can be measured adequately" (p. 1). The goal of their study was ". . . to study the laws relating situations, personal characteristics, and policies, to satisfactions and behaviors" (p. 3). The communality between the philosophy underlying the development of the JDI and the current research seemed to make this measure very desirable as an operationalization of work satisfaction.

In addition to the similarity in goals, a second most valuable aspect of the JDI was the careful and precise research that went into its development. The research took place over a period of 10 years, and national norms are available against which priests could be compared; the data from our study were compared to the scores of some 2500 men (professional and men in general) from 21 organizations throughout the United States. These norm groups permit comparisons of priests with other working men on five aspects of job satisfaction: work, pay, promotion, supervision, and co-workers.

Obviously, other kinds of comparisons may be accomplished with this instrument and with the other measures we developed. One possibility is to compare pastors, curates, and specials on these measures and see where differences and similarities exist. A second procedure might be to look at how curates change over time; one may question if across curates as a group there are noteworthy differences which can be attributed to tenure as a priest. In this latter type of analysis we will speak of these data *as if* they were longitudinal.

The former kind of analysis, comparing pastors, curates, and specials, constitutes the major reason for our enthusiasm in testing the theory of organizational careers on priests. From a research standpoint, this archdiocese was a living laboratory in which we could explore the effects of different treatments on the subjects. While a source of consternation to the priests in the system, the differences between these three work roles were dramatic. While these facts will become clearer as data are brought to bear on how these positions differ, it is sufficient to indicate at this point that *the professional specialists as a group tend to have the conditions necessary for psychological success, while assistant pastors as a group have conditions for psychological failure.* Exactly what these conditions are and what follows from these conditions constitute the subject of our book.

Making Use of the Collected Data

During the year-long project a large amount of data were collected on each priest and thus the entire diocese. For each interviewed priest there was at least a 1½-hour tape to be transcribed, coded, and summarized. For each questionnaire we eventually had 23 punch cards of data, ranging from raw item responses to factor scores. The question is raised: What does a researcher do with all of this information? In reality this is three questions: (1) How does the researcher summarize and make manageable the information available?; (2) How does he interpret the summarized data?; and (3) How does he prepare the organization so that it can make maximum use of the data he provides? In this chapter we discuss points (1) and (2); Chapter Nine discusses point (3).

Summarizing the Information

We employed two analytic techniques—content analysis and factor analysis—in bringing our data to manageable form. Once in this form, the data were treated both in terms of group averages (by position or tenure in the organization) and by correlations both within and across these groups. The results of content and factor analyses of the questionnaire respondents were analyzed together, and data were coordinated for the 72 priests for whom we had both taped interviews and questionnaires. Some hypotheses were tested only with questionnaire data, some with only interview data, and others with a combination of both.

The use of factor analysis in a piece of research, especially one in which it is used as much as the current study, presupposes a theory of behavior which has multiple variables as causative agents. Thus even one factor out of all the factors to be generated in this research has many components. It is true that our conception of behavior attributes cause both to the person and the environment in which he finds himself;

we have a multidimensional view of cause and effect of individual behavior in organizational settings. Kaplan (1964, p. 158), in his delightful and informative book on research philosophy and method in the behavioral sciences, tells the following story:

> A famous set of experiments was once carried out to determine what produced ovulation in the rabbit. One after another a series of possible causative agents was eliminated—various hormones nerve impulses, and so on—and still the rabbit ovulated, till at last it was recognized that when one source of stimulation is blocked others become more effective. The rabbit, if I may say so, does not put all her eggs in one basket, and the experimenter would be well to follow her example.

Our philosophy in conducting the research has utilized this insight in many ways. First, we have collected data through many different methods. Second, the data collected exist at a number of different levels of behavior; they range from the very specific ("How many other curates are there in your rectory?") to the global generalization ("To what extent do you feel you are using your important skills and abilities in your present assignment?"). Recently, Schneider (1973) has shown the merits of moving systematically from a specific to a general sense when examining people's work worlds. In Chapter Ten we will use this form of analysis to test the general model of psychological success.

In addition to the questionnaire and interview, we have made use of our notes and the minutes of the personnel board in our discussion of the similarities between group and individual development. As Webb, Campbell, Schwartz, & Sechrest (1966) have noted, there are clearly a number of sources of data on which one may draw for social science research. Indeed, the directory of the diocese also proved invaluable when we required information about turnover in the diocese.

At each relevant point in the chapters which follow, information specific to the use of these data will be presented, including checks on reliability of coding, internal consistency of factor scale scores, etc. At this point a general comment is in order regarding the development of the factors on which scale scores were subsequently obtained.

For most of our use of factor analysis, we were attempting to develop clusters of items which tapped some theoretical construct represented in the psychological success model. In this sense we used factor analysis to test hypotheses about the existence of constructs (Nunnally, 1967). There is a dilemma, however, in testing for the existence of constructs through factor analysis and then using these constructs as scale scores to test the theory. On the one hand, the items making up the factor were written to factor in a particular way. On the other hand, to go back and develop factor scores based on the same people used for testing one hypothesis would be taking advantage of any chance variation in the original factor scores and might result in a nonrepresentative view of true factor structure.

To compensate for this possibility of capitalizing on chance variation, a split-sample procedure was employed. All factor analyses were accomplished on a subsample of 97 priests. The factors were rotated by the Varimax procedure and, using an approximation of the criterion of simple structure, the items to be scored for the various factors were chosen. The remainder of the sample was then scored (unit weights) according to the factors developed in the subsample. Internal consistency estimates and scale intercorrelations suggested good fits between the results for both samples. For final factor scores, the total sample was submitted to an analysis based on the first subsample results.[11]

Interpreting the Data

The essence of data collection and summarizing is to allow the research scientist to understand more completely his initial problem, to examine the information collected as it relates to his initial questions. As with data collection and data summarizing, we used a number of techniques to aid us in interpreting our information. First, we had a theoretical framework, the impact of personal and situational characteristics on experiences of psychological success, to guide our interpretation. This was aided by the statement of original hypotheses. Second, we had a number of tools at our disposal, statistical and clinical in nature, which were employed as tests of the adequacy of our hypotheses and thus the usefulness of our interpretations.

There are a number of ways in which one may view the interpretations of data in the light of hypothesis testing. Confirmation or disconfirmation is but the first step in interpretation. Examination of the data with which hypotheses are tested may yield insights into the general problem under investigation that were not thought of prior to initial analyses. Thus the discovery of new hypotheses, the establishment of relationships not considered earlier, form a second part of data interpretation. For both these conditions statistical tests of significance in combination with the feelings, descriptions, and emotions expressed by the priest interviewees are utilized. The reader is reminded that the form

---

[11]In the data chapters we will present estimates of the internal consistency of the various scales we developed through factor analysis. These estimates were obtained by applying the factors developed on the sample of 97 to the remainder of the sample; the internal consistency estimates are thus not contaminated by being developed on the factor sample.

of the questions in the questionnaire was dictated largely by impressions gathered through the interviews. In a number of ways, then, the questionnaire was employed as a validation of impressions gathered in the interviews. The use of interview passages to support statistical tests of significance gives the reader a deeper sense of some of the processual or dynamic issues the questionnaire "picks at." In addition, our use of data presentation by group averages in different tenure groups will help support the concept of a dynamic, unfolding career. This procedure of supporting interview data by questionnaire and vice versa is viewed by social scientists as a condition made necessary by our relatively imperfect measurement techniques. Campbell & Fiske (1959) give a complete discussion of these points, stressing the increased faith one may place in similar findings gathered through a number of different methodological procedures. Using multiple methods also increases the understandability of statistical tests of significance; for confirmation of a finding in essentially the same way, a statistical test of significance attests to reliability.

In summary, then, our strategy was to involve the archdiocese in the research both through contacts with the personnel board and by having one of the priests help us with a third of the interviews. In Chapter Nine we detail the results of this collaboration between the board and the research team. Our second strategy was an attempt to converge, by the utilization of multiple methods and levels of data, on the important concepts necessary to test for the correlates of psychological success in organizations.

FOUR
Personal Styles and Values
of the Diocesan Priest

To begin the picture of the priest's career in the diocese studied, it seems appropriate to present the priest as a person. In this chapter we will focus on the personal characteristics of the priest, while in the following chapters we will deal in turn with the remaining three facets of the priestly career experience—work characteristics, career outcomes, and role transitions.

Family Background

Since we were primarily interested in personal qualities which would be related to work and career outcomes, we did not assess many aspects of the family background of our sample. As suggested in Chapter Two, the "priest personality" approach has prevailed, not been useful in discriminating more successful from less successful priests, and yields little information of use to organizations which wish to attack system-wide problems.

One set of data we did collect in an attempt to locate our priests in relation to other samples concerned the priest's place in his family—we wanted to know about family size. The average number of children in the family of our sample is 4.26, a figure which is the same as Fichter (1961) has reported. The pastors in our sample come from larger families (average number equals 5.26) than the younger specials (3.56) and curates (3.82). These data suggest that an average for the diocese as a whole is not meaningful; we will note this many times in the book.

More specifically, we do not find very much overlap in birth-order data between any of our three groups and the Potvin & Suziedelis data. The reasons for this may be numerous, but we assume that the major reason is the wide geographical distribution from which they drew their sample as compared to the restricted sample—a single diocese in the northeastern United States—for which we present data. Of particular interest may be the fact that the pastors, of all the groups, seem to be distributed more like the normative data sample of Potvin & Suziedelis than either of our younger samples. We have no explanation for these findings.[13]

Concerning the climate of family relationships, we must rely upon the findings of other studies since no data were obtained on this subject in the present study. However, the available data indicate that the mother of the priest tends to be rather strict and relatively dominant, the father is relatively nondominant, and the priest as a boy tends to experience a closer relationship with the mother than with the father (Neal, 1965; Potvin & Suziedelis, 1969).

The Decision To Become a Priest

The choice of one's occupational career is an important decision. The time and manner of making this career decision can be important factors in determining how satisfied and effective a person will be in his life's work. A career selection made at too early an age or one made too much in response to the influences of other people, being an immature choice, may result in low internal commitment to work. The outcome of this low commitment could be psychological failure in the career or a later switch to a different occupation. As Caplow (1954, p. 217) puts it, "In general, the earlier a choice must be made, the less equitable will be the eventual distribution of function and the less connection will there be between the individual's own interests and the occupational role chosen for him."

[13]Analyses of birth-order data in the psychological literature have yielded inconclusive data. We did not pursue our own data regarding birth order.

An approximate gauge for measuring the maturity of a career choice is found in the three phases of career decision making formulated by Eli Ginzberg and associates (1951). A period of *fantasy* choices extends from perhaps 4 or 5 to age 11, followed by a phase of *tentative* choices up to age 17. Beyond 17 the period of *realistic* choices occurs. This theory would suggest that a final career choice made substantially earlier than late high school or early college would more probably be an immature decision.[14]

In our questionnaire, priests were asked the following question, "Please state briefly how and when you decided to enter the priesthood." Of the 325 priests responding to this question, 23 reported that they had wanted to be a priest as far back as they could remember—for them, in effect, no conscious decision was ever made. Another 28 decided in childhood, before the age of 10. In all, a total of 125, over a third of the respondents, had made a definite decision to enter the priesthood by the end of grammar school. Another third (120 men) made this choice in high school. Seventy-seven people made the decision after high school.

It appears, then, that over one-third of the priests responding to this question made a life-long career commitment prior to what Ginsberg has called the *realistic* age for decision. This young age at the time of choosing, coupled with the unusually high commitment required of a priest, raises questions about how much mature thought enters into the decision to become a priest.

These age data appear to differ from those found by other researchers. Potvin & Suziedelis (1969) report that approximately 60% of the theology seminarians they sampled claimed to have made their final decisions after high school. This figure is substantially higher than the post-high-school percentage in our data (24%). The difference may be due in part to the differences in recollection of seminarians and priests. Fichter (1968) reports an average decision age of 17, which falls somewhere between our data, where the mode occurs in the high school years, and the Potvin & Suziedelis (1969) figures, with a post-high-school mode.

However, even Potvin & Suziedelis report that 24.1% of their seminarians chose the priesthood in grammar school or earlier. Fichter reports a figure of 20% for grammar school choice. Therefore, even using the most conservative data, there still appear to be a substantial proportion of priests making important and difficult career choices dur-

---

[14]It is interesting to note that a young man who enters the major seminary upon completing college or later is called a "delayed vocation." We found this term representing for us the continued attempt by the church to obtain early commitment.

ing the years more generally spent fantasizing about a wide range of careers.

In response to the second part of the question, "why you entered the priesthood," there were three major categories of response: *influence of others, desire to serve others,* and *personal spiritual concerns.*

Of the people responding to this question, by far the most frequently cited factors (248 cases) involved the influence of others, generally the clergy and other Church influences. Factors involving one's own reasons, either the desire to serve others or one's own spiritual growth, account for only 48 and 33 cases, respectively. Thus the ratio of choices made on the basis of one's own reasons to choices influenced by others is 81 to 248, roughly, 1 : 3. For approximately 75% of the priests surveyed, the decision to enter the priesthood appears to have been more passive than active.

Values

Having considered the career decision-making style of the priest, we turn to a consideration of personal, organizationally relevant characteristics: interpersonal, organizational, and task values. All three are characteristics which the priest brings with him to his priesthood but which, because of their nature, are also amenable to change as a result of individual or organizational impacts. Since there is a large general interpersonal component to the parish priests' work life, we turn to this value first.

Interpersonal Values

To measure interpersonal values, we used a sentence-completion instrument developed by Argyris (1965). The respondent is asked to provide his own conclusion to five incomplete sentences, and then his responses are coded in terms of summarizing categories.

The largest difference in response between pastors, curates, and specials occurred on the first sentence, "The effective leader is one who . . . ." The most frequent *pastor response* (34%) was a form of *unshared control* (directing, leading, controlling, inspiring, persuading). The most frequent *curate response* (40%) favored *semishared control,* in which the leader would generate a full group discussion, listen, integrate ideas, and weigh all opinions, but then make the decision himself. Among the *specials*, however, there was a shift toward *fully shared control* (42%), in which the leader creates an atmosphere for uninhibited discussion and helps the group make its own decision.

Like many other findings to be reported in this book, these data show that one strong source of difference among the three types of priests lies along the dimension of authority, as demonstrated by the finding that pastors tend to value unshared authority, curates value semishared authority, and specials are more likely to favor shared authority.

The only other dimension in which differences between groups occur concerns the issue of trust (question 2). The modal response for both pastors (60%) and curates (56%), when asked how trust can be assessed, was that trust is indicated by members' cooperation and willingness to listen to each other. Many of the curates (37%), however, and the majority of the specials (59%), felt that a willingness to be frank and open was the best measure. Thus curates and specials seem to value the open expression of views as a measure of trust more than pastors.[15]

Our results indicate that the interpersonal values of this diocese favor *rationality* and the *suppression of emotions*, a condition Argyris finds related to low interpersonal competence and low opportunities for personal growth. These data fit with the interview responses, indicating that priests tend to suppress interpersonal conflict in the rectory. This suppression continues to the point where one or more parties lose control, vent their angers incompetently, and then "forget the whole thing" later. Open discussion of negative feelings, before they reach the "explosion" point, seems to be a rarity.

Given the tendency to suppress direct expressions of interpersonal conflict, it is not surprising that conflicts in the rectory are a widespread phenomenon and that they are dealt with in a covert manner. Specifically, interpersonal tensions are often acted out in the form of *games*. One such game is ignoring conflict when both parties know it exists. In the words of one assistant pastor,

> I do admit that I do like him as a person. However, when you have to . . . fight with the man, and then sit down at [the dinner table] and play games all over again, saying nothing happened–'No, you didn't insult me, and I didn't tell you off, so let's, you know, make believe now that we are happy, we're one big happy family.' Well, that's a lot of nonsense.

Another type of covert game is communicating through behaviors rather than confronting issues and fellow priests directly. This indirect communication is often unsuccessful, as was the experience of one pastor:

[15]The other incomplete sentences to which responses were obtained, but for which no differences existed, were: "The most effective members tend to . . ."; "When disagreement erupts into personal antagonisms and hostile feelings, the best thing for a leader to do is . . ."; and "In your experience the most serious blocks to group progress in a meeting are . . . ."

> There hasn't been any open disagreement [with my curate]. . . . A month ago I was about to take over the care of what we would call the altar boys because they are *really* getting away with murder. And yet he has been with them maybe [pause], perhaps he's been with them too long. They *are* careless as to the cassock, the black dress, and surplice. I just sometimes go into the sacristy and I say, 'Oh, dear, that pile.' And I, by my own example, I thought maybe I could correct all of that by my removing them, putting them down in the cellar where they have to come looking for them—or he would.

Other games consist of the curate's manipulation of the pastor through diplomacy, secrecy, threat, or covert disobedience. The pastor's games include secretly gathering information about the curate behind his back, criticizing him and spreading rumors among the laity and fellow pastors, monitoring his behavior closely under the guise of concern for him, and giving him great autonomy and little advice so that he has enough rope to hang himself.

Given the severity of some of the conflicts and the need to keep them "bottled up" inside, it is not surprising that serious personal emotional problems occasionally develop:

> In my second appointment there was a terrible cropping up of jealousy [with the pastor]. . . . I mean, I'm not putting the blame on him, I'm just saying that my demonstration of living evidently grated on him, and, oh, he would subject me to severe criticism, even publicly. Now you can't blame anyone for becoming involved with liquor or any other vice. But, humanly speaking, I was a bit disappointed. From there on, of course, I just became involved.

Not only did this priest keep his feelings from the pastor, but he also would not even acknowledge the hostility to himself. Even his way of speaking indicate a sense of detachment from himself: "my demonstration of living grated on him," rather than "I grated on him," or (even more threatening) "we grated on each other;" and "I just became involved," rather than "I began to drink." This account is reminiscent of Bettelheim's (1958) account of concentration camp inmates who defend against anxiety by distancing themselves from the situation and ceasing to see themselves as responsible for their actions.

These actual descriptions of some possible consequences of suppressing interpersonal problems seem to be reflected in the agreement across the three groups on the most serious blocks to group progress: interpersonal incompetence, inability to listen, defensiveness, taking extreme positions, lack of trust, etc. Weak leadership was seen as another big problem—again, the authority issue. The third-ranked problem was in another category unique to the diocese: individual prominence-seeking and selfishness. This system seems more concerned about pride and individual prominence as negative qualities than most other types of organizations.

When one considers that a parish priest in an assignment with another priest eats three meals per day, sleeps, works, and watches television in the same house with that man, there are a great number of interpersonal problems which may arise. In addition to the problems which may arise, there are different value systems regarding the resolution of interpersonal problems. This seems to be a potent climate for friction. Consider the pastor–curate relationship in which the curate must, legally, follow the pastor's requirements in all ways, including work. If the pastor's ideas of what work is important are different from those of the curate, another source of friction may exist.

Task Values

We hypothesized in Chapter One that, given appropriate conditions of work, a man had a higher probability of experiencing psychological success than someone without the necessary conditions. We also suggested that part of the burden for achieving psychological success rested on the individual worker who had to stretch himself, to reach out to the environment and work for the experience. For this reason we were interested in exactly what kinds of work different priests do value and what kinds of work they do.

In our interviews (with the 95 priests) we accomplished some preliminary identification of the specific activities priests do in their work, things like saying mass, visiting the sick, supervising lay employees, etc. For the questionnaire we put together a list of 35 such activities and asked priests to "indicate (1) the amount of each activity you perform and (2) how important it is to you that you perform the activity." The defining characteristics of the scale were "above average," "average," and "below average." These items were submitted to a principal components factor analysis and rotated by the Varimax procedure (Kaiser, 1958) on a sample of 97 priests and then replicated on the remainder of the sample. A four-factor solution accounting for 42% of the variance was most interpretable and resulted in keeping 27 items which met an approximation of the simple structure criterion (see Chapter Three). The first types of activities identified in this fashion are: *parochial* duties, which are the standard church-related activities such as saying mass in church,[16]

[16]It is interesting that "saying mass" did not load on any factor, but the personnel board could not understand how we could have a "parochial activity" factor without "saying mass." The reason it did not load on any factor is that all priests see it as being of about the same importance. Since this particular item has no variability, it cannot correlate with any other item. We have retained it to give the factor more content or face validity.

performing marriages, baptisms, funerals, etc. A second cluster consisted of *administrative* activities, which involve maintaining or developing the organizational apparatus of the parish—supervision, fund raising, school administration, etc. The third important group of duties entail *community involvement*, performing various types of priestly functions outside of the formal church setting, taking them into homes and other community settings. A fourth type of activity consisted of *personal development*—improving one's personal capacities and knowledge. A complete list of the components of the four types of activities is shown in Table 4.1, with

TABLE 4.1

*Components of Four Factors of Priest Activities
with Scale Intercorrelations for Importance of Activities* [a]

1. Parochial	3. Community involvement
Saying mass in church	Ecumenical work
Marriages	Community meetings
Baptisms	Inner-city work
Funerals	Attending workshops and conferences
Religious instructions	Saying mass in homes
Teaching (nonreligion) courses in school (reverse scored)	Home visitation
Visiting the sick	Being on call outside the rectory
Parish organization meetings	Motivating the laity to become more active Catholics
Nonmarriage counseling	
Hearing confessions	
Being on duty in the rectory	
2. Administration	**4. Personal development**
Supervising lay employees	Reading
Parish administration	Private prayer
School administration	Preparation for duties
Raising funds	Training (self-improvement)
Administering diocesan affairs	
Supervising priests and/or sisters	

	1	2	3	4
1. Parochial	(61)			
2. Administration	23	(82)		
3. Community involvement	26	−01	(74)	
4. Personal development	28	−07	34	(65)

[a] Same factors and components are used for the amount of activities (see Chapter Six). Figures in parentheses are item-item correlations within the factor corrected by the Spearman–Brown prophecy formula (Ghiselli, 1964) to give an estimate of internal consistency. The intercorrelations presented are representative of those for each of the three positions, even though they were calculated on the total sample.

their intercorrelations and scale internal consistencies. Priests were encouraged to write in types of activities other than those specified in the questionnaire and some did, but the nature of these activities varies greatly from one priest to another. (See Schneider & Hall, 1972, for a detailed account of the factor analysis of task activities and work climate.)

There is a relatively high degree of similarity in basic framework between Locke's (see 1968, 1970) position regarding the process by which an individual achieves goals he sets and our conception of psychological success through autonomous and challenging work. Locke (1970, p. 487) notes, "Success on a challenging task produces not only satisfaction but a feeling of increased competency or efficacy." Locke assumes, as we do, that this desire for increased competence is a basic value which "underlies and causes the desire for success on particular tasks." Our task values are an attempt to specify which of the tasks priests value in this movement toward a sense of efficacy and competence.

The average importance attached to each type of activity is tabulated as follows:

| | | Average[a] | | |
Type of activity	All positions (N = 373)	Pastors (N = 120)	Curates (N = 198)	Specials (N = 55)
Parochial	2.27	2.32	2.29	2.11
Administration	1.75	2.15	1.53	1.65
Community involvement	2.18	2.07	2.24	2.22
Personal development	2.45	2.33	2.52	2.47

[a] Standard deviations are lowest for parochial ($\cong .25$) and about the same for the other three activities ($\cong .40$).

For the total sample, personal development is the most highly valued of the four activities, with parochial and community activities next. Administration ranks as the least desirable type of priestly function. Administration activity is also rated least desirable by Protestant ministers (Jud et al., 1970). When the sample is examined by position, important differences in task values appear. For curates and specials, the rank order of importance attached to the four functions is about the same as for the total sample, although for specials community involvement is number two while for curates parochial activities are second most important. Pastors rate administrative activities third and community activities least important. In fact, the most striking difference between the three positions is that pastors feel it is significantly more important for them to perform administrative activities than do curates or specials. Furthermore curates feel that community involvement and personal development are significantly more important to them than do pastors. These data summarize one of the central issues in the pastor–curate "generation gap": Pastors stress the importance of maintaining and expanding church structures, meeting financial obligations, and administering the parish effectively, while curates want to devote more time and energy to community development and their own personal growth. It is important to see, too, that they do not differ in the absolute importance attached to performing parochial duties; it is only on the relative importance of parochial vs. other functions that the two groups disagree.

In their agreement on the importance of performing parochial duties themselves, pastors and curates both differ significantly from priests in special assignments. This seems to be a natural consequence of the other duties which are the primary task of the special assignment.[17] This point requires elaboration. By the very nature of their assignment specials are specialists, devoting more time to, and perhaps seeing as more important, only one or two of the components which make up any one of the clusters of activities identified through our procedures. Thus under community involvement one of the activities is "inner-city work." A man on special assignment in a store-front parish may see this aspect of community involvement as very important but other components as far less important; his "score" on this factor would not be very high. A better example is the cluster of activities under administration. Here a school administrator may not feel it is important for him to do parish administration or raise funds; he may not appear to feel administration is important in our data. Given these limitations, we have chosen to retain our factors because of their parsimony and their meaningfulness to the majority of priests we studied.

Our procedure of assessing the importance of activities as well as the amount of activities performed allows us to examine the extent to which priests with different task values, but doing the same work, experience different amounts of challenge. Thus two priests doing the same thing may experience that task differently, depending upon whether they feel doing that task is important.

In addition, however, to the way valued activities interact with activities performed to result in particular outcomes, we may ask the question: Why do particular individuals value some activities and other people value different activities? What is the source of the valued activities? Although in the initial planning stage of this research we did not consider this question to be important, our subsequent data analyses and theoretical considerations resulted in a reevaluation of its role. Fortunately, we had collected information which could be used

[17]Only full-time special-assignment priests were included in this category.

for both our original purpose and as a secondary analysis to answer these questions. We called these sources of specific task values *organizational values*.

Organizational Values

The original purpose for collecting information on where priests see their organization going and where they think it should be going was to see if there are marked differences in perceptions and goals between younger and older priests. As the analyses proceeded, we began to view task values as a way for priests to implement their more global values. That is, if, as a priest, I want to see the Church become more involved with issues like racial tension or drug abuse, what are the kinds of tasks I value? Through what mechanisms do a person's goals for a total organization become translated into his behaviors to accomplish these goals? We think that this occurs by his translation of organizational-level goals into more specific action goals. One may think of this relationship as a distinction frequently made between personality and attitudes; attitudes are more specific orientations of the individual's more global or general personality. Smith, Bruner, & White (1960, p. 280) make the distinction between more global and inclusive personality and the more specific attitudes or opinions by referring to the deep dynamics of personality and the more externally oriented nature of opinions and attitudes. For our sample those aspects of a priest's orientation toward his role and career concern his values at the organizational level, while the aspect of the priest more in contact with the outside world are the tasks he feels are important for him to do. Thus task values are one component part of organizational values, that part most closely tied to action.

Because the topic of organizational goals and values was not a component of the interview, we could not assemble a series of specific items to which the priest could respond as we had done with the task values. We could have asked a number of different questions, but we chose the simple strategy of directly asking: "What would you say is (are) the most important goals(s) of the Roman Catholic Church today?" and "What would you say should be the most important goal(s) of the Roman Catholic Church?"

Once again, we constructed coding categories (shown in Table 4.2) based on the responses to the two questions, and it is by these categories that the results will be summarized. Sizable responses were recorded in only four of the eight categories we developed. The infrequently used categories were: the Church as a socialization agent, clergy growth, clergy involvement, and Vatican II and Church renewal. The four categories with sizable responses were called "Theological," "Existence," "Meaning and Relevance," and "Church and Society."

TABLE 4.2

Components of Four Categories of Church Goals

Major category 1. Theological	Major category 3. The Church: Meaning and
Bring Christ's teachings to all men (either generally or via such things as newspapers or missions)	relevance
	Find its real identity
	Become relevant to contemporary society
Help people *live* Christ's teachings — maintain and practice faith	Make religion meaningful
	Update, reform, become open; change
Salvation — administer sacraments	Church law; reform canon law
Love of God and man	Satisfaction of members
Fulfillment of man in *theological* sense	(Better) communication between clergy
Establish a Christian community	and laymen
	Active response of laity
	Solution on birth control
	Divorce, remarriage
Major category 2. The Church: Its existence	Major category 4. The Church and society
Maintain status quo	Social reforms — helping poor, oppressed;
Self-preservation, survival	civil rights
Financial and economic concerns	Bring peace, charity, justice, mercy to
Converts and growth in numbers	world (abstract rather than concrete)
Sustaining parochial school system	Rapport between Church and outsiders
Unity within system; a united front	(communication)
To govern, within the Church; in the religious world	Leadership in the secular and non-Catholic world; moral authority in the world

What Goals Are and What Goals Should Be

In all subsequent analyses regarding these goals we will use the number of responses per major category; each category is then just like a factor, and a score represents the frequency with which the priest mentioned the various goals coded into the category. Table 4.3 presents the average value scores for each of the four major categories.

Clearly, the most frequently mentioned goal area is the Theological category. The categories in which the greatest discrepancy occurs between what goals are and what goals should be are Meaning and Relevance and Church and Society. In both cases curates and specials think these goals should receive (significantly) more emphasis than is currently the case.

TABLE 4.3

*Average Response Rate to Organizational Goals
by Position with Scale Intercorrelations*[a]

	Mean scores					
	Goals are			Goals should be		
	P	C	S	P	C	S
1. Theological	1.05	.80	.85	.88	1.02	.82
2. Existence	.33	.74	.41	.17	.14	.05
3. Meaning and relevance	.16	.27	.21	.18	.51	.38
4. Church and society	.31	.18	.18	.38	.48	.41

Scale intercorrelations

	Goals are			
	1	2	3	4
1. Theological	(−)			
2. Existence	−15	(−)		
3. Meaning and relevance	−21	−09	(−)	
4. Church and society	04	−06	05	(−)

	Goals should be			
	A	B	C	D
A. Theological	(−)			
B. Existence	03	(−)		
C. Meaning and relevance	−19	−06	(−)	
D. Church and society	01	01	03	(−)

[a] Intercorrelations are for total sample of priests and are representative of the intercorrelations within each group. Decimals have been omitted. On a sample of questionnaires, four coders had an agreement rate of 82.5% on categorizing statements. The formula used for this calculation is given in Scott & Wertheimer (1962, pp. 194ff). It considers the degree of agreement between two coders corrected for the degree of agreement one would expect simply by chance.

To us the most interesting thing about these data was the *similarities* across the three groups as well as the differences. For Theological category goals there exists good agreement on "goals are" and "goals should be." All three groups agree on less emphasis on the Existence category and on more emphasis on the categories Meaning and Relevance and Church and Society.[18] It is clear, however, that curates see the greatest discrepancy between "are" and "should be."

Almost half of the curates (45%) felt the Church's goals are Existence oriented, while only one in eight (12%) indicated that this is what the

[18]These last two organizational goals seem similar to those Potvin & Suziedelis (1969) called the "Secular orientation."

goals should be. Simply stated, curates see the Church as currently having an emphasis on maintaining the status quo, being concerned with survival, finances, and presenting a united front, and they, like specials and pastors, do not think these things should be emphasized. Concerning the Church being meaningful and relevant, pastors would not make it more so, but over one-third of the curates think it should be. About one-fourth of the pastors already see the Church as being oriented toward society, while 18% of the specials and 16% of the curates would agree. Of these latter two groups approximately 40% think this is what the goals should be.

Relationships between Organizational Values and Task Values

In reality, perceptions of the current goals of the Church by priests are more an assessment of the Church than an index of the individual's values. However, what a priest thinks the goals of the Church *should be* is more an index of what the priest is than of what the Church is. The latter question is the one we consider in correlating the more global organizational values to the more specific task values.

These data suggest only minimal agreement between organizational values and task values. Only for priests on special assignment are there consistent and significant relationships. For this group, valuing community involvement tasks is negatively related to valuing Church existence ($r = -.34, p < .05$) and positively related to Church and Society values ($r = .27, p < .05$). In addition, for specials, valuing administration tasks is negatively related to feeling the Church should be moving toward Meaning and Relevance ($r = -.28, p < .05$). The most consistent finding across all groups is that the importance assigned to community-involvement activities is more highly related to organizational values than are any other task values. This consistency is reflected in the data for the total sample, where the importance of community activities is significantly correlated with both Meaning and Relevance ($r = .12, p < .01$) and church and society ($r = .17, p < .01$).

Generation Gap in the Priesthood

The data from the interviews and the material presented in this chapter suggest the existence of a strong generation gap in the priesthood. Value differences seem to lie at the heart of the split. Younger priests, the "new breed," stress the importance of shared authority, open communication, community involvement, personal development, meaning and relevance for the Church, and a closer link between the Church and the problems of contemporary society. This seems to reflect a concern for the horizontal or secular aspects of the priestly role.

Older priests, however, place more stress on obedience to authority, both divine and organizational. They also place more stress on commitment to administration and maintenance of the church organization than do curates, and they have more faith that the church already is putting its theological and social goals into action. Because these values are related to age, this split is popularly called a generation gap. However, as we will show in later chapters, the differences within the group of young priests are almost as great as the gap between young and old. It is probably more accurate to refer to a value gap than a generation gap.

Life Styles and Values

The picture we form of the personal styles of the priests we studied is one of dependence on others, deference to authority, and lack of concern for self. The manifestation of this dependence is reflected in our data regarding career choices and the kinds of interpersonal values pastors and curates hold. The source of data on deference to authority is also the interpersonal value data. This lack of concern for self fits well with the Church's views against "pride" and "ambition."

We recall, in this context, resistance from older priests to the idea that we were studying careers of priests, looking at priests as professionals. To these men, the priesthood was a call to obedience, to be a Christ figure; it was in *no way* comparable to careers of people in the secular world. Thus a style of duty and obedience, first to family and then to the Church, seems somewhat characteristic of the older priests in our sample.

This style variable seems to carry over somewhat into other kinds of interpersonal styles priests value. Generally speaking, they see effective leaders being nonemotional, rational, and not very collaborative. They are more concerned about prominence seeking (and more likely to devalue it) than are other samples of professionals—again, the ambition or self-orientation issue. It will be interesting in later discussions to explore how interpersonal issues are related to interpersonal perceptions —the perceptions of others' interpersonal style as in superior–subordinate relationships.

The community-oriented task values are most related to the global concepts of long-term goals for the Church as a whole. Younger men are broader in the goals they feel the Church should be reaching for; the differences between younger and older priests seem to involve more a question of breadth than of depth. Younger priests see more awareness of relevant priestly work as requiring their attention than do older priests. Pastors, as older priests, are more concerned with administration than in branching out into new areas of concern.

In subsequent chapters, the way these styles and values are related to the work actually performed and the work conditions actually perceived will be examined. First, however, we will examine the nature and climate of the work priests do.

FIVE
The Nature and Climate of the Priest's Work

Priest Activities

In the individual interviews we asked priests to describe what they did in a typical day, from start to finish. We encouraged them to be specific about actual behaviors and suggested that they "replay" the events of the previous day as an example.

Priestly Work: A Typical Day

After a few interviews it quickly became apparent that the work of a pastor is significantly different—in nature and in degree—from what his assistants do. And the tasks of both parish priests (pastor and curate) are unlike those of a priest in a full-time special assignment. In this sense, then, there is no such thing as "the work" of " the priest." At best, we can only speak of the work of the pastor, the work of the curate, and the work of the specialist.

67

With this distinction in mind, we will discuss separate "typical days" for priests in each type of assignment. Let us start with the pastors first. Father McCrea (a fictitious name) seems representative of pastors in large parishes. His parish includes 1500 families who are registered with him, plus perhaps 200 or 300 more who are probably living within the geographical boundaries of his parish but for various reasons are not yet registered. The "physical plant" or buildings for which he is responsible include the church, the rectory in which he and his 2 curates live, a parochial grammar school, and a cemetery. He is solely responsible for the parish's total annual operating budget. He may have just finished a building program for a new school. The building program was a 3-year effort which entailed fund-raising, planning, dealing with architects, contractors, and the diocese construction commission, hiring additional staff, getting an additional curate from the bishop to serve as school principal, and all the headaches of moving into and starting up the completed building. Although Father McCrea had lay committees responsible for various functions such as fund raising and planning as well as his curates to assist with certain areas, he always seemed to be presented with problems encountered in various phases of their work. As many pastors have said to us, "No matter how much I try to delegate these responsibilities, everything always ends up back on my desk." Like all leaders, then, the pastor is continually reminded that he is the final authority—and the chief fire fighter—in his parish. Indeed, everyone—he, his curates, his parishioners, and the bishop—does see it as "his" parish, and he experiences the full range of headaches and rewards that come with personal ownership.

In the interviews it appeared that some pastors were highly active, hard working, and involved in many different projects, while others seemed to be significantly less active. Indeed, curates reported they would greatly prefer to be with a "working" pastor than with a "nonworking" pastor. To illustrate the extremes of pastor activity we present the following composite (fictional) acount of a typical day's activities for each type.

Of course, these are only "types" that we are talking about. Most of the pastors we would consider to be workers rather than nonworkers. However, there are pastors who have schedules like the nonworkers described here. In a later chapter we will examine the differences between high-activity and low-activity priests in terms of their satisfactions, use of skills, and self-image.

It may be useful to consider the functions of social systems proposed by Parsons (1960) in this context. Once a parish is established and the structures and procedures laid out, it is possible for a pastor to *maintain*

"Working" pastors	"Nonworking" pastors
Arise between 5 and 6 AM	Arise between 5 and 6 AM
Say mass	Say mass
Breakfast	Breakfast
Spend early morning hours in office	Office work
Administrative work (pay bills, make	Pay bills, bookkeeping
phone calls, deal with banks, corres-	Correspondence
pondence, bookkeeping)	Phone calls
Write sermons	Assist people who come in
Counsel and give help in problem solving	(Hospital visits made by curates)
to parishioners who come in	
Make hospital visits — late morning until	
lunch	
Lunch	Lunch
Meet with various community organizations	Nap
Plan and initiate new parish programs	Work around the rectory and yard
Visit parishioners in their homes, participate	Play golf or tennis
in census	Cocktails
Visit parish school	Dinner
Dinner	Nap
Evening meetings — church or community	Evening meetings
groups	Counsel or give marriage instruction
Counsel or give marriage instructions	Watch television
Read	Bed
Bed	

the parish with quite a low level of effort. However, in order to actively *pursue particular goals* and *adapt to changes*, much more work is required. Thus we could call nonworking pastors "maintainers" and working pastors "goal attainers and adapters."

A somewhat different situation is experienced by the pastor in a small rural parish, with perhaps 100 or 150 Catholic families. In such a small parish the pastor would usually be the only priest assigned there, although as the census (i.e., number of registered Catholics) grows, a curate is generally assigned there in time. If the parish is located in a summer resort area (such as along the shore or near a lake), young newly ordained priests may be sent there to serve as temporary summer curates. Then in September they move on to permanent assignments in larger parishes.

This sort of rural pastorate is often a difficult one, primarily because of the twin problems of being alone: loneliness and overwork. The transition from curate to pastor is stressful in and of itself, with its sudden, jolting increase in challenge and responsibility following 22 years of nonresponsibility; this stress can be greatly aggravated when the new pastor lives by himself with no one to talk to, no source of support. As Mills (1970) has found among Protestant clergy, support—both personal and organizational—is a prime factor in a past's success or failure. It is also known that interpersonal relationships can serve as important facilitators during stressful role transitions (Evan, 1962; Hall, 1968; Mansfield, 1970). Little of this interpersonal help is available to the isolated rural priest.

The second problem of being alone is that the pastor himself is responsible for performing all of the priestly functions of his parish. He must make all the sick calls, officiate at all the weddings, baptisms, funerals, and generally be on call 24 hours a day. If he wants to take a day off—or even a few hours—he must make some sort of arrangement with a nearby priest to have his rectory covered in case of emergencies. This sudden sense of newly acquired continuous responsibility is somewhat analogous to that of parents with their first child: They simply cannot escape the fact that they are responsible for meeting that child's needs at any hour of the day; if they are going to be away, they must arrange for someone else to watch the baby, but even then they cannot escape the fact that they are the parents and they could be called home for an emergency at a moment's notice. All pastors feel this sense of ultimate responsibility for their parishes, but the rural pastor operating alone experiences more daily situations and problems resulting from this responsibility.

This is how one rural pastor describes these problems:

> When you're alone there is [much responsibility], because you're on duty 24 hours a day. There's always that anxiety, even if you go out for just a little while, whereas if you have assistants you know things are being cared for anyway. But it's a terrific responsibility.

Like pastors, curates can be found in different types of parish settings. Probably the most important factor affecting the nature of the assistant's work is the leadership style and work pattern of his pastor. If, on the one hand, his pastor chooses to share important duties and responsibilities with his curate, and if he encourages the curate to take initiatives and to innovate, then the assistant can have a rewarding job. On the other hand, if the pastor is at either of two extremes—autocratic or laissez-faire—the curate will experience the frustrations of being stifled from the first extreme or of receiving no support and help in the second.

A second important factor in the work of the curate is the size of his parish. If the parish is so small that he is the only curate, his work experiences are even more dependent than usual upon the pastor. If, however, there are other curates in the house, as is true in larger parishes, the support and assistance provided by these other men can partially offset the influence of the pastor. A seniority system operates in multicurate parishes so that the oldest curate operates somewhat like a sergeant, being responsible for the younger curates, coordinating their duties and serving as liaison between curates and pastor. The oldest curate is referred to as "first curate" and the youngest is (less frequently) known as the "baby curate." The latter term is usually reserved for especially large parishes (5 or more curates) and situations in which the youngest curate has been ordained for only a few years or less.

To illustrate the work of the curate better under various conditions, here are quotes from assistants regarding collaborative, autocratic, and laissez-faire pastors, respectively. First, a curate describes his former pastor, an autocrat:

> I was simply there more or less as a houseboy. Pretty much a phone, a door, hospital visitations, and so forth. But nothing, nothing at all was done unless the pastor knew about it, approved it, and so forth. There was absolutely no room for creativity at all.

A second curate describes how a more open, collaborative climate is developed and maintained in his dealings with his pastor:

> Priest: "[Shared authority] has to be established, of course."
> Interviewer: "How does one do that?"
> Priest: "Well, if authority has tended to be exercised excessively, well then you sit down and say, 'Hey, just a minute, Here's what I feel, here's what I am, here's what I do, here's what I expect of you, and tell me what you expect of me. Let's work it from there.' "

The third type of pastoral leadership style, laissez-faire, provided more freedom for the curate but little contact or support. This style is described by one man as follows:

> Interviewer: "How did you receive your assignments?"
> Priest: ". . . It must have happened one night, like the night I got there and he said, 'you've got CYO,' and after that there were no changes in the regime within the house. I had the CYO and I kept the CYO. I would say that that was the last kind of interference or direction, as I remember, information or advice that I received. . . . I had no experience, and I didn't do a very good job. And I suppose I might have done a better job if I had received a little more advice."

Earlier we distinguished between working and nonworking pastors. We find that the same distinction also applies to curates. Composite "typical days" for these two types of curates are as follows:

Typical day of "working" curates	Typical day of "nonworking" curates
Up between 5 and 6 AM	Up between 5 and 6 AM
Mass	Mass
Breakfast	Breakfast
Prepare for classes	Help people who come to rectory
Grade class papers	Hospital visits
Meet with class	Lunch
Hospital visits	Nap
Plan CYO activities	Meet with ladies' club
Lunch	Read
Phone and door duty	Dinner
Community meeting	Counsel or give religious instructions
Take census	
Counsel or give religious instructions	Bed
Dinner	
Club meetings	
Bed	

There is one unique position in the parish ministry which falls in between those of curate and pastor—the *administrator*. This position is created only if a particular pastor becomes disabled and is unable to continue running the parish. When this happens, the bishop may choose not to remove his title of pastor but rather to appoint another priest to serve as administrator of the parish, with all of the authority otherwise vested in the pastor. Sometimes the administrator is a pastor moved from another parish, but often he is a curate, either from that particular parish or another one. There are also occasions in which an incompetent pastor is never formally divested of his power, although his curate informally runs the parish. The disability of a pastor, then, can provide a unique opportunity for a young curate to assume responsibilities he might not otherwise receive for another 15 or 20 years. Ths opportunity is described by one curate ordained 12 years as follows:

> Obviously, I have no real authority and anything we've done, anything new, the few new things we've done, we've all talked about it, we have managed. But obviously we haven't done anything, made any extreme innovations. And the pastor, we've always communicated with him by telephone, so he knows what's going on. . . .
>
> There are some places where you could improve upon it, but on the whole I think we're fairly efficient. Maybe not an A, but we might get a B.

Because of the variety of special assignments, it is not possible to illustrate the typical activities of priests doing this sort of work. Most of the specials are either chaplains (in universities, hospitals, or homes), educational administrators, or chancery office personnel. The work is usually of a professional nature. For example, the chaplain is usually trained in counseling, the chancery official in canon law, and the school administrator in education. Their professional duties are usually superimposed upon a skeletal schedule of more traditional priestly functions, such as morning mass where they live and weekend confessions and masses for nearby pastors who need extra help. They sometimes refer to themselves as "weekend priests" because that is the main time they perform parochial duties. Sociologists refer to specials sometimes as "hyphenated priests": priest-educators, priest-lawyers, etc. (Koval, 1970). This hyphenation illustrates well the dual role—professional and parochial— of the specialist. In most cases, however, it would be more accurate to place the name of the professional role before rather than after the hyphen.

Most younger priests, curates, and specialists alike seemed to agree upon the "specialness" of the specialized assignment. It was consistently perceived as being more attractive than the job of a curate, and often preferable to that of the pastor. The two most desirable features were (1) the autonomy of having no pastor as a superior and (2) the challenge, meaning, and responsibility of the work content. One specialist describes his position as follows:

> I think the blessing of this job as chaplain is that there is no pastor. You have responsibility, you have independence, so to speak. So in regard to authority, I at 31 sort of have more authority than someone at 45 or 46 that is a curate in one of the parishes. And I think this is one of the distinct blessings of a job like a special—you don't have a pastor on your back.

Another priest on special assignment put it this way:

> It's the kind of job you can make into something. . . . It's real priestly work, in contrast to parish work, where you're collecting money, you're counting the money, you're going down to the Boy Scouts, you're answering the phone, you're going downstairs in the middle of the night to make out a mass card. These are clerical jobs that somebody else can do. In the hospital you have a job to do which no one else can do for you.

Given these general descriptions of the day-to-day world of the priest at work, we were interested in developing questionnaire measures of what they do, the psychological conditions under which they work, and the physical surroundings in which they live and work. As indicated earlier, the specific items of interest for the measures of activities were based on the interviews; this is also true for the descriptions of environmental characteristics. The work climate measures were based on both priests' descriptions as given in the interviews and our concept of the conditions necessary for psychological success.

Amount of Activities by Position

A complete list of activity items with the factor scale intercorrelations are presented in Table 5.1; these are the same as the activity categories used in Chapter Four. The amount of activities performed by priests

TABLE 5.1

Four Types of Priest Activities with Scale Intercorrelations and Averages for Amount of Activities [a]

1. Parochial

   Saying mass in church
   Marriages
   Baptisms
   Funerals
   Religious instructions
   Teaching (nonreligion) courses in school
      (reverse scored)
   Visiting the sick
   Parish organization meetings
   Nonmarriage counseling
   Hearing confessions
   Being on duty in the rectory

2. Administration

   Supervising lay employees
   Parish administration
   School administration
   Raising funds
   Administering diocesan affairs
   Supervising priests and/or sisters

3. Community involvement

   Ecumenical work
   Community meetings
   Inner-city work
   Attending workshops and conferences
   Saying mass in homes
   Home visitation
   Being on call outside the rectory
   Motivating the laity to become more
      active Catholics

4. Personal development

   Reading
   Private prayer
   Preparation for duties
   Training (self-improvement)

					Scale intercorrelations and averages			
		1	2	3	4	Total (N = 373)	Pastor (N = 120)	Curate (N = 198)	Special (N = 55)
Parochial	(1)	(70)				2.11	2.18	2.19	1.71
Administration	(2)	12	(81)			1.70	2.19	1.40	1.71
Community involvement	(3)	20	23	(78)		1.79	1.87	1.76	1.71
Personal development	(4)	−06	12	16	(57)	2.03	2.07	1.95	2.24

   [a] These are the same components as used in the value or importance of activities. The figures in parentheses in the table of intercorrelations represent the internal consistency reliability estimates of the scale scores as corrected by the Spearman–Brown prophecy formula (Ghiselli, 1964). Standard deviations = .25 for parochial and ≅ .45 for the three other activities, essentially the same as for activity importance.

in different positions is shown in Table 5.1. On the average, except for parochial duties, curates see themselves as spending significantly less time in work activities than do pastors. This feeling on the part of curates of being less busy, i.e., feeling underutilized, is a theme that will recur throughout this report.

Priests on special assignment vary in comparison to pastors and curates according to the specific activity under consideration. In addition, they wrote in a large number of other activities on the questionnaire. Compared to parish priests, specials saw themselves as participating more in these "other" activities than did either pastors or curates. They perform significantly fewer parochial functions and are involved in only moderate amounts of administrative and community activities, but spend significantly more time in personal development activities.

Work Climate

When we began our research, we had a very simple conception of work climate: the psychological atmosphere in which a person perceives himself to be. With this simple conception and specification of two of these psychological characteristics on the basis of theory (challenging work and autonomy at work), it was a simple step to operationalization. It now seems clear that we were not measuring organizational climate so much as we were assessing work climate. Thus we would distinguish between perceptions of the climate of the archdiocese as a whole from the more restricted work climate of a particular assignment. Surely, one *aspect* of organizational climate may be the work climate of assignments. However, there are other dimensions, such as racial tension, intermarriage, etc., which would be equally relevant for consideration in the more general assessment of the climate of the total organization.

The issue of the psychological conditions existing in the work life of the priest was particularly salient because of the strong impact which rectory life seems to have. On the one hand, there are relationships with the superior that priests report are relevant to their work, and, on the other hand, peer relationships and relationships with the laity were also mentioned as important correlates of satisfaction. As noted previously, the two most important aspects of work climate from a theoretical point of view concerned challenge in work and autonomy at work. From the theory, supplemented by descriptions from the interviews, a set of items were written for the questionnaire. These items were then factor analyzed and yielded four clearly interpretable factors. The components of these factors are presented in Table 5.2, with intercorrelations.

TABLE 5.2

*Components of Four Factors of Work Climate
with Scale Intercorrelations*[a]

1. Superior effectiveness

   Amount of guidance provided by superior
   Amount of direction provided by superior
   Pastoral effectiveness of superior
   Amount of constructive criticism from
     superior
   Amount of constructive leadership by
     superior
   Respect for superior
   Amount of task structure provided by
     superior
   Recognition of accomplishment by
     superior

2. Work challenge and meaning

   Feeling of contentment in work
   Opportunity to get to know people
   Feeling of confidence in work
   Amount of initiative actually exercised
   Workload
   Amount of challenge
   Amount of responsibility
   Being accepted by other priests in rectory
   Amount of priestly meaning in work

3. Personal acceptance

   Feeling of being accepted by laity as a
     priest
   Feeling of being accepted by laity as a
     person
   Adequacy of seminary training
   Amount of assistance provided by fellow
     priests

4. Supportive autonomy

   Opportunity to express ideas
   Willingness of pastor to accept ideas
   Feeling of contributing to decision
     making
   Amount of discussion of work with
     superior
   Amount of friendship with superior
   Congeniality of life in rectory
   Amount of authoritarian control by
     superior (reversed scoring)
   Feeling of being treated as an equal by
     superior
   Discussion of things other than work with
     superior
   Opportunity to exercise initiative
   Encouragement to exercise initiative

	1	2	3	4
1. Superior effectiveness	(86)			
2. Work challenge and meaning	36	(91)		
3. Personal acceptance	22	49	(88)	
4. Supportive autonomy	64	61	24	(85)

[a] Figures in parentheses indicate the reliability (internal consistency) estimates calculated on the basis of item-item correlation averages within each scale and corrected by the Spearman–Brown prophecy formula (Ghiselli, 1964).

The four factors were called *Superior effectiveness* (including items like "Amount of guidance provided by superior" and "Pastoral effectiveness of superior"), *Work challenge and meaning* (including items like "Amount of challenge in my work" and "Amount of priestly meaning in my work," as well as items regarding peer relationships with other curates), *Personal acceptance* (with items such as "Feeling of being accepted by the laity as a priest" and "Feeling of being accepted by the laity as a person"), and *Supportive autonomy* (with items such as "Opportunity to express ideas" and "Feeling of being treated as an equal by superior").

The fourth category, supportive autonomy, was especially interesting to us because it seemed, in its most positive sense, to represent the balanced type of leadership that most curates interviewed seemed to be seeking—a balance between the autocratic and the laissez-faire. It seemed that many pastors were at one of two extremes: (1) supervising curates too closely and allowing little autonomy (i.e., autocratic) or (2) abdicating virtually all responsibility and concern for the work of the curate, leaving him completely on his own, with no help, support, or guidance (i.e., laissez-faire). What the curates seemed to prefer was a pastor who would give them freedom and responsibility for their own work and would also be available to discuss and help with that work if the curate wanted to seek him out. Similarly, pastors expressed concern for less control by the bishop and his committees in some areas (requiring permission from a diocese commission for expenditures of more than $1000) but more help in other areas (establishment of parish councils). The supportive autonomy factor seems to measure this desired style of leadership behavior—available, but not abdicated nor authoritative.

Campbell *et al.* (1970) have reviewed the literature on organizational climate and synthesized the data from approximately ten different sources. They conclude (p. 393) that four factors seem to be common across investigations:

1. Individual autonomy. This is perhaps the clearest composite and includes the individual responsibility, agent independence, and rules orientation factors found by Litwin and Stringer, Schneider and Bartlett, and Kahn et al., respectively, and Taguiri's factor dealing with opportunities for exercising individual initiative. The keystone of this dimension is the freedom of the individual to be his own boss and reserve considerable decision-making power for himself. He does not have to be constantly accountable to higher management.

2. The degree of structure imposed upon the position. Litwin and Stringer's structure; Schneider and Bartlett's managerial structure; Taguiri's first factor dealing with direction, objectives, etc.; and Kahn et al.'s closeness of supervision seem similar enough to be lumped under this label. The principal element is the degree to which the objectives of, and methods for, the job are established and communicated to the individual by superiors.

3. Reward orientation. Another meaningful grouping included Litwin and Stringer's reward factor; Schneider and Bartlett's general satisfaction factor, which seems to convey reward overtones; Kahn et al.'s promotion-achievement orientation; and Taguiri's being with a profit-minded and sales-oriented company. These factors do not hang together quite as well as the previous two groups and seem to vary a great deal in breadth. However, the reward element appear to be present in all.

4. Consideration, warmth, and support. This dimension lacks the clarity of the previous three. Managerial support from the Schneider and Bartlett study

and nurturance of subordinates from Kahn et al. seem quite similar. Litwin and Stringer's warmth and support also seems to belong here since apparently this is a characteristic attributable to supervisory practices. Taguiri's mention of working with a superior who is highly competitive and competent does not fit quite so easily, but nevertheless seems to refer to the support and stimulation received from one's superior. However, the human relations referent is not as clear as in the factors derived from the other studies.

It is tempting to label a fifth group and include Litwin and Stringer's "tolerance of conflict," Schneider and Bartlett's "presence of conflict," Taguiri's "working with cooperative and pleasant people," and Kahn et al.'s "universalism." All these factors seem to represent interpersonal relationships between peers, but from somewhat different perspectives. The Schneider and Bartlett and the Taguiri factors appear to fall on opposite ends of the same continuum, a kind of "cooperativeness" dimension, while the Litwin and Stringer factor reflects more of a willingness to be honest and open about interpersonal conflict, and the Kahn et al. factor represents the effect of group identification on how interpersonal relationships are handled.

In terms of these summary categories, it appears that our dimension of supportive autonomy contains elements of Campbell and his co-workers' individual autonomy and consideration. Supportive autonomy reflects more the degree of collaborative, mutual authority in the superior–subordinate relationship than the complete independence of the subordinate. As one might expect theoretically, mutual authority requires both interpersonal supportiveness and a respect for subordinate self-direction on the part of the supervisor (McGregor, 1960).

Although, as the dicussion by Campbell et al. suggests, it is not possible to establish "tight" connections between various climate analyses, our factor of superior effectiveness has strong overtones of superior guidance, which makes it somewhat similar to the structure category of Campell et al. Interpersonal acceptance falls in their fifth category, covering interpersonal relationships. Our personal development factor and work challenge seems to have no counterpart, however, in the analysis of Campbell et al.

It is instructive to note that the two factors in our analyses which have considerable overlap with the summary of Campbell et al. concern supervisory style. It is easy to speak of supportive autonomy as the consideration or human relations orientation and of superior effectiveness as structure or task oriented. These two dimensions occur in such wide-ranging types of interpersonal settings that they may almost have reached the status of a law. They appear in studies of small laboratory groups (Carter, 1954; Schneider, 1970), foremen in machine shops (Fleishman, Harris & Brutt, 1955), and other groups in industrial settings (Korman, 1966), and basketball teams (Fiedler, 1967) and are the basis for the most often-used technique for sensitivity training (Blake & Mouton, 1964).

We know of no other climate research to consider work challenge explicitly as a variable in climate; however, it is important for our conception. In contexts other than organizational climate such a dimension has been found, especially where the concept of job involvement has been the major focus of research (Lodahl & Kejner, 1965). The measure developed by Lodahl and Kejner has been used in many settings and has also been conceptualized as a factor in organizational identification (Hall, Schneider, & Nygren, 1970; Schneider, Hall, & Nygren, 1971). Also, it seems that job or work challenge is not the same as job or work satisfaction (Lawler & Hall, 1970). In later chapters we will explore this relationship. For the present we turn to our data on climate and then to the relationship between task performance and climate perceptions.

Work Climate by Position

Average work climate scores for the three types of assignments are shown in Table 5.3. Again, as in the data describing activities, there are consistent differences in the way pastors and curates assess their current assignments. Pastors rate their assignments significantly higher than curates on all four dimensions of work climate.

TABLE 5.3

Work Climate of Present and First Assignment [a]

Dimension	Present assignment			
	Overall	Pastor	Curate	Special
Superior effectiveness	1.82	2.00	1.67	2.15
Work challenge	2.27	2.39	2.13	2.63
Personal acceptance	2.22	2.28	2.17	2.32
Supportive autonomy	2.06	2.14	1.92	2.51
	First assignment			
Superior effectiveness	1.80	1.97	1.69	1.85
Work challenge	2.27	2.34	2.21	2.36
Personal acceptance	2.30	2.38	2.23	2.38
Supportive autonomy	1.83	1.93	1.71	2.07

[a] Standard deviations $\cong$ .50 with two major exceptions: for First assignment, Personal acceptance = .38 and Supportive autonomy = .60.

Interestingly, priests in special work rate their assignments even higher than pastors. The specials score significantly higher than pastors on the amount of challenge and meaning and personal acceptance they find in their work. Again, then, the specials appear to have the most positive perceptions of the nature of their work.

Another interesting aspect of the data in Table 5.3 is the comparative rankings of the four work climate dimensions. For people in all three types of assignment, the lowest average climate score is given to superior effectiveness. For pastors and specials, the next-lowest average describes another aspect of the superior's style—supportive autonomy. These data make clear the impressions we gathered from the interviews about the feelings priests in different positions have regarding the psychological nature of their work. The most impressive information provided by the data is the relatively negative way in which curates evaluate their pastors' supervisory effectiveness and style.

Work Climate Factors–First Assignment

As we have said before, career research indicates that a man's initial job assignment in an organization is an important determinant of his later effectiveness, involvement, and satisfaction in that system. The interviews had also indicated that the first assignment is critical in the development of a priest, and it seemed useful to poll the entire diocese on the issue. Therefore, in the questionnaire we also asked priests to describe the work climate of their first assignment.

To obtain the priests' views on the importance of the first assignment, we asked them the extent to which they agree with the idea that the first assignment is a critical one. The overwhelming majority of responses were either "Strongly agree" or "Agree." Therefore, we decided to examine their descriptions of their own first assignments. The same four climate factors were used for the first assignment that were used in the preceding section to describe the present assignment. The data are shown in Table 5.3.

Again it is seen that the curates score lower than the other two groups. However, the difference between the curates and the pastors is significant on only one dimension, supportive autonomy. The curates' scores are significantly lower than the specials on all four dimensions of work climate.

Since these are retrospective ratings, it is difficult to say how much they represent real difference in first assignments and how much they are distorted by one's experiences in later assignments. One might think that the curates are rating the first assignment lower because they are closer to it, yet the specials are only an average of 4 years older than the curates and are therefore not much further away from it. Given the great similarity in the patterns of the means for first and present assignment, with the curates' means displaced slightly downward, our suspicion is that the first assignments were roughly similar and that the curates' perceptions are being affected by their perceptions of their subsequent assignments.

Task Behavior and Work Climate Perceptions

By examining the interrelationships of task activities performed and work climate, an understanding of the interdependence of the two may be gained. Given the differences between the groups on amount of activities and climate descriptions, we are specifically interested in the ways these two levels of data are related within position. These correlations are presented in Table 5.4.

TABLE 5.4

Intercorrelations of Task Activities and Work Climate by Position[a]

Climate	Activities				Climate	Activities			
	Total sample (N = 373)					Pastors (N = 120)			
	A[b]	B	C	D		A	B	C	D
1[c]	−03	22	−02	11*	1	13	12	−05	07
2	04	33**	29**	22**	2	20	25*	06	09
3	05	12*	04	09	3	12	01	−11	−06
4	−06	26**	14**	14**	4	−04	21	24*	06
	Curates (N = 198)					Specials (N = 55)			
	A	B	C	D		A	B	C	D
1	19**	14*	03	−01	1	−09	−21	−26	−03
2	29**	30**	42**	15*	2	−03	13	19	15
3	17*	14*	15*	10	3	−08	−12	−26	03
4	20**	28**	18**	06	4	−03	−10	−03	02

[a] These correlations are only concerned with the intersection of two different levels of data. For the intercorrelations within the tasks see Table 5.1; for the intercorrelations within climate see Table 5.2.

[b] Task activities: A, parochial; B, administration; C, community involvement; D, personal development.

[c] Work climate: 1, superior effectiveness; 2, work challenge and meaning; 3, interpersonal acceptance; 4, supportive autonomy.

* $p < .05$.

** $p < .01$.

It is clear from these intercorrelations that different patterns exist for different groups. For curates, climate and task behavior are consistently intertwined, with 12 of the 16 correlations being significant. Work challenge, however, is most strongly related to work activity, especially to community involvement ($r = .42, p < .01$). For pastors there are only two significant relationships: The more work involves administration, the more challenging it is seen ($r = .25, p < .05$); and the more community-related activities are engaged in, the more positively the bishop's giving of supportive autonomy is described ($r = .24, p < .05$). Perhaps this occurs when the bishop has provided the pastor with a number of assistants, which allows the pastor more time to engage in community activities.[19]

For specials there are no significant relationships between activities and climate, and those which approach significance are negative. These negative correlations regarding work activities for specialists may be a function of how the activity factors were derived. As we mentioned before, we collected a list of the activities priests perform most frequently. Because the work of specialists is, as their title implies, specialized, there were few common activities they all shared; for parish priests, however, there were numerous similarities in the work duties performed in different parishes. Therefore, our activity factors are more relevant to parish work than special work. The more of these duties the specialist performs, the more similar his work would then be to a parish curate's.

Focusing now on the intercorrelations for the total sample, we note the two climate dimensions most strongly related to task activities are work challenge and supportive autonomy. Six of the 8 significant correlations concern these two factors, the two characteristics of work climate which are, we theorize, most important for psychohological success. At this point in our analysis we do not know whether task performance causes climate or vice versa; we will consider this issue more fully in later chapters. For the present, we now consider another characteristic of the priest's work world—the physical environment in which he works.

Environmental Characteristics

One suggestion which arose in the individual interviews was that priests should be allowed to live outside the rectory. This suggestion was presented as one possible solution to the problems of the pastor–curate relationship. It was felt that one reason why pastors or curates did not openly confront each other and openly acknowledge conflict was that open conflict would make it extremely difficult to live in the same house.

[19]We will explore the questions of direction of causality in these relationships in Chapter Eleven.

Because of the salience of this issue, we were interested in the percentage of priests who would prefer to live outside the rectory. The data are as follows:

Percent of Priests Who Would Prefer to Live Outside Rectory

Pastors	3%
Curates	30%
Special	8%

It appears that it is primarily the curates who would prefer to live outside the rectory. Only a handful of pastors and specials would prefer this arrangement for themselves. However, 60 of the curates responded positively to the idea. These results come very close to those of Fichter's survey, which reports that 33% of the full-time curates polled felt that priests should have a choice of separate residence (1968, p. 121).

The desire to live outside the rectory may be attributed to poor interpersonal relationships. The pastor, as we have said, is the final authority in his parish. When the pastor–curate relationship is poor, two specific issues seem to symbolize the pastor's authority and the curate's resentment of it. First, the rectory is perceived as "the pastor's house," his territory, in which the curates often do not really feel "at home." The fact that so much of the curate's life revolves around the rectory, as a place of work and residence, aggravates this problem.

The second issue which aggravates the curate's perceived lack of authority is the fact that the rectory housekeeper is often seen as more influential with the pastor than the curate is. Problem housekeepers are often viewed as a major threat to a happy house. The following is a representative view:

> Interviewer: "Do you feel that she [the housekeeper] in some way really interferes with your functioning as a priest?"
> Curate: "Oh, sure! Because she tells him [the pastor], she dictates to him. The hierarchy is her, him, and me, and if there were a dog, it'd be between him and me."

The following comments express the views of many assistants who would prefer to live outside the rectory:

> "Whether I have to live by myself or with Father ———, fine, but, the living, let's have it homey and everything, but at the same time, I'm a professional man, to a degree, so therefore let me have my professional privacy, and I believe in this. And in a rectory you just don't have it, you just don't have it. That's because you've got this guy [the pastor] and her [the housekeeper] breathing down your neck."

One curate's conclusions about rectories were a bit more extreme, however. He stated,

"I have a theory about rectories—it's that they're about the most atheistic places in the parishes. If there is any place where God does not exist, it's in the rectory."

Another issue of interest regarding more physical assignment characteristics was the proportion of priests who would prefer to work in special assignments. At the very beginning of our study, we were under the impression that many people would prefer special work to parish work because of greater perceived opportunities for autonomy, challenge, and responsibility. The interviews indicated that this was not true. Most parish priests said they preferred parish work. Neal (1965) reports a similar finding as an index of assignment satisfaction. We found, however, that most dissatisfactions seem to stem from the *conditions* (pastor–curate relationships, other rectory relationships, restricted duties) of parish work, not from the intrinsic content of the work to be done in a parish.

We asked how many priests would prefer a special assignment:

Percentage of Parish Priests Who Would Prefer a Special Assignment

Pastors	1%
Curates	16%

There is certainly a larger percentage of curates than pastors who would prefer to do specialized work, but 16% does not represent a number approaching the majority of the curate population. The size of this figure does allow for the possibility that those curates preferring special work might be accommodated without disturbing the parish needs of the diocese. This prospect seems especially realistic when one considers that 50% of the men now in special work do not indicate that they prefer this type of assignment.

Environmental Satisfaction

For pastors, the most frequently mentioned preferred and extant characteristics are: living in the rectory (59%), having younger and older parishioners (51%), adequate telephone facilities (44%), rectory near the church (50%), and a suite of rooms in the rectory (43%). For curates, the items which a large percentage now have and prefer are: rectory near the church (69%), both younger and older parishioners (56%), suite of rooms in the rectory (50%), and living in the rectory (50%).

For specials, the highest ranking characteristics are: both older and younger parishioners (56%), adequate telephone facilities (46%), and a suite of rooms (46%). Thus there seems to be a great deal of agreement on the most satisfying environmental characteristics for pastors, curates, and specials.

Environmental Dissatisfaction

For pastors, the environmental characteristics they would most prefer but do not have are: full-time housekeeper (16%), settled parishioners (15%), suite of rooms (14%), younger parishioners (14%), and a small parish (14%). For curates, they want: telephone answering service (56%), full-time secretary (47%), small parish (44%), and living accommodations outside the rectory (30%). These data from the curates support the interview impressions that many of them feel dissatisfied with routine activities such as answering the telephone, watching the door, or performing clerical duties. They feel a telephone answering service and/or secretary would be desirable replacements.

For the specials, the features they most frequently want but do not have are: telephone answering service (33%), settled parishioners (25%), living inside a rectory (27%), and a full-time secretary (27%). Thus specials, too, feel the need for relief from certain routine activities.

Another salient characteristic of these data is that the percentage of curates experiencing dissatisfaction with environmental characteristics of the assignment is far higher than that of the pastors. Here, then, is more support for the idea that one of the areas of dissatisfaction for curates is the working conditions of the parish assignment.

Analysis of Assignment Characteristics

Using the psychological success model, it should be possible to predict the relative satisfactions and self-perceptions of the the three position groups on the basis of their assignment characteristics. To do this, it is necessary to see which groups perceive their assignments as coming closest to meeting the conditions for psychological success.

It seems clear that the curates rank consistently below the specials and pastors on the four necessary conditions. They report the lowest job challenge and meaning, the lowest supportive autonomy, and the lowest correlation between valued work activities and activities actually performed of the three groups. The assignments of the specials rate generally higher than the pastors on these dimensions. The work of the specials appear to be of a more professional nature than parish work; if one views the specials as professional specialists, it is not surprisng that their work contains more autonomy and challenge than that of the pastors.

On the basis of these differing assignment characteristics then, we would predict that specials will generally rank highest on the career experience criteria of satisfaction, self-image, and skill utilization, pastors a close second, and curates a distant third.

SIX
Outcomes of Psychological Success and Failure

The focal point of our book is individual experiences of psychological success. In Chapters Four and Five attention was focused on the conditions for psychological success experiences that exist for priests in different roles. In this chapter we begin a detailed examination of the outcomes of psychological success experiences—the priest's work satisfactions, the way he sees himself, and his general feeling of being actualized in his work role as priest. We have already considered the personal and situational conditions existing for priests in different roles. In this chapter we will utilize the questionnaire and interview data regarding career outcomes for these same priests. The individual interview quotes will identify some of the ways in which priests express these outcomes.

The Outcome Measures

Actual measures of psychological success were not employed since this experience is not conceptualized as being continual or sustained over long periods of time. However, given the appropriate personal and situational characteristics (i.e., the conditions for psychological success), we can infer that such experiences have occurred by examining the outcomes of successive experiences. The momentary experience itself is a hypothetical construct (MacCorquodale & Meehl, 1948) which is inferred from a set of prior conditions and the consequent outcomes.

As suggested earlier, the focal point of our book is individual experiences resulting from psychological success and failure; it is the experience we have assumed is an important goal for individuals to seek and for organizations to facilitate. Our model of career development, however, does not as clearly specify the outcomes of psychological success as it does the conditions under which these positive career outcomes may be experienced. We have claimed that individuals who experience psychological success will (1) experience greater satisfaction in their work, (2) be more committed to their work and organization, (3) feel that their important skills are being utilized, (4) feel a sense of competence and self-esteem. From these general descriptions, we have chosen specific measures to serve as operational definitions.

Satisfaction with work was assessed by a measure of job satisfaction developed by Smith et al. (1969). This carefully developed measure assesses satisfaction with work and four other facets of the work world: supervision, pay, promotion, and co-workers.

Each of the five sections of the questionnaire contain sets of evaluative and descriptive words to which the respondent indicates whether ("yes") or not ("no") the item is descriptive of the aspect of his work world being rated. He is also permitted to indicate that he is undecided as to whether or not the word describes his job by placing a question mark beside the item. The entire questionnaire is reproduced in Appendix A, but samples of the various sets of items are presented at the top of page 89.

The choice of the Job Descriptive Index (JDI) as a technique for assessing organizational commitment is based on the extensive literature linking satisfaction to job involvement (Lodahl & Kejner, 1965) and turnover (Brayfield & Crockett, 1955; Herzberg, Mausner, Snyderman, 1959; Vroom, 1964), studies showing the positive relationship between satisfaction and identification with the organization and its goals (Hall et al., 1970), and studies showing the relationship between positive job characteristics (challenge, involvement) and organizational identification (Schneider et al., 1971). Another strength of the JDI was the national normative data available against which priests could be compared. Thus we were able to compare our sample of priests to men in general, men

Work	Pay	Promotion
Fascinating	Income adequate for	Good opportunity for
Routine	normal expenses	advancement
Satisfying	Barely live on income	Opportunity
Boring	Bad	somewhat limited
(Total number of		Promotion on ability
items = 18)	(Items = 7)	(Items = 9)

	Supervision	Co-workers
	Asks my advice	Stimulating
	Hard to please	Boring
	Impolite	Slow
	Praises good work	Ambitious
	(Items = 18)	(Items = 18)

of different ages and men in different kinds of jobs ranging from unskilled workers to professionals.[20]

Commitment to the organization was also measured by coding the interviews for the extent to which the person seemed to identify with the organization in its present state. We first coded the extent to which each priest accepted the organization. This was done on a three-point scale, with a 3 given if he seemed to accept the organization (both goals and procedures) as is, 2 if he wanted to reform the organization (accepting the basic goals but attempting to change the procedures), and 1 if he generally rejected both the goals and the procedures of the Church. Data on commitment will be presented in Chapter Eight.

Psychological success experiences are subjective sensations, and to tap their outcomes one should have a measure of how the person sees himself, such as his self-esteem or sense of competence in his environment. Our concept of self-esteem is not a narcissistic view of man in a vacuum. As we have consistently argued, psychologists have tended to view man as if he existed in a world of his own, as if his self-esteem existed as a construct independent of others. The concept of subidentity in career development demands that self-esteem be viewed as the individual sees himself in different role relationships. For example, men may see themselves in one way in their role as husband and another way in their role as businessman. Scientists see themselves differently

[20]These comparisons in our original report (Hall & Schneider, 1969) were made possible through the generosity of Patricia C. Smith, who permitted us to utilize her data prior to the publication of her book (Smith *et al.*, 1969). Note that for the pay dimension of the JDI we used seven items, although the scale contains nine items. The two items we did not use were "insecure" and "satisfactory profit sharing." This fact was accounted for in scoring the JDI.

when writing a paper than when supervising men in the laboratory. Because of the apparently great impact of different relationships on priests, we were interested in how they see themselves in those different relationships—in their subidentities as subordinate to a superior, as priest to parishioner, and as friend to friend.

Self-image was assessed by the semantic differential technique (Osgood, Suci, & Tannenbaum, 1957) originally designed for the measurement of the meaning of words and concepts. In the present research the concept to be assessed is the self: in general; in relationship to the superior; in relation to friends and in relation to superior. This instrument is shown in Section 5 of the questionnaire in Appendix A. The items chosen for this section of the questionnaire came both from the interviews and from previous semantic differential self-descriptions (Schein & Hall, 1967).

The 29 adjectives in our sample were submitted to a principal components factor analysis which resulted in three dimensions of self-image. The factors were titled *supportive* (e.g., sincere, kind, informal, etc.), *intellectual* (creative, intellectual, clear thinking, etc.), and *involved* (active, sensitive, involved, etc.). A complete list of the items is as follows:

1. Supportive	2. Intellectual	3. Involved
Sincere	Enthusiastic	Active
Kind	Creative	Sensitive
Informal	Intellectual	Concerned about people
Helpful	Clear thinking	Committed
Trusting	Bright	Involved
Obedient	Knowledgeable	Expresses emotion
Friendly	Industrious	
Cooperative		
Approachable		
Considerate		
Available		

The third criterion measure was the extent to which the individual priest felt his important skills and abilities were being utilized in his present assignment. This was ascertained by simply asking the following question: "To what extent do you feel you are utilizing your important skills and abilities in your present assignment? (Circle the number on the scale which most clearly reflects your opinion.)" Responses ranged from 1 ("not at all") to 5 ("a great deal"). The response to this seemingly simple question suggests the extent to which, in a global sense, the individual is experiencing a sense of actualization. The concept of self-actualization has been at the foundation of modern motivation-based theories of organizational behavior [Alderfer (1969, 1971), Argyris (1957, 1964), McGregor (1960, 1967), and Maslow (1943, 1954)]. More than any other concept, it has led to a humanizing force in organizational life. In our study it serves as an important outcome of psychological success.[21]

Results

The hypotheses we were testing are rather straightforward. Since they have fewer opportunities for psychological success experiences as described in Chapter Five, curates should have lower criterion scores on all measures. In most relationships, particularly the superior–subordinate relationship, curates should have lower self-esteem scores than pastors or specials have in their superior–subordinate relationships.

Utilization of Skills and Abilities

In our interviews we sensed great disparity in the degree to which priests were called upon to fully utilize their capabilities. On the one hand, young pastors were asked to take a geographical location and turn it into a fully functioning parish; this included the building, the raising of funds, visiting the potential parishioners, etc. On the other hand, this same man as curate might have been told by his pastor what time to be in at night, which community groups he should join, how much money he had for CYO expenses, not to take marriage cases which belonged to the pastor, and when to turn on the heat in the morning. While not a usual state of affairs, the latter condition for curates symbolizes the conditions for underutilization. A 47-year-old curate awaiting his appointment to pastorate put it as follows:

> If I ever thought about leaving the priesthood, I thought about it then. I felt I was in a prison. You didn't even leave the house to get a haircut . . . no freedom, no communication. You couldn't talk to him [the pastor]. . . . And you were constantly behind closed doors, when there was so much work to be done but you couldn't do it, because he wouldn't let you go out. I had to answer the phone, which rang very little, but you had to be there. . . . And so therefore you're not getting full benefit of the talent of any priest because of the fact that he's held back by the pastor.

A curate, ordained 6 years, suggests the sense of incompleteness he feels in his role as an assistant pastor—

[21]It is clear in the psychometric literature that the use of a single question to measure a construct is fraught with problems ranging from reliability to comprehensiveness. However, in the present research the question serves as a focal point and was so frequently a topic of priests' conversations in the interviews that the use of the global rating item was deemed justified.

> It's just that no matter what you do, no matter what project you embark on, or think you would like to embark on, you just have the feeling that it is not your own. You know it's not you doing it, speaking as an assistant now. Whereas in 20 years when you're no longer an assistant, if you're still alive, you will at least, as they say, 'have your feet under your own table.' And you don't feel that you have to answer to somebody who lives in the same house right away. That's what I find most depressing, and I can't say I fully realized it before ordination.

He explained some of the possible consequences, saying,

> I think living under circumstances like that over a period of time can have a very, very depressing effect. You know, sort of an attitude of carelessness after a while. I don't think you get excited over anything. That's what I found in my 6 years.

It almost seems like a cycle: Curate is ordained with high expectations; curate is sent to pastor who treats him as child; curate feels frustrated and shows little enthusiasm for work; curate acts like a child; pastor treats him more like a child, and so forth. A pastor spoke about his curates as follows:

> . . . Fortunately for me and for themselves and the parish, they are very fine priests. Therefore, each one knows what he's supposed to be doing and his definite duties each day. One day a week they may have some special thing. Well if they neglect it I have to speak to them about it. Fortunately, they do not fail. They're also this kind, who I talked about earlier, observe certain parish needs—this should be started or that should be started. Well it's up to me, I can impede it or I can give permission in that regard. Like the boss of anything, I guess, they're supposed to ask permission and, like good priests that they are, they do.

One of the curates in this situation is 42 years old.

In response to the question "To what extent do you feel you are utilizing your most important skills and abilities in your present assignment?" only 5.6% of the curates responded "a great deal." Table 6.1 presents the comparable response figures to the same question for pastors and specials—41.5 and 46.7%, respectively. Another way of summarizing these data is to combine the two most positive response categories ("a great deal" and "fairly much") and the two most negative response categories ("comparatively little" and "not at all") for the three types of assignments. Eighty-two percent of the pastors and 82% of the specials are positive about their skills being utilized, while only 5.4% of the pastors and 5% of the specials respond negatively. The contrasting figures for curates are: 37% positive and 24% negative. It also is of interest to note that a comparison of means indicates specials to be more positive than pastors and both these groups to feel significantly more use of their skills and abilities than do curates. We are reminded of one curate who suggested that "having a curate do some of the things pastors tell them to do is like using a 50-pound gold ingot as a doorstop—it does the job but what a waste."

TABLE 6.1

Perceived Use of Skills and Abilities, by Position
(Percent Responding)

	Pastor (N = 120)	Curate (N = 198)	Special (N = 55)
A great deal	41.5	5.6	46.7
Fairly much	40.7	31.3	35.0
To some degree	11.9	39.5	13.3
Comparatively little	5.4	21.0	5.0
Not at all	0	2.6	0
Overall mean	4.02	3.13	4.11
S.D.	1.14	.97	1.05

Self-Image

Our theory of psychological success and failure suggests that an individual's self-esteem is related to the opportunities his environment offers for autonomous, challenging work. We have shown that pastors and specials feel their roles offer more of these opportunities than the climate in which curates work. Given these differences in the three assignments, we expected to find similar discrepancies in our measures of general self and self-image in three kinds of relationships: friends, laity, and superior. (Table 6.2 presents these data, by position.)

Only in the subordinate subidentity (self-image vs. superior) are consistent significant differences between positions obvious. As one might expect with the interviews presented previously, curates significantly more often than pastors and specials see themselves less supportive and intellectual in relation to their superior. So far as feeling involved is concerned, curates see themselves significantly less involved than do specials. Indeed, specials' intellectual self-image is significantly higher than pastors and also (nonsignificantly) higher than pastors on the other two dimensions as well.

The following quote comes from a curate ordained 6 years and speaks to his feeling of inequality vis-a-vis his pastor:

"[Before ordination] I had no awareness at all of any kind of inequality, of injustice, between a pastor and a curate. . . . The work of a priest was so idealized in my mind that this unfortunate aspect just didn't hold too much water until after I was ordained. Then it began to hold a lot of water."

One curate, ordained 3 years, was aware of the problems while he was in the seminary:

> We used to kid in the seminary about some of these strongarm rulers as pastors in the archdiocese. There are some names that come up that are almost legendary. It's a big laugh.... Well, I got my letter in September when I was in ———, and one of my classmates ... in another suburbia resort parish, I called him up right away. 'Got my letter.' 'What did you get?' 'I hit the jackpot.' 'Did you get so and so?' I said, 'No.' 'Then you must have gotten so and so.' And I said, 'Yes.'. ... There had always been a long history of newly ordained priests who had been sent to him.

This assistant pastor remained in the parish for approximately 2 years. His description of life in the parish runs uninterrupted for ten typewritten pages or one-fourth of a 1½-hour interview.

Pastors seem to have a different kind of relationship with their superior, the bishop. For one thing, he is not immediately available, either as a threat of punishment, or a source of support. A pastor described his relationship with the hierarchy as follows:

> ... they give a man a job, they expect him to do it. The same way with myself; I give an assistant a job, I don't want to be bothered every five minutes. ... There are certain things, permissions and certain things you have to communicate. There are certain spiritual things, dispensations. For example ... a mixed marriage, you have to get permission—that's no problem—just don't marry them without getting the proper dispensation from the bishop. Certain amounts of money. If you were going to spend money beyond a certain figure, a thousand dollars, you're supposed to get permission. And I can see that.

Another pastor, recently promoted to the pastorate, was not as convinced about the necessity for such close scrutiny:

> I cannot sign any kind of financial paper of any importance without direct approval. I would not purchase a piece of land. I can knock my brains out now and have this all set up and present it to the chancery and they can say, 'Sorry.'

Whether or not there is agreement on the extent of control, the pressure of the authority is clear.

It is difficult to find specials speaking about their superiors. Earlier we quoted one priest on special assignment who indicated that he does not have the kind of job in which someone stands over him. On the questionnaire we asked priests to indicate who their immediate superior was. In response to the question, all but 10 curates (or 94%) indicated a pastor as immediate superior, 98 pastors (or 81%) indicated the bishop was their immediate superior, and 16 indicated themselves or another (administrators were included with pastors). However, 50% of the specials responded that their immediate superior was someone outside the Church hierarchy. Most other specials indicated the bishop as their superior.

We have devoted considerable time to the impact of the pastor on the curate but have looked less at the impact of the bishop on his priests. In the interview we asked priests to describe the way they perceived their relationship with and the impact of the chancery office and bishop. By content coding, a set of categories regarding the chancery and bishop were developed. These data indicate that pastors and specials feel less separation from the chancery and bishop than do curates—almost one-half (47.5%) of the curates had a basically negative response, especially regarding being treated as an individual, to the hierarchy. Pastors and specials, however, tend to feel more closeness to the hierarchy—freedom to contact them (28.6% pastors, 10% specials), a feeling of being "in" with them through friendship or classmates (20% pastors, 30% specials), and a sense of the bishop as being kind, charitable, and concerned (22.9% pastors, 20% specials). Specials, indeed, have a strong sense of being listened to, even though at the same time they do not feel they have much impact (35% of specials, 12.5% of curates, and 2.9% of pastors). This increased sense of positive contact with the superior may be a contributing factor to the generally higher self-image on the part of specials in relation to their superior. They simply know more people there.

In this context of knowing more people, the only other self-image relationship in which significant differences appear is self-image in relationships with close friends. In these relationships curates see themselves as more supportive and involved than pastors see themselves. These data, in combination with the fact that curates' self-image on these two dimensions suffers greatest when in contact with the superior (see Table 6.2), support the idea that the curates feel more at ease in relationships with close friends than in any other relationships. The same phenomenon appears to occur for the other two groups as well since the self-image scores tend to be higher in relations with close friends than in any other relationships. Thus pastors and specials, possibly because they feel they have more friends (classmates, etc.) in the chancery office, do not reveal the large drop in their self-image in relationship to superiors.

Friends are an important part of priests' lives, and they tend to be chosen from the ordination class. Ordination class is clearly the most inclusive piece of information one can know about a priest. It indicates who his friends are, what position he holds in the diocese, when he will be (or was) promoted to pastor, who he can vote for in diocesan elections, and provides much other information which will be discussed in Chapter Eight.

TABLE 6.2

Summary of Self-Image in Different Relationships by Position [a,b]

	General	Laity	Friends	Superior
Supportive				
Pastor	5.90	5.92	5.99	5.71
Curate	5.91	5.90	6.18	5.42
Special	5.81	5.86	6.02	5.83
Intellectual				
Pastor	5.42	5.63	5.51	5.11
Curate	5.25	5.54	5.50	4.86
Special	5.40	5.78	5.58	5.50
Involved				
Pastor	5.54	5.65	5.51	5.08
Curate	5.51	5.52	5.80	5.05
Special	5.51	5.60	5.62	5.47

[a] See Table 6.5 for scale intercorrelations.

[b] 7 = high, 1 = low. Standard deviations are essentially the same across relationships but within roles there are differences: Pastor S.D.'s ≅ .95; Curate ≅ .85; and, Specials S.D. ≅ .80.

A curate, asked about his relationships with men about his own age, responded:

> Well again that depends pretty much on your assignment, where you are as to whom you come in contact with. I would say it wasn't very good up until the last six months or so because there were just none that I knew too well, none of my class around the area. Whereas now there's three or four, and that's, I would say, very important, very helpful to have those your age available that you could be with say on a day off or something.

Another fact which Table 6.2 brings out clearly is the consistency with which priests evaluate themselves most highly on the supportive dimension. Some additional insight into this fact is derived from the fact that priests, when asked to indicate "the five (5) characteristics you feel are *most* important in your conception of the *ideal priest*" most frequently used the adjectives priestly, kind, concerned about people, sincere, dedicated, and approachable. Sincere, kind, and approachable are scored as part of the supportive dimension; concerned about people is part of involved. The remaining two adjectives did not have clearly interpretable factor structures. In summary then it is the priest's self-image in relation to his superior which seems to most reflect other differences we have noted between the three positions.

Job Satisfaction

Table 6.3 shows that, compared to men in general, the average priest is about as satisfied with his work world as is the average worker. Compared to professionals, he is less satisfied than two-thirds of them. Of more interest in the context of the present study is the relatively low standing for curates: less satisfied than two-thirds of the men in general sample and less satisfied than 83% of the professional sample. Pastors and specials, of course, stand relatively better.

TABLE 6.3

Percentile Rank on Satisfaction Variables Compared with Men in General, Professionals, and Middle Managers[a]

	Pastor	Curate	Special	All priests
Men-in-general sample				
Work	70	33	63	55
Pay	68	60	75	68
Promotion	60	30	60	50
Supervision	45	14	63	41
People	37	23	45	35
Average	56	33	61	50
Professional-men sample				
Work	40	10	30	27
Pay	53	38	60	50
Promotion	48	15	48	37
Supervision	30	8	45	28
People	28	15	33	25
Average	40	17	43	33
Middle-management-men sample				
Work	60	25	55	47
Pay	63	54	75	64
Promotion	58	20	58	45
Supervision	45	18	63	42
People	40	25	50	38
Average	53	28	60	47

[a] The men-in-general sample is 2000 men at various job levels, while the professional sample is 300 men at the upper-management level (masters and Ph.D. degree holders) working in industry. The middle-management sample is 250 men.

On every dimension pastors and specials are significantly more satisfied than curates. If we remain with comparisons to the professional sample in Table 6.3, curates are least satisfied with supervision (8th percentile), then work (10th percentile), and then promotion and co-workers (15th percentile) and most satisfied with pay (38th percentile). Pastors are least satisfied with their co-workers (28th percentile) and promotion (48th percentile) and most satisfied with pay (53rd percentile). Specials are also most satisfied with their pay (60th percentile), then (as with pastors) promotion, then supervision (45th percentile), and then co-workers (33rd percentile) and least satisfied with their work (30th percentile).

In different ways we have more or less discussed each of these dimensions of job satisfaction. Of course, we have concentrated more on the question of supervision than the other four dimensions. For the curate, though, supervision seems tied up in his feelings regarding promotion, his work and his co-workers, one of whom is usually a pastor. We will consider each of the areas separately.

Pay. We heard very little in the interviews regarding the question of pay. As evidenced in our data, this is the area in which, relative to others, priests are more satisfied than any other aspect of their work world. We asked some additional questions on the questionnaire regarding salary: "How important to you is the issue of salaries?" and "How adequate do you feel your present salary is?" The responses were consistent with the data from the JDI, with specials being most satisfied (feeling their pay is most adequate) and curates being least satisfied.

Promotion. Curates, while not happy with the promotion-by-seniority system in the diocese, were unsure about how to remedy the system which required them to wait 22 years for the promotion to pastorate. Three major recommendations were made: Make smaller parishes, enforce early retirement, and do away with the pastor–curate relationship. A curate ordained less than 10 years expressed his feelings this way:

> . . . I have classmates ordained with me from ——— who live in another diocese and are pastors now. Now that's not to say they're pastors of huge parishes with all kinds of responsibilities, but they are pastors and they are independent and they are on their own.

When asked about early retirement as a solution, he said,

> I personally feel that as long as a priest has his health and faculties and abilities that he shouldn't have to retire. . . . I don't see retirement as a solution to my

situation, I see a change in the canon law of the Church, or a change in parish structure. To give the young man something more satisfying to do.

An interesting contrast to the desire to become a pastor comes from a newly ordained curate whose pastor became very ill shortly after the initial assignment. In the interview he described how he "runs the whole show" and his exhilaration when a new program worked: "Like I put a whole new program in of study for the CYO and things like that. I'm not sure whether it was really going to work. It turned out tremendously." With all this activity he feels more empathy with older pastors, wants to get back to being a curate, but enjoys his role now. "As soon as I get a pastor back my application goes in for permanent third curate the rest of my life. They can take their pastor. I don't mind it, I enjoy it."

Specials speak more about demotion to the curacy than promotion to the pastorate. Occasionally, although feeling in a "rut" over the assignment, the priest on special assignment would speak of "jumping out of the frying pan into the fire."

The most depressing comments regarding promotion were directed at a sense of being "too old," or "all washed up," or "too tired" by the time the promotion came. The priest waits so long for his name to move to the top of the list that it becomes an object of great attention—it may affect what he does, what he says, who he says it to, etc. The following conversation transpired at the start of one interview:

Interviewee: "I want to ask a question, is this being recorded? I don't know what you're going to ask, it's not going to be published what we say?"
Interviewer: "No it's completely confidential. . . ."
Interviewee: "Because you know you want to express your opinion, but on the other hand. . . ."
Interviewer: ". . . absolutely nothing to do with your name."
Interviewee: "Because you know, after all, getting up there close to. . . ."

Questions regarding promotion satisfaction covered one aspect of the assignment situation in the archdiocese. As indicated earlier, at a more basic level was the whole question of assignments: how they are made, by whom they are made, and on what basis they are made. Perhaps some additional light may be shed on the differences in satisfaction with promotion by examining the results of another portion of the questionnaire which was specifically designed to assess opinions on the way assignments should be made. The results to this section of the questionnaire are presented in Table 6.4.

TABLE 6.4

Opinions on the Ways Assignments Should be Made[a]

	Pastor	Curate	Special
1. With consultation of the priest involved	4.14	4.70	4.40
2. With consideration of (taking into account) interests and abilities of the priest involved	4.42	4.76	4.66
3. Based upon psychological testing	2.75	3.43	3.21
4. Based upon professional guidance	3.06	3.79	3.60
5. Based upon an interview with the priests	3.97	4.49	4.24
6. Based upon performance in previous assignments	4.28	4.06	4.37
7. Based upon a survey of all priest's interests and talents	3.88	4.04	4.17
8. With the opportunity for special training where necessary	4.31	4.68	4.76
9. As at present	2.43	1.56	1.73
10. By a new committee of priests whose main function is the development and assignment of priests	2.40	3.38	3.16
11. Based on the needs of the diocese	4.24	3.95	4.40
12. Based on the needs of particular parishes or other diocesan functions	4.23	4.06	4.26
13. With routine periodic evaluation of each priest's performance	3.75	4.02	4.02
14. With routine periodic evaluation of each priest's suitability for his assignment	3.77	4.19	4.11
15. With evaluation of a priest's suitability for an assignment only at the priest's request	2.79	2.64	2.52
16. Based on the interests and personal characteristics of the pastor in the new assignment	3.28	3.27	3.30
17. Based on the interests and personal characteristics of the other assistant(s) in the new assignment	2.93	3.20	3.15
18. With the opportunity for special training or further education where necessary	4.06	4.57	4.58
19. With the guarantee that reasons for not granting requests for a certain assignment or special training would be discussed with the priest involved	4.18	4.42	4.22
20. Taking into account the specialized training (and/or lack thereof) of the priest involved	4.16	4.55	4.58
21. With a *maximum* time allowed in the assignment	3.52	3.68	3.18
22. With a *minimum* time allowed in the assignment	3.14	3.39	2.75
23. With the opportunity to refuse reassignment without prejudice	3.14	4.06	3.49
24. With the opportunity to express a desire for a particular assignment	3.76	4.40	4.38
25. Based on consultation with the laity	1.74	2.70	2.34
26. Based partially on seniority	3.58	3.46	3.73
27. Based solely on seniority	2.29	1.48	1.59
28. Based partially on merit	3.75	3.87	4.13
29. Based solely on merit	2.64	2.46	2.36

[a] Note: The figures presented are averages (means) from a five-point scale ranging from "Definitely agree" (5) to "Definitely disagree" (1).

As the responses to question 9 indicate, the large majority of priests do not want assignments made as they are now. On the contrary, all of the averages for questions 1 and 2 regarding consultation of the priest and consideration of his abilities are toward the "definitely agree" side of the scale. Therefore, there is much agreement that priests want to be considered before they are given a new assignment. There is no doubt that there is strong sentiment in favor of a change in the process of making assignments.

It is of interest to note that there is generally agreement about *what* should be done in making the assignments. The areas in which there is disagreement concern *who* should be doing these things. For example, there is general agreement that assignments should be made (1) with consultation of the priest involved (item 1); (2) taking into account his interests and abilities (item 2); (3) with the opportunity for special training (item 8); (4) based on the needs of the diocese and particular parishes (items 11 and 12); and (5) based on the interests and personal characteristics of the pastor in the new assignment (item 16).

There is disagreement on who should be taking these things into account and providing these opportunities. Should professional guidance people be used (item 4)? Pastors tend to be uncertain, while curates tend to agree. Should there be a new committee of priests whose main function is assignment and development (item 10)? Curates are little more than uncertain, but pastors tend to disagree with this idea. Should the laity be consulted (item 25)? Curates are uncertain, while pastors think not. The conclusion is that priests know how they want assignments to be made, but they cannot seem to agree on who should be doing it.

During the interviews many younger priests said that seniority should not be the only criterion for the promotion to pastorate; they felt that if the pastorate was a minimum of 22 years away, then the value or merit of a man's performance should be considered in the opportunity for promotion. On the questionnaire we asked the priests, "How and by whom should merit be judged?" Data on the "how" part of the question are contained in Table 6.4, items 26-29. In that table there seems to be good general agreement on the fact that assignments should be made based partially on seniority and partially on merit. The "by whom" part of the question was responded to in essay form and then content analyzed.

Pastors and curates think merit should be judged on the basis of past assignments and performance, with the second most important characteristics being intelligence and abilities. For those on special assignment, the most important criterion for merit would be intelligence and abilities, with the degree of dedication, openness, and extent to which one is approachable being the second most important consideration. On the basis of these data, there seems to be good agreement that past performance, ability, and dedication-openness-approachableness are criteria that might be tried.

It is interesting to note the kind of priest who is likely to favor a certain method of judging merit. Through correlation analyses which will not be reported here, we found that priests desiring to have merit judged by a board or committee of priests:

Have been more recently ordained.

Engage in fewer administrative activities.

See administrative activities as being less important.

See community involvement as being more important.

Rate the effectiveness of their superior as low, on both first and present assignment.

Rate supportive autonomy as low on the first assignment.

Have low work and supervision satisfaction.

Priests desiring that the bishop make judgments tend to:

Engage in more administrative and more community activities.

See administration as being more important.

Feel the work they perform has challenge and meaning in their present assignment.

Be satisfied with their work and the people they work with.

Co-workers. Ten percent of parish priests (pastors and curates) report no co-workers, 24% report 1, 39% report 2, and 12% report 3 or more.[22] Priests on special assignment account for the remainder with 9% reporting no priest co-workers, 5% reporting 1, just under 1% reporting 2 priest co-workers, and 5% reporting 3 or more. The number of fellow workers seems relatively unrelated to satisfaction with co-workers ($r = .12$, $-.08$, and $-.14$ for pastors, curates, and specials, respectively) so that co-workers satisfaction is more likely related to qualitative rather than quantitative characteristics.

Our impression from the individual interviews was that priests talk about two kinds of interpersonal relationships: those having to do with

_____

[22]We should express a caution at this point regarding the measure of co-workers satisfaction: It is possible that some respondents expressed their opinions about all the people (parishioners included) they encounter in their work, not just co-workers. This may have happened because the directions for this section of the JDI are: "think of the majority of the people that you work with now or the people you meet in connection with your own work." With these instructions, it is possible that the broader interpretation was made by some respondents because instead of the title "co-worker" for that section we used the title "people on your present assignment."

superior–subordinate issues and those dealing with friends. The mention of co-workers did not seem to be usual. Even when asked about the quality of relationships with other priests, fellow priests in the same rectory were not often mentioned. When other priests were spoken about, it tended to be in reference to the pastor—about the pastor getting them all to cooperate or the pastor causing divisiveness. In addition, of course, the seniority issue is present among curates. A curate refers to himself as a "second" or "third" curate, depending on his age. Even when there is a good working relationship, this tends not to carry over into a social relationship—the classmates dominate this type of relationship. A young curate put his relationship with his fellow curates this way:

> They were helpful, supportive. I'd say fine, mature, adjusted men. My being here didn't bother them at all, you know. They just were helpful in any way they could be. They were great! Relating as far as doing things together, we didn't do an awful lot together. It was just the way things were. Because the pastor didn't pull things together.

The seniority issue not only seems to have an impact on social encounters but affects the kinds of tasks that a given curate might perform. Earlier we saw how the pastor might determine the kinds of cases he would handle; e.g., the pastor may want all the marriage cases. In some cases the most senior curate might also have more choices and influence over his activities than would the younger man. This leads to a situation where the young curate is in an even more untenable position than might occur in a 1-curate rectory. A priest on special assignment awaiting his pastorate had this insight into the issue of co-workers:

> I say the most difficult assignment in the priesthood I think would be when you have two curates who don't agree, because they're together all the time. Whereas if you don't agree with the pastor you won't see him as much as the curate.

Another older curate felt that having different-aged curates in the same rectory created some problems. Even though he was able to get along with others, he felt he had to give up something in order to maintain peace.

> ... Since it's our home I would rather be—get the lesser end or lose out so to speak, like keeping quiet if it meant peace in the house because I think after you do a day's work you should be able to come back to a home where there is no tension. So that's the philosophy I always use. ... So I got along pretty well with most of the priests that I've ever lived with following that philosophy.

Work. The remaining two dimensions of the JDI, work and supervision, have been left for last because they are more central to the psychological success framework than the others. It is through work that we assume individuals have their psychological success experiences, and it is supervision which facilitates or inhibits the opportunity for success. Thus we would view particular kinds of supervisory styles as moderating the challenge inherent in a given task and thus affecting work satisfaction. Work satisfaction, in turn, should most likely precede satisfaction with one's supervision, for it is on the basis of the outcomes of supervision that supervision is evaluated.

Priests, especially curates, frequently indicated the extent to which their talents were not being used, "even with so much challenging work yet to be done." Their explanation for not "taking up the challenge" concerned their superior or the system. In fact, while psychologists have tended to look at the personality of priests for explanations of priests' behavior, priests tend to look at "the system" as the explanatory variable. It is too easy for the researcher to find himself concentrating on a similarly unidimensioal explanatory concept. In the case of priests, this would seem to be an issue of authority.

Authority seems to be the one constant in the priest's life in that the magnitude of direct superior–subordinate contact varies so obviously from rectory to rectory and role to role. In addition, until the pastorate is attained, this contact is subject to change at a moment's notice.

It might be argued that a sense of the divine, the spiritual aspect of the priesthood, is the one most important constant in a priest's life, and we would agree. It is his sense of closeness with God and the spirit of working with God for mankind's salvation that separates the priest from other men. However, this source of difference seems not so important in explaining differences in the career outcomes of priests in different roles.

Examples of Psychological Success

To provide a better sense of what psychological success means in the daily lives of priests, we have summarized here three pastor–curate relationships in which both members experience success. (Examples of failure will be presented in later chapters.) We have interviewed both the pastor and the curate in each pair, so we could compare their reports.

1. Father K. (administrator,[23] ordained 20 years) is an active supervisor. He has had a course in counseling and would like to take additional

---

[23] An administrator handles the affairs of the parish as a sort of interim, acting pastor. He often has all the formal authority of the pastor without the title and job security.

courses. He feels strongly about the needs of the urban poor who live in his parish. He and his curate, Father C., work together developing programs for the inner city. The administrator provides high autonomy for his curates, in fact perhaps a bit too much, according to Father C., because he thinks each curate can go his own way too much. However, Father C. thrives in this atmosphere, identifying strongly with the needs of the parish and the goals of the pastor. He is taking a counseling course, is active in the parish council, and has a different activity for each night of the week.

2. Father D. (a pastor, ordained 25 years) has had a history of challenging assignments and was an administrator before becoming a pastor. He is a hard worker, feeling it is important to keep active, young, and alive. In a conflict situation he "blows his stack" first and then discusses the matter with the other person. He provides high supportive autonomy for his curate, Father F. (ordained 1 year): "I give him a job, let him work independently, *and* I talk things over with him." He backs up his curate when Father F. needs help. He likes the ideas of younger men and values having them around, especially in times of change. The curate values his relationship with his pastor and feels that the pastor values his skills and abilities. The assistant is happy about his work, which includes "anything and everything."

3. Father O. (a pastor, ordained 31 years) works hard and values success and achievement. His curate, Father T. (ordained 1 year) calls him "one of the best pastors in the business." The pastor attends many seminars or conferences on subjects he needs for his work. The curate organized the parish council, among many other activities, and is enthusiastic about the level and quality of lay involvement they have in running the parish. Both pastor and curate practice and value openness in their relationship. They discuss things, plan, and work together as a team. The curate feels very successful about the degree of lay involvement and his relationship with the people and the pastor. He reports he and the pastor are "just about ready to make the parish a real dynamic place."

There was a total of 17 pastor–curate pairs for which both members were interviewed. We examined them in detail, using the general criteria of the members' skill utilization, satisfaction, and self-image, and gave each one a global rating of "good," "moderate," or "poor." Relationships were rated poor if one or both parties reported extremely low skill utilization, satisfaction, or self-image. (The three described here, of course, were all rated good.) Of the 17, we found the following distribution:

    Good pastor–curate relationships: 5
    Moderately good pastor–curate relationships: 5
    Poor pastor–curate relationships: 7

Interrelationships of the Outcome Measures

It is important for us to look at the statistical interrelationships of our outcome measures to examine the extent to which authority pervades the other measures. Clearly, the superior–subordinate relationship has an affect on the self-image of curates. Similarly, curates are less satisfied with supervision than are pastors and specials. However, they are also less satisfied on the other satisfaction measures. The question we now ask is: Does satisfaction with supervision pervade all other outcome measures to the extent that all we are measuring is satisfaction with supervision?

Let us approach the question of criteria intercorrelations by asking a series of questions: How is supervision related to the way I see myself in general and in different relationships? How is supervision related to the way I describe my satisfactions? How is supervision related to my feelings that I am actualizing myself in my present assignment? Of course, these questions can be answered not only by comparing the impact of supervision for the different positions but by comparing which variable(s) seem to predominate or are most central to the other outcome variables. Similarities in the pattern of relationships are also of great interest, for these lead to useful generalizations.

One such generalization is as follows: For all priests the way they see themselves in relationships with their superior is less related to their general self-image than is either of the other subidentity self-images. This can be shown in the following way: For each subidentity, take the average of the correlations of the three self-image dimensions to the general self-image.[24] Vis-à-vis the way they see themselves in general, priests see themselves least that way in relationships with their superiors

---

[24]For this discussion the use of average correlations for the three dimensions does not reflect the fact that in general the three dimensions tend to show the same patterns of correlations with each other in the different subidentities. It is clear from Table 6.5 that the three dimensions are assessing different aspects of self-image. This can be seen by examining the intercorrelations of each dimension with the same dimension in other subidentity relationships. In almost every case the correlations in what Campbell & Fiske (1959) call the validity diagonal are the highest in the matrix. These relationships are highlighted in the table.

TABLE 6.5

Intercorrelations of Criterion Measures for Total Sample[a]

	1	2	3	4	5	6	7	8	9	10	11	12	13	14	15	16	17
1. Use of skills and abilities	53																
2. Work satisfaction (JDI)	14	22															
3. Pay satisfaction (JDI)	26	40	16														
4. Promotion satisfaction (JDI)	26	44	16	33													
5. Supervision satisfaction (JDI)	42	44	16	24	45												
6. Co-worker satisfaction (JDI)	32	49	12	20	47	29											
7. Supportive (superior)	30	33	08	26	33	22	60										
8. Intellectual (superior)	27	33	01	04	27	21	55	68									
9. Involved (superior)	27	27	27	-07	0	20	50	29	33								
10. Supportive (friends)	04	01	-07	07	-09	-03	48	47	34	51							
11. Intellectual (friends)	09	08	-09	02	-14	01	21	35	46	61	63						
12. Involved (friends)	-01	0	-10	03	-0	-01	23	47	30	65	48	47					
13. Supportive (laity)	10	11	04	14	-0	13	36	50	37	42	69	52	67				
14. Intellectual (laity)	18	19	02	09	-0	12	31	30	44	45	48	51	68	71			
15. Involved (laity)	16	19	05	09	01	10	38	38	55	51	67	52	75	55	54		
16. Supportive (general)	16	20	04	04	-01	10	48	32	33	71	47	51	81	58	58	56	
17. Intellectual (general)	18	09	-02	10	-01	08	27	54	37	38	73	50	55	75	53	58	61
18. Involved (general)	09	15	0	10	-09	03	19	37	37	44	52	75	52	58	78	58	61

[a] Decimals have been omitted. Sample size is approximately 373 but varies due to incomplete data on some measures. Highlighted correlations are intercorrelations within a scale and suggest the relative independence of measures within a set. See appendix C for intercorrelations for each position.

(r_{overall} = .53) and most like that in their subidentity with parishioners (r_{overall} = .82). Between these two values lies the correlations between how priests see themselves in general and when they are with their friends (r_{overall} = .74). These results hold up when compared separately by position. The data lead to the general conclusion that priests feel least "themselves" (i.e., least like their general self-image) when they are in the subordinate subidentity, dealing with their superiors. For the interest of the research-oriented reader, the intercorrelations among all the criterion variables are shown in Table 6.5.

The only aspect of self-image which relates to the satisfaction dimensions and use of skills is self-image in relation to superior. General self-image and self-image in relation to the laity and close friends are not strongly correlated with skill utilization or satisfaction. Again we see how the superior–subordinate relationship plays a key role in determining the priest's various job gratifications and psychological success.

Of the five dimensions of job satisfaction, satisfaction with the work itself seems to be the most central, as indicated by its high intercorrelations with the other dimensions. The next most central satisfaction dimension is supervision, followed closely by co-workers. These results are consistent with our earlier assertions about the critical role of the work itself and the superior–subordinate relationship in the psychological success of the priest.

Conclusion

We conclude that authority is the central explanatory concept in understanding the amount of psychological success the priest experiences. This conclusion is based on the fact that priests, especially curates, are almost unable to describe any aspect of their careers without considering authority. Even in cases where supervision or authority seems to have the least impact on the positive outcomes of a career, it enters the world of the priest on special assignment. This is especially paradoxical because specials are more satisfied with the supervision they receive than are the curates. We accounted for a number of relationships by identifying the *general* self-image as both an outcome variable and a personal variable and speaking of the various role relationship self-images as more subject to cyclical and situational influences.

In a sense there was only one surprise: General self-image is the same for priests on all three assignments, despite the considerable differences in the task activities, work climate, and satisfactions of pastors and curates. This suggests that general self-image may be a rather stable personality characteristic in the long run. There is evidence that self-image does respond to role transitions or environmental changes in the short run (Hall, 1968), but in time it may return to its previous characteristic level.

We would also conclude from their mean scores on skill utilization and work satisfaction that the average level of psychological success among assistant pastors is quite low. Because of these low scores, and because curates are the largest group of priests in the diocese (constituting over 50% of our questionnaire sample), much of our data and discussions will deal with failure rather than success; this, we think, reflects fairly the state of the system we are studying.

However, there is a difference between the *level* of success (or failure) and the *relationship* of success to various personal and organizational conditions. In Chapter Seven we will discuss levels of success and failure in terms of the changing roles of the priest. In Chapter Eight we will look at the relationship between success (or failure) and the priest's organizational commitment. In Chapter Nine we will examine the changing levels of success and failure in the personnel board and how they affected the board's performance. In Chapter Ten we will consider how various organizational conditions affect (are related to) the priest's sense of success or failure. In the chapters dealing with levels of career outcomes, the tone will probably be more failure oriented than success oriented. Those covering relationships will identify factors which help explain differences between priests experiencing psychological success and those encountering failure.

SEVEN
The Changing Roles of the Priest

In Chapters Four, Five, and Six we have reviewed the personal characteristics, the work environment, and the outcome experiences of priests. Considerable similarity in the conditions underlying the decision to enter the priesthood were shown. However, especially as regards the work world and psychological success, consistent and significant differences have been shown to exist between the three roles of the diocesan priest. These analyses, however, have not permitted us to examine the changes which probably occur, e.g., in the years between ordination and promotion to the pastorate.

Career Stages of Priests

As an individual progresses through different phases of the life cycle, changing patterns of development tasks, career concerns, modal activities, values, and needs seem to arise during particular age ranges. Super (1957), following Buehler (1933), proposes that the adult career years contain four distinct stages: exploration, establishment, maintenance, and decline. Careers of professionals appear to contain an early phase of gaining recognition in a field, then gaining advancement within the profession, and then, for the more successful members, administrative or leadership responsibilities (Caplow & McGee, 1958; Glaser, 1964; O. Hall, 1948). Such a pattern has been found in samples of Protestant ministers (E. Mills, 1970), research scientists (Glaser, 1964), physicians (O. Hall, 1948), and managers (Hall & Nougaim, 1968). It seems safe to say, then, that a person's position in the life cycle is an important determinant of career issues.

In our interviews we wanted to learn more about the subjective meaning of the unfolding life cycle of the priest. This process of identifying particular career stages and turning points presented special problems. First and most important, we were attempting to measure a dynamic process with data obtained at one point in time. Second, we had little notion of what the appropriate dimension or even concepts (needs? values? activities?) might be for measuring career stages. Third, we faced the problem of what method to use to question priests about stages and turning points in their lives.

The method we finally decided upon was the straightforward process of incorporating the priest into our inquiry as a collaborator. We simply told each interviewee what we were trying to accomplish (identifying identity stages and turning points in the career of the priest); we explained what we meant by the terms stages and turning points; and we asked him to try to identify and describe some of these in his own life. The vehicle for describing his own life experiences was an unmarked straight line running from margin to margin across a piece of paper. The instructions were to illustrate his perceptions of his life experiences by subdividing and labeling the line.

The responses to the life lines were content analyzed, which enabled us to obtain quantitative measures with a basically exploratory instrument. This solved the administration and dimension problems. The need for longitudinal data is still unmet. However, the retrospective approach does give some sense of changes over time for each person, although perhaps distorted in some ways; introducing some sense of intraindividual change does yield advantages over straight cross-sectional data (i.e., data describing only present time for different age groups).

Since the life line form inquired into areas more personal than many others covered in the interview, we decided to use it at the end of the interview after the necessary trust and rapport had been established. Unfortunately, many of the interviews ran over the allotted 1½ hours, and it was necessary to ask many men to complete the life line form at home and return it by mail. Because a number of interviewees did not do this, we can report results on only 51 completed forms, summarized in Table 7.1.

TABLE 7.1

Coding Categories and Frequencies for Life Line[a]

Turning points				
Institutional		**Personal**		
Birth	3	Found vocation		2
Entered seminary	7	Decision to become a priest		6
Ordained	21	Decision to enter seminary		3
First assignment	11	Began/ended education		7
Changed assignment	10	Important meeting with a priest		6
Vatican II	3			
Pastorate	8			
First Mass	2			
Other institutional event				
(award in seminary, etc.)	9			

Stages				
Institutional		**Personal**		
Altar boy	4	Family	2	
Grammar school (childhood	14	Priest	6	influences 12[a,b]
High school	6	Faculty	2	
Minor seminary	8	Other	2	
Major seminary	17	Relationships with pastors		
First assignment (not specified)	9	Good		3[c]
Parish	6 } 18	Poor		6[c,d]
Special	3	A satisfying period (general)		11[d]
Other assignment (not specified)	5	Satisfying work		6[c]
Parish	3 } 16	Good pastor–curate relation		3[d]
Special	8	Disillusionment (general)		6
Military service	3	due to pastor–curate relationship		6[d]
Pastorate	4	Concern for personal growth;		
Retirement	2	introspection		19[c,d]
Future	5	Question becoming or remaining		
		a priest		5
		Concern for role of Church		3
		Concern for role of priest		3

[a] This table is based on 51 life lines. Numbers are frequency of response. Letters are periods when most frequently mentioned:

a, high school (major seminary)

b, major seminary

c, early curacy (first assignment)

d, later curacy

No superscript, likely to occur in any period

A dominant theme in the interviews was the priest's relation to authority and the extent to which he felt control over his life. The life-line responses also contained evidence of this theme, and it was possible to make distinctions between *institutional* experiences, in which the organization was the initiator, and *personal* events, in which the priest himself was actively responsible for the experience. Within each of these two general sources of career influence, specific categories were derived empirically through content analysis. However, because of the *small* sample size, we will only present data on the more general categories.[26]

These analyses revealed the almost overwhelming reliance of the respondents on institutional rather than personal stages and turning points as being characteristic of their lives. The most important experiences in priest's lives seem to be the regular institutional experiences that all other priests go through—grammar school, seminary, ordination, first assignment, subsequent assignments, pastorate, and retirement —rather than personal events.

We were fortunate to have some data on a group of ministers collected with the same measure against which to compare the information provided by priests. Differences between the two groups were most noticeable in their explicit use of the word "decided" (chose, opted). Priests describe turning points without using this word, while ministers[27] use the word quite frequently. This difference in the tendency to use the word might be explained by the religious backgrounds of the individuals. We feel, however, that the data from the interviews, substantiated through the questionnaires, indicate a relative dependency of priests on the system, and a system that makes many of the decisions for the individuals.

Educational experiences (especially grammar school—a time of career choosing—and the major seminary) stand out in the memories of priests. Also, important memories involve authority figures known in childhood and youth—family, priests, and faculty. The first assignment stands out more frequently than all subsequent positions. This fact, coupled with the frequent mention of ordination, makes the transition into the priesthood perhaps the most salient memory of the priest's career.

Some idea of the different attitudes on the priest's career is provided in the data for the personal aspects of the life stages. Most of the particularly salient attitudes tend to occur during the years the priest is a curate. This tends to be a period of either strong disillusionment or satisfaction about priestly work. Pastor–curate relationships, either good or bad, are also very much on the curate's mind. Also during

[26]In a trial sample of 15 cases, the authors agreed on the category designations of 62% of the experiences recorded by the priests.

[27]Data on ministers were obtained at talks presented by the authors to the Ecumenical Continuing Education Center, New Haven, Connecticut, May 1968 and January 1969.

this long period of reportedly low challenge and responsibility he remembers doing considerable introspecting and thinking about his personal growth (or lack of it).

Role Transitions of Priests: Interview Data

The roles of the active priesthood are bordered by the role of seminarian on the preordination or preparatory side and the role of retired priest on the older or postwork side. Given these four roles, there are three major role transitions which can be observed during the priest's career: (1) seminarian to curate, (2) curate to pastor, and (3) pastor to retired priest. The transition on which we have data is curate to pastor, but we can present data on changes which occur *between* ordination and the pastorate and *between* the pastorate and retirement. Thus we will be able to examine the extent to which the previously documented differences between pastors and curates occur abruptly at promotion to the pastorate or change gradually over the years of the curacy. Of course, we can also examine the extent to which "the pastorate" is homogeneous or changing as well.

It is important to realize that age differences could arise in at least two different ways. First, people could be changing over the years. Second, the younger groups could represent a different type of person (the so-called "new breed", perhaps) than is found among older priests, which would suggest that the differences do not represent personal changes but rather stable intergroup differences. And, of course, the age differences could reflect both of these effects simultaneously. We will speak about differences over time as if they represent the same group followed from ordination on. The ideal method of measuring developmental changes is to follow a group of priests through a number of years of their priesthood in a combination cross-sectional–longitudinal design (Schaie, 1965).

We will consider the transition process that unfolds as a priest moves through his career as if we had followed the same priests over a period of 40 years. We will speak of our data in terms like "early in his priesthood . . . , while later he . . ."; of course, we are speaking about *different* priests assessed at the same point in time. However, the attempt will be to provide the reader with a sense of what priests are and how they change over time, to provide an identity for priests.

In all analyses, the following tenure (amount of time since ordination) groups will be used: curates 0–5 years ($N = 56$), curates 6–10

($N = 47$), curates 11–16 ($N = 55$), curates 17–22 and over ($N = 35$),[28] pastors 22 and under[29] to 25 ($N = 20$), pastors 26–30 ($N = 35$), pastors 31–35 ($N = 24$), pastors 36–40 ($N = 21$), and pastors 41 and over ($N = 18$).

Our sample of specials was too small to break down into these age groups. Therefore, no special assignment priests were included in this analysis.

Generally, we are using 5-year intervals, with certain exceptions. The 17- to 22-year group was used because this is a period in which curates are currently anticipating appointments as pastors, and the interviews indicated that this is a very special period. The 22- to 25-year period was used because this is the time immediately following the appointment to pastor.

We will speak of the age groups 0–5, 6–10, 11–16, and 17–22 years ordained as representing various stages of transition in the curacy. Based upon the interview descriptions, we have called this period *accommodation to the curacy*. The age groups 17–22, 22–25, 26–30, and 31–35 years ordained will be presented to show the transition into the pastorate and will be referred to as *growing into the pastorate*. The final phase is the adjustment to retirement, as shown by the groups that are 36–40 and over 41 years ordained and will be called the *decline into retirement*.

Accommodation to the Curacy

In most professions there is a certain amount of strain experienced by the individual as he moves from an educational/training institution into his first occupational assignment. Since one function of an educational system is to facilitate societal innovation by creating and transmitting to students new knowledge, concepts, and techniques, the student must inevitably bear the brunt of the clash between the innovative system (the school) and the established one (his employer). Therefore, the "reality shock" of the transition from school to work has been identified in many professions: law (Lortie, 1959), education (Wright & Tuska, 1968; Walberg, 1968), management (Schein, 1968; Mansfield, 1970), medicine (Becker *et al.*, 1961; Merton, Reader, & Kendall, 1957), and nursing (Olesen & Whittaker, 1968). This shock is equally present for the priest as he moves from seminary to parish.

---

[28]There were 7 curates in this group who had been ordained more than 22 years. Only 1, however, had been ordained more than 23 years.

[29]There were 3 pastors in this group who had been ordained less than 22 years.

The reality shock for the new priest seems to operate in two phases. First, he experiences the joy of ordination, the end of seminary life, and the first flush of anticipation of the respect and authority represented by his newly acquired roles. With "the oil still moist on his palms," the priest's initial experience of being addressed reverently as "Father" by strangers on the street is described as a heady experience.

This postordination joy often carries over through the temporary summer assignment, since this post involves little in the way of parish organizations or projects to work with and few of the problems and headaches of larger parishes. The main tasks are the parochial activities that must be performed for the vacationers: Masses, confessions, baptisms, etc. The new curate does not get too involved in such a parish and generally has few problems. However, it is not a very challenging time either. The curate often sees it as a period of "marking time" until he gets his permanent assignment in September.

The second phase of the postordination reality shock occurs after the new curate reports to his first permanent parish—and his first permanent pastor. For the first time he becomes fully aware of the differentiation within the priesthood—all priests are not equal, and it is being a pastor, not being ordained, that really counts.

As a result of this first assignment jolt, priests report that their concept of the priesthood changes in four ways. First, they move from being rather *idealistic* to being more *realistic* about the priesthood. They realize that priests are, after all, human beings, subject to just as many flaws as most other people. This de-idealization of the priest is expressed as follows by a man ordained for 6 years:

> I was pretty much unaware all through elementary school and high school, and pretty much through the seminary, too, of the human element in the priesthood and the weaknesses that are there, and that I think are in every group. And it's only since I've been ordained, and since I've been out and actually lived with priests and been in situations that I see that the human nature is very, very strong and very real. And that has kind of tempered my zeal in a way.

The two experiences which affected this man so strongly were being assigned to an alcoholic pastor and being transferred by another pastor for staying out of the rectory later than 11:30. (There is a formal time deadline for returning to the rectory, but it is rarely enforced.)

A second change is the sudden appreciation of the *interpersonal or political* aspects of the priesthood, in addition to the more technical or theoretical aspects covered in the seminary. Many men reported that the technical emphasis of the seminary education left them completely unprepared for the interpersonal problems they would have to face as working priests (problems with other priests as well as the laity).

A rather extreme interpersonal experience was reported by one young assistant as follows:

Respondent: "I was brand new, I was just ordained, see? So, you come out at the beginning, the first two months, being that I was brand new, [my pastor] never talked to me, not once. You know, that's a little hard to take."
Interviewer: "He *never* talked to you?"
Respondent: "Never, never. . . ."
Interviewer: "Why wasn't he talking?"
Respondent: "Because he figured you've got to put the worker in his place, you see? It's a game, it's a game. . . . And it wrecked some fellows. It wrecked the last curate that was there because he just wasn't the same temperament as me. . . ."

A less extreme experience is the following, reported by a senior curate awaiting his first pastorate assignment:

When I was a young priest coming out of the seminary I was really shocked at some of the behavior of the pastor and then the uncharitableness which existed among the priests. I didn't think that existed, because St. [seminary] always gave the picture of the ideal priest, charity reigned and everything else. So, as I say, after 1 month there I thought I was tricked into some kind of association in which the real picture was kept hidden from you because of this behavior. Of course now that I look back it's all due to human frailty, and I understand.

A third change is from a state of enthusiasm for creating innovations in the Church to a strong awareness of difficulty of change because of the rigidity of organizational rules and procedures and/or because of the resistance of the pastor. Even when the pastor provides autonomy for his assistants, he often effectively prevents innovation by withholding financial support for new projects.

Many young priests appear to give up after a few attempts to create change. Only a few realize that the real challenge lies precisely in the problems of overcoming the sources of resistance to change. One assistant, ordained 7 years, described curates' tendencies to overestimate the difficulty of influencing his pastor as follows:

A lot of the curates, almost all the curates that were with him, have been afraid of him, and I think this is to their detriment, too. You have to assert yourself a lot of times in a diplomatic way. I think I can do that.

In Chapter Eight we will examine the strategies curates use in influencing pastors and creating change. These include collaborative problem-solving, trickery, diplomacy, threat, informal, covert rule breaking, and open defiance.

A fourth theme of this first-parish letdown is dismay at the low challenge and underutilization of the new curate's competencies. For some curates their only nonparochial responsibility was supervising the altar boys. No wonder that in time one reported he began to feel like a "glorified altar boy" himself:

> Respondent: "I think one of the great frustrating areas today is in part or in whole, mostly in part for us, where there would be priests involved in work that isn't priestly. It's just as frustrating as having a guy come out of medical school and go through a year of internship and years of residency and have him handing out aspirins. I mean, this is—what a waste! Like using your tape recorder for a door stop."
> Interviewer: "Not related to its natural function."
> Respondent: "Yeah, it'll work, but so would the Hope diamond, but what a waste!"

It is clear that our conception of the curacy is dominated by the priest's early experiences—e.g., his first assignment. Clearly, changes occur from the first assignment to the promotion to pastorate, but they do not stand out as clearly in our minds as we write this narrative. Perhaps when we turn to the more formal data analyses, the changes during the curate years will become more clear. For now let us turn to the narrative portion of this chapter describing the growth into the pastorate.

Growing into the Pastorate

The transition into the pastorate seems to have four general phases. First comes *anticipation* during the last curate years. At this time the priest is largely looking forward to the independence and authority of his own parish, and many of the variables we measured showed sharp increases here. Immediately following the advancement to pastor, there appears to be a *decline* on many measures. This is a period of disillusionment, a second "reality shock" perhaps, when the priest becomes aware of the problems of the pastorate as well as its benefits.

Following the decline is a *recovery* period during which the young pastor learns to cope with the greatly increased challenges and responsibilities of the job. This recovery results in a peak period, approximately 30–40 years after ordination, when the pastor seems to experience the highest levels of career outcomes of his working career, even though the characteristics of his assignment are not greatly different from other times in the pastorate.

Our impression of the pastorate is one of status quo; not many things change once the man becomes a pastor. The day-to-day tasks remain at a constant level and the burden of responsibility is a steady companion. Pastors tended to speak less about the kinds of experiences they had as pastors than they spoke about their times as curates or than curates spoke about their own experiences.

One area in which pastors expressed their feelings was the length of time it took to be promoted to the pastorate. A man who had been a pastor for 3 years said,

> ... Let me put it this way. If I had been given it [the pastorate] a few years earlier, I think I could have brought to it a little more youth, a little more physical zeal maybe. I don't think spiritual or emotional zeal could be any more than it is.

Another issue of concern to some pastors is the lack of time they had to spend with the parishioners because of the responsibilities placed on them to administer the parish. Some pastors spoke about their desire to have the autonomy of the pastorate but to be doing the "real" work of the parish priest. A priest promoted to the pastorate less than a year put it as follows:

> ... tied down with administrative things, [the pastor] would be delegating the more spiritual and more vital areas to the curate. So that in a sense it's less of the administrative and material concerns he [the curate] would have, and more of the actual, vital priesthood. . . .

It was interesting to note that curates spoke more about pastors than pastors spoke about curates. One could come to the conclusion that curates have more trouble getting along with their pastors than vice versa. We think such a conclusion would be a mistake. Generally speaking, we had the feeling that pastors did not view curates' problems with concern—that since they the pastors had suffered through the curacy, it was now the curates' turn to suffer. In this context we heard words like "obedience" and "dedication" as traits that were uncharacteristic of the younger men: "They think they have all the answers."

Decline into Retirement

As we will show later in the chapter, there appears to be a rather sharp drop in most measures we have taken toward the end of the priest's career, the period of career decline. Retirement is a new concept for priests, and in the diocese we studied it has only been in effect for a few years, the mandatory retirement age being 70. Since we did not speak with priests whose retirement was imminent, for the most part we will have to depend on the questionnaire data to clarify some of the issues associated with the end of the career.

The impact of the decision to have retirement at all, however, was clear for priests of all ages. A young pastor put his feelings in the following way:

> ...when they first started talking about retirement it struck me as a funny deal. I never considered myself as coming to retirement from the priesthood.... The first thought of returning you to secular areas to live and so forth seemed a little incongruous, but it has become the accepted thing.... But I never thought of it in those terms in the old days.

This priest's response was typical. The general feeling seemed to be that a mandatory retirement age does not allow for differences and that someone should take the burden of responsibility for determining who should retire and when instead of fixing this age by regulation. No one in particular was suggested as the person or board which should have this responsibility.

Role Transitions of Priests: Questionnaire Data

We now turn to the questionnaire for more data on changes in assignments, personal characteristics, and career outcomes for priests over time. The data will be presented in graphs on which each variable will be plotted vs. time (in years) since ordination. Each graph will show all the years of the priest's work career. Significance of the differences between the age groups *within* each position will be tested by one-way analyses of variance. We will begin by examining personal characteristics, assignment characteristics, and career criteria vs. time for the transition into the curacy.

Personal Characteristics vs. Tenure

The personal factors most related to time in the priesthood are the importance which priests attach to various activities and values about and perceptions of Church goals. On the other personal factors reported earlier, interpersonal values and decisions to enter the priesthood, few pastor–curate differences were found; therefore, these measures will not be reported here.

Average scores for valued activities vs. age are shown in Fig. 7.1. Because of the strong pastor–curate differences reported in Chapter Four, the personal factor we would have expected to be most relevant to time in the priesthood is the importance which priests attach to various activities, and this expectation is corroborated by Fig. 7.1.

One of the greatest differences between pastors and curates was in the value they attach to administrative activity. Note in Fig. 7.1 that this difference is not due to an abrupt change, but that the importance of administration increases significantly during the curate years ($p < .05$). Curates begin to value administration long before they actually begin to perform administrative duties.

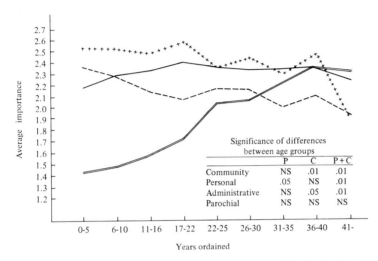

		Significance of differences between age groups	
	P	C	P+C
Community	NS	.01	.01
Personal	.05	NS	.01
Administrative	NS	.05	.01
Parochial	NS	NS	NS

Fig. 7.1. Activities: importance to perform vs. years ordained. Single solid line, parochial; pluses, personal development; dashes, community involvement; double solid line, administration.

The importance of parochial activities shows a slight but nonsignificant increase during the curate years, while the value of community involvement decreases significantly ($p < .01$). The youngest curate group (0–5 years ordained) rated community involvement higher than parochial activities. They were the only group to do so. This relative stress on community involvement seems to be an important characteristic of the so-called "new breed" of priests and is probably less likely reflective of age-related changes than the curves for the other activities.

For pastors, there exists a significant change ($p < .05$) over time in the importance attached to personal development. However, the value pastors attach to performing the three other activities does not change significantly over time.

As was shown in Chapter Four, there are some differences between curates' and pastors' views of what the goals of the Catholic Church should be. The greatest difference here is on the issue of the Church's meaning and relevance to contemporary society, with curates seeing this as a more important concern than pastors. Not surprisingly, then, there is a tendency for curates to attach less value to meaning and relevance as they acquire more seniority (see Fig. 7.2); however, these changes from younger to older assistants are not significant. In fact, there are no Church goal dimensions on which the values of curates differ significantly among age groups.

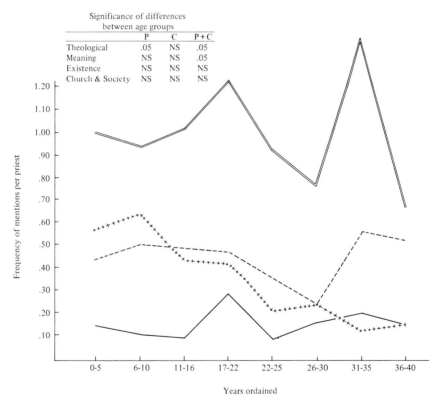

Significance of differences between age groups			
	P	C	P+C
Theological	.05	NS	.05
Meaning	NS	NS	.05
Existence	NS	NS	NS
Church & Society	NS	NS	NS

Fig. 7.2. Desired church goals vs. years ordained (goals should be). Double solid line, theological; single solid line, existence; pluses, meaning and relevance; dashed line, Church and society.

More differences are found among different age groups when we explore priests' perceptions of what the goals of the Church actually are, as shown by Fig. 7.3. Curates see theological goals as being less in evidence than pastors; at the same time, they are more likely to see

Church existence as a goal than are pastors. Perceptions of theological goals increase significantly over the curate years ($p < .01$).

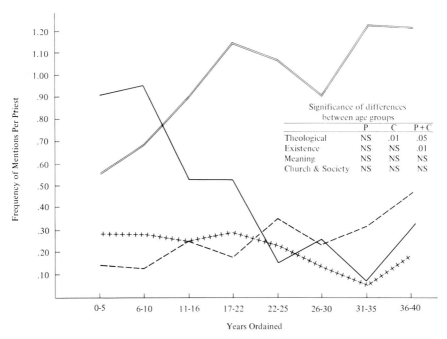

<figure>

Significance of differences
between age groups

	P	C	P+C
Theological	NS	.01	.05
Existence	NS	NS	.01
Meaning	NS	NS	NS
Church & Society	NS	NS	NS

</figure>

Fig. 7.3. Perceived church goals vs. years ordained. Double solid line, theological; single solid line, existence; crosses, meaning and relevance; dashes, Church and society.

The greatest change in Church values and perceived Church goals during the pastor years involves theological goals. For the pastor groups ordained 22–25 and 26–30 years there is a decrease in perceptions that the Church goals should be ($p < .05$) and are (NS) theological in nature. However, closer inspection of Figs. 7.2 and 7.3 indicates that most types of goals were mentioned less frequently during this period. It would appear that the pastor is so busy during the 22- to 30-year ordained period that he simply gives less thought to the organization's goals than he can during less active periods.

Again, these differences fit with the general nature of the generation gap in the priesthood and in other social systems; younger members see the institution as straying from its primary or pivotal goal (theology in the case of the Church) while becoming overly preoccupied with internal maintenance of the present structure and the status quo. In other words, the older members have more faith that the system, in practice, is actually living up to its basic stated values, while the younger people are more disillusioned and see a more substantial gap between values and actual organizational practices. The decrease in this gap over time between desired and perceived Church goals is shown in Fig. 7.4, illustrating the process of socialization, the increase in person–system goal congruence.

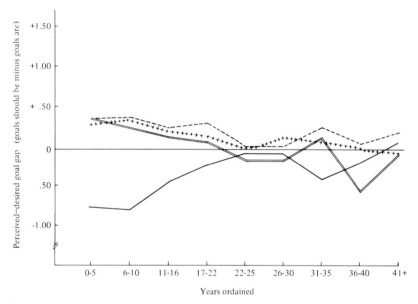

Fig. 7.4. Congruence in perceived and desired goals vs. years ordained. Double solid line, theological; single solid line, existence; pluses, meaning and relevance; dashed lines, Church and society.

There is also a significant tendency for younger priests to describe Church goals, both desired and actual, in more complex terms than pastors.[30] Presumably, these complexity ratings are an indication of how

[30]Coding of complexity was accomplished concurrently with content coding. The coders used a four-point scale for coding complexity where a score of 1 represented an "outline list of goals." This list included "nothing about *means*, rank order, explanations of why goals are *important*, or of what *means* can be used to achieve the goals. No verb. Very simple response." A 2 had to meet the following requirements: "Some description of the goals. *Verb* in sentence is required for score of Two. Some thought represented. Still no means or importance of goals." A score of 3 represented "evidence of thought, some feeling about *importance* of goals. Comparative, relative discussion of goals. Must have means for accomplishing goals." A score of 4 required "very specific discussion of means that are important. Evidence of very strong feelings."

much thought the priest has given to the goals of the organization, a measure of how salient the issue of goals per se is to him. By this reasoning, then, we would conclude that the younger members of this organization have thought through general value and organizational goal issues to a greater extent than their senior colleagues. This may be because, as curates, they experience such a sharp discrepancy between (1) the priestly work they value and which they entered the priesthood to perform and (2) the work which they find themselves and other priests actually performing. Also, they have not been as fully socialized as have pastors into seeing a better fit between their values and the actual present state of the Church.

Activities Performed vs. Tenure

We have seen in Chapter Six that there are striking differences between the work activities and work climate of curates and those of pastors and specials. Do the pastor–curate differences arise abruptly following advancement to pastor, or is there a period of anticipatory socialization during the final curate years in which the curate's work gradually begins to resemble that of the pastor? Data for all activities over time are presented in Fig. 7.5

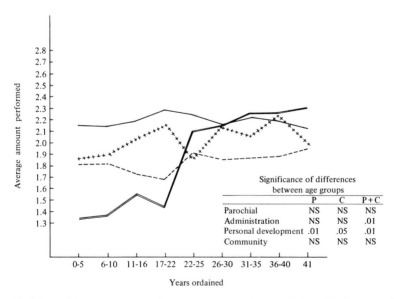

Fig. 7.5. Activities; amount performed vs. years ordained. Single solid line, parochial; pluses, personal development; dashed line, community involvement; double solid line, administration.

This figure indicates that the change in administrative work is a discontinuous one. There is little change during the curate years but a large change once the priest becomes a pastor. Perhaps this curve illustrates why so many pastors stressed the complete lack of preparation for this new role. There seems to be little indication that there is an opportunity to acquire skills in administration before one has the responsibility of an entire parish.

Frequently, new pastors are assigned to new parishes which are being created from part of a larger parish. In this case the heavy administrative demands involve creating an entire parish rather than maintaining one. This building function often appeared to us to be more demanding than running a larger, preexisting parish. The job of parish building is described by a newly appointed pastor:

> I was given a new parish, newly formed parish, which is a cutoff of the large existing parish. And I have four boundary lines and about a thousand people. And now within those boundary lines I must find a place to live, which I have done within the midst of my people, a normal family house that I am trying to make serve as a parish house or rectory, place to live for myself, a place for an office, and a small chapel to work out of. I'm conducting mass on Sunday in a public school auditorium in the confines of the area that I have. And now I have been engaged in trying to find land. When I find land I'll proceed to build a church, I think, if by that time churches are the things that are wanted and needed.

Later in the interview he goes on to describe his specific activities as he builds his parish.

> My typical day is a day in which I have not been able to do half the things that I intended to do, hoped to do, wished I could do, and should do. . . . Answering the telephone, which in my capacity involves not only parish . . . , involves also business now of which I'm involved a lot in from the bank or from the town hall or from appraisers trying to buy land, real estate people. I have spent a lot of time doing that. Having mass in a school means that I don't have a lot of the other religious contact with the people. I've been having to spend of necessity a lot of time now buying furniture, looking for a housekeeper, all the necessities of setting up a home, and setting up an office, and setting up a church—two churches actually, the one where I do say mass on Sunday and one daily.

This rapid increase in administrative work seems to occur at the expense of the new pastor's personal development; this latter activity takes a sharp downturn immediately after the appointment to pastor and then increases in subsequent periods ($P < .01$). This is ironic since it may be precisely during this period that the priest is *most* in need of time for personal development. This activity seems to be resumed in the 26–30 year period, however.

Personal-development activity during the curacy increases steadily, while community involvement declines. In the interviews, it often sounded as if this increase in the curate's personal-development activity was in reaction to the low degree of stimulation and challenge he found in his work. This reaction often seemed to take the form of "I don't really mind having nothing to do; I just do a lot of reading."

There does not appear to be a great deal of variation in the amount of parochial work a priest performs over the years. Interviewees described this activity as basic "priestly work," and it seems to be fairly constant. During the pastor years, then, activities do not change greatly over time, with the exception of personal development. Administrative, parochial, and community activities seem to be generally constant, regardless of the pastor's age.

Work Climate vs. Tenure

We have seen that there is some accommodation to the curacy in terms of the activities curates value and the activities they perform. However, the dimensions of the work world on which the greatest differences between pastors and curates existed had to do not so much with the work being accomplished but with the climate in which the work was done. Fig.7.6 thus presents the perceptions of work climate by priests in the different age groups.

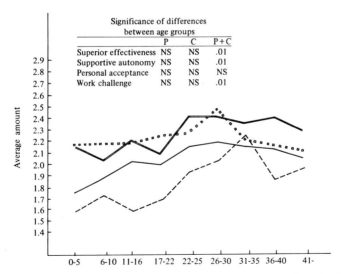

Fig. 7.6. Climate characteristics of present assignment vs. years ordained. Single solid line, supportive autonomy; dashes, superior effectiveness; double solid line, work challenge and meaning; squares, personal acceptance.

In this figure the dimension of work climate which seems to change most during the curate years concerns the amount of supportive autonomy received. Thus as the curate becomes more senior, perhaps the pastor is more likely to treat him as an equal in matters having to do with the parish; he consults with him and considers his suggestions. Also it is noted that curates' ratings of their pastors' effectiveness as superiors reveals a sharp increase in the 17- to 22-year period. The interviews indicated that older curates tended to have closer relationships with their pastors; indeed, some older curates may have served in different parishes with their present pastors when both men were curates. These curves indicate that as this closeness increases, the curates see their pastors in a different light. Also, perhaps anticipating their own appointments to the pastorate, the older curates are beginning to identify more with their own pastors and are becoming less critical of them.

For many curates this 17- to 22-year period is very much a matter of "biding their time"—they don't work too hard or become too critical of their boss or the system. This "early retirement" phenomenon is illustrated in the following remarks between the interviewer and a priest awaiting his first parish:

> Interviewer: "How important is it to you to develop new skills and abilities?"
> Respondent: "I'm not at that stage of the career. When *new* challenges come, well, *then*, maybe."
> Interviewer: "I see what you mean!" [laughter].

The early retirement phenomenon was rarely discussed directly and openly. However, it is tacitly accepted as being well-earned by older curates, and such a person is rarely criticized for taking advantage of the opportunity. One young curate described his older fellow curate as follows:

> The other curate that's with me is waiting to become a pastor. He's worked hard all his priesthood, so he doesn't really have the young approach—I think in fairness I could put it that way. He doesn't get out very much. He's the nicest person in the world to live with.

It is interesting that superior effectiveness and work challenge and meaning seem to vary inversely with each other during the curate years. For the first 10 years, work challenge drops and superior effectiveness rises. Then work challenge becomes higher during the middle curate years, and superior effectiveness decreases. Finally, at the end of the curacy challenge decreases and superior effectiveness rises. This may be due in part to a tendency for experienced curates to be assigned occasionally to parishes with ailing, old, or otherwise less effective pastors. In such a situation the curate would have a more challenging experience and rate his pastor relatively low on effectiveness.

As would be expected, there is an increase in most work climate ratings, especially work challenge and meaning, in the first period of the pastorate (22–25 years after ordination), although the priest's work climate does not change significantly during the pastorate. The dimension with the smallest increase after the transition from curate to pastor is personal acceptance, which may be related to the sense of personal decline, the career outcomes he experiences during this period; this decline will be discussed later.

Personal acceptance reaches a peak in the 26- to 30-year group and then declines. This finding fits with interview comments indicating that the older pastors often felt a sense of interpersonal distance from both their curates *and* their parishioners. In fact, it appears that often one kind of power the curate can enjoy over the pastor is this greater closeness to parishioners and thus greater effectiveness in dealing with them. Under these conditions, the pastor is forced to depend on the curate and to make better use of his talents.

On the one hand, work challenge and meaning and supportive autonomy appear to remain fairly constant over all of the pastor years. Perceptions of the superior's (i.e., bishop's) effectiveness, on the other hand, appear to continue rising. In the diocese we studied, the bishop was in his seventies, and this increase may reflect the fact that older priests knew him better and felt closer to him than younger men. *It appears that the nature of priestly work, both climate and activities, changes mainly as a function of position, not of time.*

Career Criteria vs. Tenure

The extent to which priests see their skills and abilities utilized as a function of time in the priesthood stays low during the curate years in relation to the pastor years. The changes in feelings of skill utilization are markedly discontinuous as one goes from curate to pastor, although there were some interesting fluctuations within positions. There is a slight but not significant increase in feelings of skill utilization during the middle years of the curacy (6–16 years). However, during the 5 years immediately preceding the appointment to pastor (17–22) this figure drops. Apparently, the older curates are either (1) chafing under the strain of still being curates when they are so close to the pastorate or (2) have "temporarily resigned" and are biding their time until they become pastors. Our interviews contain evidence of both reactions.

The most dramatic change in the transition from curate to pastor is the great increase in perceived use of skills and abilities. This change illustrates the great discontinuity in the personal demands made by curate and pastor assignments because the change in feelings of skill utilization is not gradual at all. After the new pastor has begun to adjust to the demands of his job, perceived skill utilization drops off slightly but later reaches a peak in the 36- to 40- year period.

Fig. 7.7 shows an increase in most areas of job satisfaction during the curate years. Satisfaction with supervision encountered on the job rises sharply during the initial years ($p < .05$). Even though these scores are quite low compared to national norms, it is significant that they do tend to increase. This suggests that particularly during the early years the curate does learn to make some sort of accommodation to the authority problems in his assignment. (The result of this accommodation may be that the curate learns how to be less dissatisfied rather than more satisfied.)

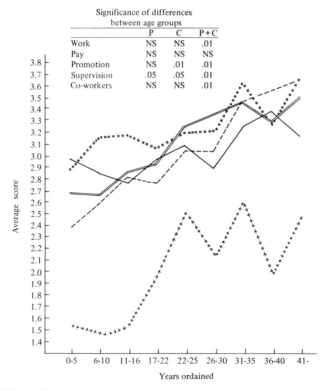

	P	C	P + C
Work	NS	NS	.01
Pay	NS	NS	NS
Promotion	NS	.01	.01
Supervision	.05	.05	.01
Co-workers	NS	NS	.01

Fig. 7.7. Satisfaction vs. years ordained. Squares, co-workers; single solid line, pay; dashes, supervision; double solid line, work; pluses, promotion.

This accommodation is described by one priest, ordained for 6 years, in his reaction to two bad experiences with problem pastors:

> I think that has sort of put me on a downward realistic turn. 'Just don't get excited, don't get upset over anything.' Some priests don't, and I think they're as well off. Because if you're too conscientious, you'll end up on the funny farm if you take things too seriously as you go along.

This comment suggests that the de-idealization of the priesthood may lead priests to lower their aspiration level regarding work climates. Another reason why satisfaction may increase in the face of basically unchanging curate assignments is that the young priests become more competent in coping with the problems of their role. This learning to deal with psychological failure is expressed by the priest just quoted, as he describes how older curates would be affected by a difficult pastor:

> . . . those kind of [difficult] pastors needed older assistants, because they would be much less likely, or they wouldn't bother an older man at all, say a man ordained 10 or 15 years. . . . Well, he at least would have the experience in back of him not to get upset or not to be troubled by it.

Satisfaction with promotion opportunities increases sharply in the curacy ($p < .01$), especially in the later curate years (17–22). This increase is important because it demonstrates that *promotion is in fact a relevant issue for priests.* If it were not, promotion satisfaction would not change in such a meaningful way. This graph and the interview data show that it is a problem to a young priest that he has to wait 22 years before he can have a parish assignment with significant responsibility and challenge. The increased status associated with a promotion may not be important or relevant in this system, but apparently the work opportunities are.

Job satisfaction continues to rise during the pastorate, as it did during the curate years, although the only significant increase occurs for satisfaction with supervision ($p < .05$). Some of the sharpest increases occur just as the transition takes place from curate to pastor, between the 17- to 22- and 22- to 25-year periods. Again, consistent with the work climate changes, the smallest increase occurred in satisfaction with co-workers in the assignment. The changes in assignment characteristics—climate and activities—show that the pastor's job is far more demanding than the curate's. Thus the priest experiences a great increase in the demands placed upon his skills and abilities. While this increased self-utilization indicates growth and is satisfying, it also tends to detract from his self-image.

As discussed in an earlier chapter, there were few self-image differences between pastors and curates. Changes in self-image seem to occur in a more complicated but consistent pattern, as indicated by Fig. 7.8, which is representative of the data for the other subidentities but shows a significant change for curates on the supportiveness ($p < .01$) dimension in relationship to superior. During early and middle curate years (0–16) there is a gradual decline in self-perceived supportiveness and involvement. Again, this change is consistent with the interpersonal "reality shock" experiences in the transition from seminary to parish, the realization that priestly fellowship is not all love and helping. One result of this kind of experience may be that the priest withdraws a bit from people and in time finds himself acting less supportive toward others.

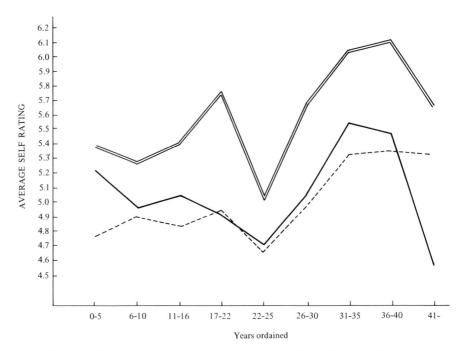

Fig. 7.8. Self-image in relation to superior vs. years ordained. Single, solid line, involvement; dashed line, intellectual; double solid line, supportiveness.

Later, as the older curate gets closer to the appointment to pastor (17–22 years), there is a rapid increase in his self-image of supportiveness in relation to his superior and close friends and in general. The changes in involvement during this period are not as consistent or strong. It appears as though the older curate has recovered from his initial interpersonal reality shock and now regards other people more positively, although his actual involvements with people may not have followed suit.

In contrast to the increases in satisfaction and work activities upon transition into the pastorate, there is, surprisingly, a consistent series of decreases in various aspects of the new pastor's self-image. As we saw earlier, as the older curate gets closer to the appointment to pastor (17–22 years), there is a rapid increase in his self-image of supportiveness. However, immediately after the appointment to pastor (22–25 years), there is a drop in self-perceptions of supportiveness and intellectual competence. These self-ratings gradually increase, though, and reach a peak after the 30-year mark. These self-image changes are found in all three role relationships (self-image regarding friends, laity, and superior) and in the general self-image; however, the only significant differences were found in the pastor's self-image in relation to his superior (intellectual, $p < .05$; supportiveness, $p < .01$).

This phenomenon of the prepastor increase and postpastor decrease in self-image was sometimes mentioned in the interviews with pastors. It appears as if the person is full of self-confidence and thoughts of the positive side of the pastorate—greater autonomy, authority, responsibility, and challenge. However, once he is actually in that long-awaited position, the reality of its *negative* aspects becomes evident—lack of real preparation and training, harder work, often being alone in a small country parish, and being held accountable for what goes on in the parish. During these years the priest becomes aware of the headaches of authority as well as its rewards.

These negative aspects of the first pastorate are logically related to decreases in self-perceived supportiveness aand intellectual competence. The decrease in supportiveness seems linked to the change in the interpersonal climate of the man's new parish. Indeed although most measures show increases after the appointment to pastor, both the climate dimension of personal acceptance and the criterion measure of co-worker satisfaction showed the least change of all dimensions on their respective instruments. The reason for these people problems is that the new pastor is assigned to a small one-priest parish, i.e., one with no curates and often no housekeeper. Such parishes are often located in rather remote rural areas with relatively low Catholic populations. Under these circumstances the priest's opportunities for social interaction and relationships are probably restricted in comparison with his previous parishes. Probably for the first time in his life the priest now may be living alone. This can be a significant deprivation for a person from a large family who may have spent 20 years in larger rectories with at least two or three other people. It is known that social interaction is important to the maintenance of one's self-image (Bennis, Schein, Steele, & Berlew, 1968; Cooley, 1956; Wylie, 1961). Research on brain-washing and social deprivation has shown how a person's self-image, especially his self-concept as a caring, supportive person, can be eroded by reduced opportunities for interpersonal contact and affiliation (Bettelheim, 1958; Schein, 1961). Furthermore, social interaction and support can aid a person in the transition through stressful experiences (Schachter, 1959; Hall, 1968). Therefore, since the new pastor is often deprived of supportive relationships—or at least experiences fewer of them—it seems understandable that his self-image would suffer, especially in the area of interpersonal supportiveness.

In the interviews, this personal change was expressed in terms of the pastor's *loneliness* in the one-man parish. To be sure, it is not uncommon for a leader in any pyramidal organizational structure to experience loneliness because of the status barrier between himself and his subordinates and because of the burden of final responsibility which is his alone. This loneliness of leadership is compounded for new pastors by the facts that (1) their position is new and they have not completely learned to live with their own authority, and (2) they are often physically alone in their rectories.

This loss of interpersonal support in the one-man parish was put strongly by several pastors, one of whom said several times, "It just isn't right to put a man all by himself out there." Indeed, some priests found at this stage in their careers that bad relationships were better than no relationships at all.

The decrease in self-image is also logically related to the task demands of the initial pastorate. Because the pastors' responsibilities and challenges are greater than those of the curate, they might easily feel less capable as administrators than previously; this reduced sense of capability could be reflected in lowered self-perceived intellectual competence.

Another problem with being alone is that all of the work has to be done by the pastor. For several pastors interviewed who live and work alone, the main concerns expressed throughout the interviews centered around their need for a curate in their parish. It is important to have someone to share the work and the time spent "on duty." The pastor in a one-man parish is not able to leave the parish unless he arranges for another priest to cover it for him; or if he cannot get someone else to cover, his visit might be interrupted by an emergency at home at any time.

It is interesting that priests describe their two greatest role transitions—seminarian to priest and curate to pastor—in similar terms. In each case they become suddenly aware of the human problems of the priest. Similarly, as pastors, they become aware of the negative aspects of authority. Furthermore, priests at both transition points report the same sense of lack of preparation and training. In the one case, priests report that the seminary did not adequately prepare them for the interpersonal problems of the priesthood; in the other, new pastors report a lack of training in administration.

Decline Into Retirement

The preceding discussion has focused on the curate and pastor years, the most active working years of the priest. Like the early years, the final years of the priest's career seem to be an especially critical and difficult transition period, as the priest approaches retirement and begins to disengage himself from a near-total investment in his work. Because of its uniqueness, we are examining the questionnaire data on this stage in a separate section.

Assignment Factors vs. Tenure

Characteristics of the assignment do not appear to change greatly as the end of the priest's working years (36–40 and over 41 years ordained). The climate characteristics and activities performed stay about the same as in the middle pastor years. The one exception to this constancy is personal-development activity, which drops off in the group ordained over 40 years.

Personal Factors vs. Tenure

Consistent with the drop in personal development in the oldest group, there is also a large decrease in the value of personal development in this group. This finding was confirmed in the interviews by the tendency of older priests to feel that they are too old to be concerned about acquiring new skills or abilities. The value attached to performing other activities does not change greatly for the oldest pastor group.

Perceived *and* valued Church goals changed in ways that are difficult to interpret. Perceived theological goals decreased sharply in the 36- to 40-year group, while the value of goals regarding Church and society, existence, and meaning and relevance increased somewhat.

Career Criteria vs. Tenure

Perceived use of skills and abilities continues to drop between the 36–40 and the 41 years and over groups, related perhaps to the decreased concern for personal development. Job satisfaction, however, continues generally to increase.

The greatest and most consistent declines are those in the older priest's self-perceptions. General self-image and self-image in relation to superior, close friends, and the laity all decline among the priests ordained more than 40 years. Again the greatest change is in self-perceptions in relation to superior. On all four aspects of self-image, the sharpest decreases are in the area of involvement. These decreases are of the same or greater magnitude as those which occurred just after the advancement to pastor. This indicates that the transition into retirement is a significant and probably stressful one. The fact that impending retirement is associated with being less active, involved, committed, concerned about people, etc. (all components of the involved peak) must make retirement an unpleasant prospect, to say the least.

Summary

The changes in assignment characteristics, personal characteristics, and career outcomes are summarized in Fig. 7.9. In the most general terms, qualities of assignments generally are at their lowest in the initial curate years, rise slightly during the later curacy, and then rise more sharply upon advancement to pastor. After this advancement, the perceived climate stabilizes in the middle and late pastor years. Work activities also start low and tend to stay low during the curacy. They, too, rise sharply with advancement to pastor and then also level off in the middle and late pastor years. The most important exception is parochial activities, which change very little over the entire career of the priest.

Among the personal factors, there is a general increase in the importance of community involvement over the career of the priest.

Among the career criteria, skill utilization starts low, increases slightly, and then decreases in late curacy. It rises sharply upon advancement, peaks in midpastorate, and then declines. Work satisfaction generally increases over the career years, although promotion satisfaction rises most dramatically just before and just after promotion to pastor. Self-image ratings decline during the early curate years, rise in the late curacy, drop sharply in the early pastor years, peak in midpastorate, and decline near retirement.

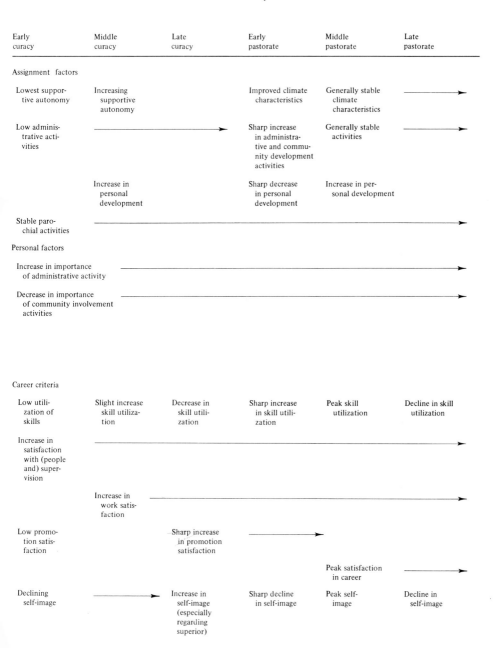

Early curacy	Middle curacy	Late curacy	Early pastorate	Middle pastorate	Late pastorate
Assignment factors					
Lowest supportive autonomy	Increasing supportive autonomy		Improved climate characteristics	Generally stable climate characteristics	⟶
Low administrative activities	⟶		Sharp increase in administrative and community development activities	Generally stable activities	⟶
	Increase in personal development		Sharp decrease in personal development	Increase in personal development	
Stable parochial activities					⟶
Personal factors					
Increase in importance of administrative activity					⟶
Decrease in importance of community involvement activities					⟶
Career criteria					
Low utilization of skills	Slight increase skill utilization	Decrease in skill utilization	Sharp increase in skill utilization	Peak skill utilization	Decline in skill utilization
Increase in satisfaction with (people and) supervision					⟶
	Increase in work satisfaction				⟶
Low promotion satisfaction		Sharp increase in promotion satisfaction	⟶		
				Peak satisfaction in career	⟶
Declining self-image	⟶	Increase in self-image (especially regarding superior)	Sharp decline in self-image	Peak self-image	Decline in self-image

Fig. 7.9. Summary of role transitions of the priest.

The impressive quality of these time-related differences is how strongly they are affected by the formal roles of the priest. The interviews and life lines similarly indicated that the most crucial career experiences seem to be the same from one priest to the next: seminary, ordination, first assignment, later assignments, and pastorate. The striking characteristic of these experiences is that they are all standard, *institutional* events; they occur in the career paths of all priests in a regularized progression. The career of the priest is thus a series of *regularized status passages* (Strauss, 1959, 1968).

Because the differences between the roles of seminarian, curate, pastor, and retired priest are so great and so distinct, most of the priestly career can be described in terms of these two positions—either transition into these roles or incumbency of them. Indeed, in a career characterized by such powerful roles and precise and common transition points, they provide clear definitions of career stages. In careers characterized by interorganizational mobility and less distinct positional sequences, stages may be more difficult to identify.

EIGHT
Failure Outcomes
and Organizational Commitment

We have seen that the opportunities and outcomes related to psychological success are less available to parish assistants (curates) than to pastors or professional specialists in the diocese. It is clear from these data that assistant pastors operate under a strong structural disadvantage in their quest for vocational fulfillment. They enter the priesthood with sincere and high goals of doing God's work, helping their fellow man, being "another Christ" (in the sense of practicing His teachings); then they encounter the reality shock of the first parish, and they find that by some mystical process answering telephones and doorbells has been spiritualized into "God's work." As a result, the parish assistant finds less satisfaction in his work than 85% of a comparable group of professionals in other occupations.

How does a person adapt to this failure to attain his aspirations when he has made a career commitment as deep and permanent as entering the priesthood? What kind of orientation does he develop toward himself and the organization that has stifled his hopes? Does he change his aspirations? Does he try to change the organizational conditions that are frustrating him? Does he tend toward "dropping out?"

A related question is how does the person adapt when he is put into a more fortunate position, one with greater opportunities for psychological success? Does he tend to feel more accepting of the organization, or does his orientation toward self and system tend to remain unchanged, fixed by 22 years of frustration in the failure-prone assistant pastorate?

A More Global Career Criterion—Organizational Commitment

The relationship between the individual and his organization may be viewed as an implicit *psychological contract* (Argyris, 1960; Berlew & Hall, 1964; H. Levinson *et al.*, 1962, Schein, 1965.

Berlew & Hall (1964, p. 31) describe this unwritten set of reciprocal expectations as follows:

> Between every individual and the organization for which he works is a "psychological contract," defined by the expectations of the individual and of the organization. . . . The relationship between the individual and the organization can be viewed as an on-going series of contract negotiations which attempt to maintain a balance between (1) the company's expectations of the individual and the individual's fulfillment of those expectations, and (2) the individual's expectations of the company and the company's fulfillment of those expectations. When expectations are not met there is a disequilibrium which, under certain conditions, can be viewed as a source of stress.

H. Levinson *et al.* (1962) defined this process of honoring mutual personal and organizational expectations as *reciprocation*. According to Levinson, if the terms of this reciprocal agreement become violated by either party, the other may tend toward terminating the relationship; i.e., the person, if frustrated by the organization, may be more likely to quit or the organization, if dissatisfied with any employee, may fire him.

Berlew & Hall (1964) confirmed Levinson's prediction. They found that young managers in their first 5 years who left the organization had a significantly greater incidence of contract nonfulfillment than men who remained. However, Berlew and Hall also found that terminating the relationship was not the only means of adapting. They found that both the company and the person tended to adjust unmet expectations. Not surprisingly, the tendency for the person to modify his performance was stronger than the tendency for the company to alter its expectations.

The attitude about the organization developed by the individual in response to the fulfillment of the psychological contract can be termed his *organizational commitment or identification*, defined as the degree of emotional attraction he feels for the organization. It is generally held that this attraction develops as the goals of the individual and those of the organization become increasingly integrated or congruent (March & Simon, 1958; McGregor, 1967, Simon, 1957, Tolman, 1943)—i.e., as the psychological contract is mutually fulfilled.[31]

Organizational commitment differs from the career criteria we have been using to this point in two important respects. First, it refers to the person's orientation toward the organization rather than his particular work assignment. Second, because the priest spends his entire career in one organization—the Church—the concept of organizational commitment is more global and describes more of a total *career orientation* than his responses to any particular assignment.

Schein (1965, p. 13) describes maintaining the psychological contract and member commitment as one of the four major issues in organizational psychology.[32] He summarizes this issue in terms of the other organizational processes with which it is centrally connected:

> To summarize, a second major psychological problem of organizations involves the nature and effects of the psychological contract between the organization and its members. Issues such as the nature of authority, the possibilities of influencing the system, the patterns of motivation and expectations of employees and managers, the incentive systems generated by management, the management patterns that create loyalty and commitment as opposed to alienation and disaffection—all are part of this general problem.

Individual Adaptations
in Organizational Commitment and Alienation

One of the earliest and most persuasive cases for the basic incompatibility in the goals of bureaucratic organizations and healthy individuals was presented by Chris Argyris in his book *Personality and Organization*. Because of this incompatibility, Argyris argued (1957, pp. 78–79), the employee generally finds himself in a situation structured for psychological failure. Earlier we indicated how the healthy individual attempts to minimize his feelings of failure:

[31]Becker & Carper (1956) consider organizational commitment together with commitments to task, occupational title, and social position as the four general facets of identification with an occupation.

[32]The other three are (1) recruitment, selecting, training, and placement, (2) integration of system components, and (3) adaptation to change.

1. Withdrawing emotionally from the work situation by lowering his work standards and becoming apathetic and uninterested.

2. Placing increased value on material rewards and depreciating the value of human or nonmaterial rewards (as a result of his apathy toward the work itself).

3. Defending his self-concept through the use of defense mechanisms.

4. Fighting the organization.

5. Attempting to gain promotion to a position with greater prospects of success.

6. Leaving the organization.

In response higher management tends to increase its formal controls, but these organizational responses tend to increase the employee's sense of failure and his failure-avoiding coping behavior; again management responds with additional controls, and a downward cycle is created. From the organization's point of view, the employee is engaging in deviant behavior, but to the individual his behavior is maintaining his mental health.

Merton (1957, p. 132) also argues that the behavior of bureaucracies can create unintended dysfunctional consequences. He describes his general thesis as follows:

> Our primary aim is to discover how some social structures exert a definite pressure upon certain persons in the society to engage in nonconforming rather than conforming conduct. If we can locate groups peculiarly subject to such pressures, we should expect to find fairly high rates of deviant behavior in these groups, not because the human beings comprising them are compounded of distinctive biological tendencies but because they are responding normally to the social situation in which they find themselves. . . . Should our quest be at all successful, some forms of deviant behavior will be found to be as psychologically normal as conformist behavior, and the equation of deviation and psychological abnormality will be put in question.

Merton (1957, pp. 140–157) goes on to describe five general ways of adapting to a given social structure. Acceptance of both system goals and the established means or procedures is termed *conformity*. Acceptance of the goals but rejection of the present means is labeled *innovation*. Rejection of the goals but acceptance of the procedures is called *ritualism*. Rejection of both goals and means Merton terms *retreatism*. Finally, rejection of present procedure and goals and substitution with new ones is defined as *rebellion*. The last four ways would, of course, be seen as deviant behavior by the social system.

There is a tendency for psychologists to speak of commitment and identification, while sociologists use the terms alienation or deviance, when actually both groups are dealing with the same concept. Identification as we have discussed it so far is the opposite of alienation. In terms of Merton's typology we would say that rebellion reflects low organizational commitment, while conformity represents a high degree of commitment.

McKelvey (1969) recasts Merton's four types of deviant adaptation in terms of two more basic dimensions: (1) whether the person expresses positive sentiments toward the organization and a sense that he is in control of his career advancement (called idealism-cynicism) and (2) whether he takes an active or a passive stand vis-à-vis the organization. Using these two dimensions, McKelvey (pp. 22–23) presents the Merton categories as follows:

	Activity	Passivity
Idealism	Innovator[a]	Ritualist
Cynicism	Rebel[b]	Retreatist

[a]Termed the crusader by McKelvey.

[b]Termed the insurgent by McKelvey. McKelvey states that his two dimensions somewhat change the meaning of the adaptation styles, thus necessitating the somewhat different labels. However, we consider the connections strong enough to maintain Merton's terms.

Categories of Organizational Commitment and Deviance in the Present Study

The development of a typology of adaptive behavior for the present study was an empirical process. Because assistant pastors were in the position most oriented toward psychological failure, the typology was created by examining the interview protocols for the 39 assistant pastors and recording each man's dominant strategy for relating to the organization. This list of strategies was reduced to successively shorter and more general lists.

Eventually, it became apparent that the coping behaviors could be described in terms of two dimensions. The first, termed *organizational acceptance*, reflected the extent to which the man accepted the organization *in its present state* (at the time of the interview). Three subcategories of acceptance were noted, the *acceptor*, the *reformer*, and the *rejector*.

The second dimension we called the *active–passive* dimension. In addition to the definition implied in the common use of the dimension name, it also entails, as an operational criterion, the extent to which the person's values or beliefs are integrated with his behavior vis-à-vis the organization. Therefore, the accept–reform–reject continuum is a measure of the person's alienation from the organization, while the active–passive dimension taps his alienation from himself.

The two dimensions can be combined to generate six types (and degrees) of person–organization integration:

	Active	Passive
Accept	6	5
Reform	3	4
Reject	1	2

Post hoc, this typology fits well with those of Merton (1957) and McKelvey (1969). Our "active accept" type (cell 6) is the equivalent of Merton's "conformity," which is, of course, nondeviant behavior. Our passive-acceptor (cell 5) is the equivalent of Merton's and McKelvey's ritualist. The active-reformer (cell 3) is the innovator, the active-rejecter (cell 1) is the rebel, and the passive-rejecter (cell 2) is the retreatist.

Interestingly, however, the present typology creates one form of adaptation not found in the Merton analysis: the passive reformer. He is the person who generally accepts the organization's goals; he does not accept the present procedures for attaining these goals, but he does little to bring about change. Perhaps the emergence of this form of coping is a function of the high level of passivity, relative to other types of systems, of the members of the priesthood. However, the passive-reformist orientation is undoubtedly an important one; at the societal level, this is the group to which liberals, reformers, *and* conservatives generally direct their appeals and calls to action; presumably, under the right circumstances, the passive reformer could swing toward either active reform or passive acceptance.

The six types of organizational adaptation were operationally defined as follows:

Active accept—Personal values congruent, with goals and means internalized; some indication of enthusiasm for, advocacy of, or involvement in present culture and structure of the Church.

Passive accept—Compliance but not agreement with organizational procedures; person "goes along," "keeps the peace," "doesn't make waves." Basically accepts the organization's goals. Does not advocate changing the organization since he has learned to live with it as it is.

Passive reform—Talks a lot about reform, gives specific suggestions for how change might be achieved, but takes little action to bring about change.

Active reform—Has general orientation toward changing one or more of the four key elements in his relationship with the organization: (1) the organization as a whole, (2) his superior, (3) his job assignment, or (4) himself (e.g., by acquiring new skills). Is both a "talker" and a "doer" regarding change.

Passive reject—Highly negative attitude toward the organization with few or no ideas about how it could be improved. Highly alienated.

Active reject—Actively fights the organization in its present form; works toward new organizational goals and procedures; takes the radical view that the organization may have to be largely torn down before it can be properly reconstructed.

In coding the interviews it became evident that often a person had orientations relevant to more than one type of adaptation in the coding system. The solution was to code the person according to what seemed to be his *dominant style*.

Two coders scored a sample of 15 interview protocols for a test of interrater reliability. On the acceptance dimension the coders agreed in 12 of 15 cases, for an agreement of .80. On the activity dimension they agreed on 11 cases, for a .73 rate of agreement.

To obtain a single scale, we rank ordered the six cells in terms of the extent to which they indicate commitment to the Church organization in its present form. This is admittedly a risky and crude statistical process, but it seemed worth trying so that all six types could be used in a correlational analysis. The scores attached to each type of coping, those used earlier as cell identification numbers are shown at the top of p. 146. It is important to remember that we are measuring commitment to the organization in its present form, which is why passive reform is rated higher than active reform.

Coding reliability on the combination of the activity and acceptance dimensions (i.e., on the six types of orientation) was 8/15, or 53%. Since this index of reliability was not as high as we would have preferred,

Organizational commitment	
Score	Type of orientation
6	Active accept
5	Passive accept
4	Passive reform
3	Active reform
2	Passive reject
1	Active reject

both coders read each interview protocol and arrived at joint agreement on the orientation scores.

Organizational Orientations of Pastors, Assistants, and Specialists

In a study of professionals in the United States Forest Service, in which members are known to manifest a high degree of organizational identification (Kaufman, 1960), Hall *et al.* (1970) and Schneider *et al.* (1971) examined personal and organizational factors which appear to lead to high commitment. This study will be used as a basis for predicting differential levels of commitment by priests in the present study. Although the missions of the two organizations are obviously quite different, the Forest Service and the Catholic Church share the following important structural similarities:

1. Both are service organizations (Blau & Scott, 1962), placing stress on interpersonal relationships and helping.

2. Both systems have strong policies of promotion from within, with little or no lateral entry at middle or top organizational levels. This means that most members spend their entire work careers in one organization. This is the classic one-organization bureaucratic career orientation described by Weber (1947).

3. Perhaps as a result of point 2, members in each system generally exhibit a high level of organizational commitment.

4. There is much geographical movement of personnel around the organization, hindering the development of local community ties and enhancing the members' ties to the organization.

5. Subjects in each study could be considered professionals—professional foresters and ordained priests.

6. Both are large systems, geographically decentralized, with flat organization structures (i.e., wide spans of control). Therefore, at the

local administrative level, the organizations had to depend upon their professionals' acceptance[33] of basic organizational goals and policy.

There are obviously many differences between the Catholic Church and the Forest Service, but the following are among the more important career-relevant contrasts:

1. Professional foresters are in great demand at much higher salaries outside the Forest Service, in private industry. Priests find their skills difficult to transfer to other organizations, and there is still considerable stigma attached to leaving the priesthood. A priest is literally ordained a priest for life. Therefore, it is far easier to leave the Forest Service than the church.

2. One central Church value is obedience, stemming from the concept of a single divine authority. A central value in the Forest Service is professional autonomy, and decision making is based on shared responsibility across levels. In terms of corporate philosophy (or theology) and managerial style, the Forest Service tends toward Theory Y and the diocese tends toward Theory X (McGregor, 1960).

3. The work of priests, of course, has a large spiritual component. The Forest Service is purely a secular institution. Religious beliefs may affect the relationship between our predictors and organizational commitment in unknown ways. (As the data will indicate, this secular–sacred difference appears unimportant as far as commitment is concerned.)[34] For example, old Church beliefs, such as absolute authority, may enhance organizational commitment, while new Church beliefs, such as collegial authority, may undermine commitment to the Church in its present state.

Hall *et al.* (1970) found that the following factors were associated with high member identification:

1. High job challenge and involvement.
2. The person's length of service in the organization (tenure).
3. Organizational position. (However, position was also highly related to tenure. When tenure was held constant, the effect of position on identification disappeared.)

---

[33]Of course, acceptance or internalization of organizational goals is not essential, but it undoubtedly strengthens the local representative's performance.

[34]Some might argue that the Forest Service philosophy of public service and multiple-use management of public land might be just as strong a force in the work of a forester as is Catholic theology in the work of a priest. This would not imply that public service and land management principles are equivalent to a religious belief system—only that each may have equivalent amounts of influence on the daily work behavior of the individual priest or forester.

4. The individual's value for a pivotal organizational goal, public service.

5. The individual's self-image (on the supportive and involved dimensions).

6. The individual's need for affiliation and security.

With these findings in mind, we examined the effects on the priest's organizational commitment of the following factors: work assignment characteristics (particularly challenge), tenure, position, values, and self-image. (No measures of personal needs were included in the present study design.)

Orientation vs. Position. The basic assumption of this analysis is that in response to the significantly lower opportunities for psychological success in their work, assistant pastors would adapt by showing less commitment to and acceptance of the organization than would pastors or specialists. We see that the Forest Study data do, indeed, support this assumption in that commitment among foresters is related to job challenge. However, the Forest Service study shows that other factors are also related to commitment. To provide a better idea of what to expect in the present study, let us examine the three priest positions in terms of the commitment-related factors reported by Hall *et al.* (1970) and Schneider *et al.* (1971).

Influences on commitment	Pastors	Specialists	Assistant pastors
Challenge	High	High	Low
Tenure	High	Moderate	Low
Self-image		No difference	
Position	High	High	Low
Values (fit with organizational goals)		Few significant differences	

Curates are either the same or lower on all predictor variables. Because of their shorter length of service, it would be expected that specialists would show somewhat less commitment than pastors; however, because tenure is the only dimension on which specialists differ from pastors, the differences in organizational identification would probably not be sizable.

The distribution of types of organization orientation, along with comparisons of mean scores on the commitment-related dimensions, is shown in Table 8.1. Scores for the acceptance dimension were defined 3 for acceptors, 2 for reformers, and 1 for rejecters.

TABLE 8.1

Organizational Orientations of Pastors, Assistant Pastors, and Specialists[a]

	Pastors					Assistant Pastors			
	Active	Passive				Active	Passive		
Accept	15	14	29	(88%)	Accept	10	6	16	(41%)
Reform	2	2	4	(12%)	Reform	7	11	18	(46%)
Reject	0	0	0	(0%)	Reject	1	4	5	(13%)
	17	16	33	(100%)		18	21	39	(100%)
	(52%)	48%)				(46%)	54%)		

	Specialists			
	Active	Passive		
Accept	8	4	12	(60%)
Reform	4	4	8	(40%)
Reject	0	0	0	(0%)
	12	8	20	(100%)
	(60%)	(40%)		

Dimension	Pastors	Specialists	Assistants	Pvs S	Pvs A	Svs A
Organizational acceptance	2.87 (.33)[c]	2.60 (.50)	2.33 (.66)	$p < .05^b$	$p < .01^b$	NS
Organizational commitment	5.27 (.83)	4.80 (1.19)	4.28 (1.37)	NS	$p < .01^b$	NS
Activity (proportion who are active)	.51	.60	.46	NS	NS	NS

[a] Interview sample, $n = 92$.

[b] Degrees of freedom corrected for unequal variances, after Welch, quoted in Ferguson (1966).

[c] Figures in parentheses are standard deviations.

As Table 8.1 shows, the hypothesized differences in organizational orientation for pastors, specialists, and assistants are generally observed. The assistants have proportionately fewer acceptors and more reformers and rejecters than either of the other, more rewarding positions. Furthermore, only among the assistant pastors are any priests found who appear to reject the Church, and this group amounts to 13% of the assistants interviewed. Forty-one percent of the assistants accept the organization as is, and 46% are oriented toward reform.

This nearly even split between acceptance and reform among the assistant pastors illustrates an often-forgotten aspect of the generation gap in organizations today: The split *within* the generation of young employees may be as important and as significant as the difference *between* the generations. The variances in the scores for both organizational commitment and organizational acceptance were significantly greater for assistants than for pastors ($F = 3.99$ and 2.72, respectively; $p < .01$). Although a bare majority of assistants want reform, a sizable proportion are just as strongly behind the present authority structure as are the majority of older priests—their pastors.

Table 8.1 shows that pastors are significantly more accepting of the present Church organization than assistants ($p < .01$). Eighty-eight percent of the pastors interviewed were acceptors, as contrasted with 41% of the assistants. It was reasoned that the pastors show more of the characteristics which predict high commitment: long tenure, high position, and high job challenge.

Also as predicted, possibly because of their relatively low tenure, the specialists' organizational acceptance and commitment fell between that of pastors and assistants. Further, the acceptance level of specialists was significantly lower than that of pastors ($p < .05$), but it was not significantly different from that of the assistants. On commitment, the specialists did not differ signficantly from either of the other positions.

In contrast to the interposition differences on acceptance and commitment, there were no differences between pastors, assistants, and specialists on how active or passive they were. However, there was a tendency, across all groups, for the majority of the acceptors to be active and for the bulk of the reformers and rejecters to be passive, as is seen in the following combined totals:

	Active	Passive
Acceptors	33	24
Reformers and re-jecters	14	21

This relationship between activity and acceptance represents a force toward organizational stability—most of the active priests tend to be active in support of the organization in its present from.

Coping with Psychological Failure. Returning now to the assistant pastors, it appears that one way they cope with the psychological failure in their assignments is by developing orientations toward changing some aspect(s) of their organization or in extreme cases, by rejecting the organization.

Two factors probably explain why there are not more passive acceptors among assistant pastors. The first is that social change is a major part of the contemporary ethos. Many people accept as axiomatic the notion that organizations need reforming, a feeling which is heightened when one experiences frustration working in the world's oldest and perhaps largest and purest bureaucracy. Thus even priests are increasingly placing the blame for their failures on the Church rather than thesmelves; i.e., they are passive reformers rather than passive acceptors.

A second factor is that the "don't make waves" orientation takes time to develop. The literature abounds with examples of professions and occupations in which people begin their careers full of zeal, energy, and thrust for change. Then as they gain experience, encounter frustrations, and grow older, they become less zealous and idealistic and more accepting of the status quo. We will see evidence of this process occurring in the present sample through the "reality shock" of the first assignment.

Correlates of Organizational Orientations

We have seen that low organizational commitment and acceptance characterize the assistant pastors in the diocese. We have argued that this low commitment develops partially in response to the psychological failure the assistants experience in their work. However, we have also hypothesized that low commitment is related to the position of the assistant, but we have not established that the work climate of a position is directly related to low commitment. We now examine how a number of factors, including work climate, are statistically related to organizational commitment.

Five general types of variables will be examined as possible correlates of organizational commitment: tenure, work characteristics and outcomes, position,[35] values, perceived organization goals, and self-image. Tenure has been predicted by March & Simon (1958) to lead to commitment. Glaser (1964) and Hinrichs (1964) found changes in the values and orientations of scientists over time which suggest increasing organizational commitment. The literature on job enlargement (Hulin & Blood, 1968) and normative organization theory (Argyris, 1964; Likert, 1967; McGregor, 1967) either suggests or strongly implies that rewarding job

[35]Position was scored a 1 for assistants and a 2 for specials and pastors. The equivalence for the latter positions is based on consideration of previous data.

experiences will generalize to satisfaction with and thus commitment to the organization. Hierarchical position is known to be related to need satisfaction (Porter, 1961) and might therefore logically also relate to commitment. Self-image seems like a reasonable predictor since commitment is a function of the fit between the person and the organization; self-image has been found to be a key variable in measuring person–environment fit (Holland, 1966; Pervin, 1968). The fit between a person's values and the perceived goals of the organization is, of course, a key theoretical indicator of person–organization integration (Argyris, 1964; March & Simon, 1958; McGregor, 1967).[36]

All of these variables were found to be important predictors of organizational identification in the United States Forest Service (Hall et al., 1970). It is hypothesized that the same variables will correlate with commitment and acceptance in the present study. For comparative purposes, the results of the Forest Service study are shown in Fig. 8.1.

The relationships for priests between the types of organizational orientations and the predictors are shown in Table 8.2. The strongest correlates of organizational commitment and acceptance are two aspects of job satisfaction, satisfaction with supervision and satisfaction with the work itself. Most dimensions of work climate also relate to commitment and acceptance, but since climate is so highly related to supervision and work satisfaction (median $r = .54$ and $.48$, respectively), it appears that the influence of climate operates through job satisfaction. In the next chapter the causal sequence of these relationships will receive detailed attention.

Tenure and position both relate to commitment and acceptance. However, tenure is a stronger correlate of both organizational attitudes, and as in the Forest Service, the impact of position disappears when tenure is held constant ($r_{\text{pos., acc. (ten)}} = .10$, NS; $r_{\text{pos., comm. (ten)}} = .07$, NS). However, with position held constant, the effect of tenure is still strong (partial $r = .32$ for acceptance, $.29$ for commitment; both $p < .05$). Therefore, length of service, not position, in the organization is the stronger correlate of commitment. People in higher positions tend to have greater tenure than those in lower positions, and this is why higher-ranking members show greater commitment and attraction. (This makes the

[36] Adapted from Hall et al. (1970). Value–goal fit was based upon the number of categories in which the priest responded for "goals should be," number of categories for "goals are," and the number in which there was overlap or agreement between the two. The formula was:

$$\text{Value–goal fit} = \frac{2X \text{ (number of categories used for both "goals are" and "goals should be")}}{\text{(number of categories used for "goals are")} + \text{(number of categories used for "goals should be")}}$$

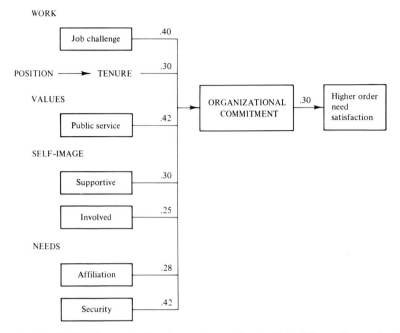

Fig. 8.1. Model of organizational commitment in the United States Forest Service. Numbers are correlations or median correlations, in the case of multiple relationships $N = 141$, $p < .05$ in all cases. Adapted from Hall *et al.* (1970).

impact of tenure especially significant here because in this organization virtually all of the other variables we have studied are more strongly affected by position than by length of service, as we have seen in earlier chapters.)

The amount of activities performed does not generally relate to orientation, except for one—the more administration one performs, the more committed he is. However, we know from previous data that pastors and specialists do more administration than assistants, and this may account for the apparent effect of administrative activity.

Of the value items, the importance attached to administration was also positively related to organizational ties, but again this predictor is strongly related to tenure ($r = .49$). Community involvement importance, however, was negatively related to commitment and acceptance, as well as being less strongly linked to tenure ($r = -.29$). Therefore, independent of tenure, priests who value community involvement—perhaps the "new breed"—tend to be less strongly committed to the present Church system than those who do not value community work. In a similar vein, those who value meaning and relevance as a Church goal

TABLE 8.2

Correlates of Organizational Attitudes[a]

	Organizational acceptance	Active–passive orientation	Organizational commitment
Assignment climate			
Superior effectiveness	31*	−03	30*
Work challenge and meaning	26	26*	27*
Interpersonal acceptance	32*	14	26*
Supportive autonomy	26*	07	29*
Activities performed			
Parochial	08	−01	08
Administrative	28*	09	28*
Community involvement	05	09	−03
Personal development	02	32*	02
Utilization of skills	32*	23	34**
Work satisfaction			
Work itself	55**	18	51**
Pay	−09	03	−06
Promotion opportunities	23	15	15
Supervision	51**	06	50**
Co-workers	30*	10	24
Position	37**	08	32*
Tenure	47**	02	42*
Values			

Parochial importance	17	-12	16
Administration importance	26*	11	31*
Community involvement importance	-27	-06	-30*
Personal development importance	-11	04	-16
Theological goals	17	-06	15
Existence goals	12	17	13
Meaning and relevance goals	-20	07	-26*
Church and society goals	-01	-01	-13
Shared authority	-26	-08	-27*
Perceived organization goals			
Theological	34	-01	32*
Existence	-29	06	-31*
Meaning and relevance	-05	10	-04
Church and society	15	04	04*
Value – perceived goal fit	25	00	25*
Self-image			
Supportiveness (general)	07	19	-01
Intellectual (general)	04	32*	02
Involved (general)	03	27*	-05
Supportiveness (superior)	24	-04	13
Intellectual (superior)	22	21	08
Involved (superior)	17	15	07

[a] Total interview sample, $n = 92$. Questionnaire data available on 72. Minimum $n \approx 60$. To be conservative, probability estimates are based on $n = 60$.

* $p < .05$, two tail.
** $p < .01$, two tail.

155

tend to be less committed as well ($p < .05$), although not significantly less accepting. Still another "new breed" value, shared authority, is also negatively correlated with organizational commitment and acceptance. All of these findings support the idea that priests who hold "new breed" values tend to be alienated from the organization in its present form.

Two types of perceived organizational goals correlated with acceptance and commitment. Priests who felt the Church is working toward theological goals report higher commitment and acceptance than men who do not see theological goals in operation. (The issue here is not whether theological goals are *relevant* to the Church but whether they are *practiced*.) However, priests who feel that the Church is motivated by concerns for internal maintenance and existence tend to be *less* committed and accepting of the system. Again these data fit with our general impressions of the concerns of "new breed" priests as opposed to moderates and conservatives. On the one hand, the "new breed" priest is likely to be cynical about the organization; he sees it as *not* practicing what it preaches about theology, being instead concerned with self-maintenance. More moderate and conservative priests, on the other hand, who are presumably more identified with the present organization, have faith that the organization is attempting to apply its theology and that Church existence *per se* is not an overriding concern.

The priest's general self-image was unrelated to commitment or acceptance. However, his image of himself as he relates to his superior was correlated with organizational commitment. In earlier chapters we have pointed out the heavy hand of authority in the Church, so it is not surprising that it is self-image *in relation to authority* which is the key self-image concept for commitment.

Interestingly, general self-image was one of the few concepts which was related to the active–passive dimension. The general self-image dimensions which were positively and significantly related to activity were the intellectual and involved components. The other predictors of the active–passive dimension were a cluster of job challenge and personal growth-type variables—work challenge, amount of personal development activities, use of skills, and global success conditions. Therefore, activity vis-à-vis the organization seems to be less a matter of person–organization fit than it is a function of one's personal style (self-image) and the extent to which one's assignment is a "stretching," challenging one.

When the data were analyzed within each of the three groups (pastor, professional specialist, and assistant pastor), we found that each position had somewhat different routes to commitment. Assistant pastors had the most significant predictors: work climate, values, and self-image.

For pastors, only values were related significantly to commitment. Specialists had a small sample size in this analysis, and there were few significant correlations. Elsewhere in this study, it was found that the impact of the work itself on the priest's satisfaction and self-image declines as he gets older and that at these later stages personal values predict satisfaction and self-image better than do the priest's job characteristics. This is consistent with the declining role of the work itself on organizational identification as the priest's career advances.

Another Form of Adaptation—Leaving the Organization

Another way to identify the components of low organizational commitment is to study employees who have voluntarily left an organization, on the assumption that those who leave are those who are less committed. Such an analysis was possible in the present study, as 13 assistant pastors had left the priesthood approximately a year and a half after the data were collected. By contrasting the personal, assignment, and career criterion variables for dropouts and those who remained, it was possible to approach commitment from another point of view. We can assume that all of the men who left did so as their own choices since the Church virtually never forces a person to leave the priesthood[37]; in fact, by canon law, the priest is ordained for life.

Unfortunately, we interviewed only four of the men who left, 3 curates and 1 specialist. Therefore, it is not possible to compare coded organizational orientation data for those who left and those who stayed. We will instead have to infer evidence of low commitment for the terminators by seeing if the correlates of leaving are the same as those of low commitment.

The data comparing terminating with nonterminating assistant pastors showed that the assistant who leaves the priesthood is younger (31½ vs. 36) than his colleague who stays; the dropout sees theological goals as less important to the Church and to himself, and he consequently performs fewer parochial functions than the nonterminating priest. The terminator's career outcomes are significantly lower than the nonterminator's—the dropout experiences lower satisfaction with the work itself and with his superior, and he experiences lower feelings of skill utilization in his assignment (all $p < .05$).

---

[37]Of course, a man may feel he was driven by organizational pressures to the point where he felt he had no alternative but to "choose" to leave. We do not necessarily equate the *choice* to leave with ultimate *responsibility* for being confronted with the choice.

Another intriguing characteristic of the dropout is that his pastor in his first assignment was viewed as less effective and less collaborative than the nonterminator's first pastor. This finding is especially striking in view of the fact that there were no differences in climate ratings of the present assignment. Thus the effectiveness and leadership style of the priest's first pastor seems to have a continuing impact upon the young priest.

Comparing the data on terminators with the correlates of commitment, we find that three key career criteria are strongly related to both turnover and commitment: utilization of skills, job satisfaction with the supervisor, and satisfaction with the work itself. Also, seeing the Church's goals as being theological is related to both high commitment and remaining in the priesthood. Further, we had interviewed four of the terminators, and they were all scored as either reformers or rejecters, whereas most of the total sample were scored as acceptors. Therefore, although our data do not bear directly on the point, it appears that leaving the organization is an outcome of low organizational commitment.

Earlier, we hypothesized that the first assignment would also be of great importance in forming the young priest's attachments to his organization. Therefore, we correlated the climate of the first assignment with the priest's organizational orientations, partialing out the climate of the present assignment.

In tracing the impact of the first assignment we also wanted to include whether or not the priest encountered surprise or "reality shock" in his first assignment. We coded the interviews, and gave each priest a score of 2 if he indicated first assignment reality shock and a score of 1 if he did not. Intercoder agreement was .90[38] on a sample of 15 protocols. For descriptive purposes, 37% of the priests interviewed reported initial reality shock; by position, the percentages are 57% for curates, 20% for pastors, and 23% for specials. Because the incidence of initial reality shock was significantly related to position ($r = -.36$, $p < .01$), the correlations between reality shock and organizational attitude were partials, with position held constant. Similarly, since present assignment was related both to first assignment ratings and to organizational attitudes, it, too, was held constant in computing the correlations between initial climate rating and organizational attitudes.

The partial correlations showing the impact of first assignment characteristics on attitudes toward the organization are shown in Table 8.3. Understandably, the person was more likely to experience reality

[38]Using the following equation:

$$\text{Rate of agreement} = \frac{2X \ \text{(number of agreements)}}{\text{(number coded by A)} + \text{(number coded by B)}}$$

shock if he had an unfavorable assignment, particularly one with an autocratic, ineffective pastor and unchallenging work. Table 8.3 also shows that if the priest experienced reality shock in the first assignment, it most likely still affects his present attitudes toward the Church. Not only will he be less committed and accepting, but he will also tend to be more passive vis-à-vis the organization.

Summary Comments on Organizational Identification

The agreement between the findings of the Forest Service and Church studies is surprisingly high. The following relationships have been found in the Forest Service and replicated in the priesthood:

1. Certain relevant personal characteristics, values, and (to a lesser extent) self-image incline a person to identify with his organization.

2. People with challenging jobs are more likely to be committed to the organization than those with less challenging jobs.

3. Identification grows as a function of the person's length of service. People in higher positions are more committed as well, but the effect of position appears to be due to the greater tenure of the incumbents.

In the Forest Service study it was found that appropriate personal needs are related to commitment, and that commitment, in turn, is related to higher order need satisfaction. The priest study showed that satisfaction with one's job is an intervening variable in the relationship between a good work climate and high organizational commitment.

Why does length of service lead to identification? One obvious response is that over time a person's values, self-image, or needs may change to become more congruent with the goals of the organization. However, in both of the present studies, although values were related to tenure, the relationship between values and commitment held up even with the effects of tenure partialed out. Self-image and needs were generally not related to tenure, which rules them out as explanatory factors.

Turnover and self-selection might be another explanation. The less committed people may quit early, leaving only the more committed in the more senior groups. However, turnover figures in both systems have been historically low, (although the dropout rate for priests is now increasing), and this does not support the self-selection argument.

What probably happens with length of service is that the person accumulates a complex network of positive and rewarding experiences which becomes associated with membership in the organization; these eventually may generalize to the organization itself (the "halo" phenome-

TABLE 8.3

Organizational Orientation vs. First Assignment Climate[a]

First-assignment variables	First-assignment reality shock	Organizational acceptance	Active–passive orientation	Organizational commitment
Zero-order correlations				
Superior effectiveness	-.41**	.37**	.14	.32**
Work challenge	-.50**	.32**	.11	.37**
Interpersonal acceptance	-.26*	.29*	.08	.29*
Supportive autonomy	-.56**	.32**	.17	.33**
First-assignment reality shock[d]	—	-.35**	-.25**	-.37**
First-order partials[e]				
Superior effectiveness	-.34**	.28*	.16	.22*
Work challenge	-.43**	.25*	.02	.31**
Interpersonal acceptance	-.14	.16	.01	.19
Supportive autonomy	-.47**	.24**	.15	.24*
First-assignment reality shock[d]	—	-.25**	-.23*	-.28**

[a] Minimum *n* = 60.

* *p* < .05, one tail.

** *p* < .01, one tail.

[d] Based on data from the total interview sample, *n* = 92. For first assignment reality shock, present position level was held constant since present level and reality shock were correlated at *r* = -.36.

[e] For the four first-assignment variables measuring climate (superior effectiveness through supportive autonomy), each corresponding present assignment variable was held constant.

non) so that organizational membership eventually becomes functionally autonomous as a motivating factor. Thus we have found that over time the priest's self-image becomes increasingly correlated with his organizational commitment, as did the forester's self-image (Schneider *et al.*, 1971). When one combines this increasing identity investment with (1) the declining number of outside opportunities as one gets older and (2) the dissonance-reducing process of assuring oneself that he has chosen his commitments wisely (Vroom, 1966), it seems reasonable that time would lead to increasing identification.

We find, then, several avenues, through which high organizational commitment can develop: *time, work, values,* and *personal style.* Let us briefly consider the implications each has for organizational effectiveness.

Time-based commitment is still a mystery here since the underlying psychological processes are unknown. If, however, it is a matter of becoming more emotionally invested in the organization, then it may eventually seem more like entrapment than commitment. The person may become highly dependent upon the organization and highly threatened by any organizational changes which may affect his position, making him a source of resistance to change.

Another source of either resistance to change or of strong reformism can come from the person with value-based commitment. He may be in accord with his perception of the organization's goals, but his perceptions may not match those of top management. Thus he may work doggedly at cross-purposes with the organization, convinced that he is pushing the organization in the "right" direction. Both the "new breed" of younger priests and the "old guard" frequently show this kind of behavior. An example of this problem was the case of one older priest who thought the second Vatican Council was completely wrong in accepting shared authority. His response was, "If we accept shared authority, we'll be Protestants, not Catholics!"

Another problem with values is that they may lead to subgroup identification rather than to organization-wide commitment. Excessive subgroup identification (e.g., to one's own district or parish) may lead to harmful intergroup competition which could undermine total organization cooperation and performance.

Personal style-based commitment can be most troublesome as the personal qualities leading to commitment become less task relevant. For example, a high need for achievement (nAch) salesman may be a good and productive fit with a challenging sales organization. The fit of the young MBA who loves the life style associated with his New York advertising agency may be less directly productive, but is probably, at the worst, neutral regarding performance. However, what if the firm wanted to move him to Omaha? Another problem arises if the personal style characteristics leading to commitment are deficiency- rather than growth-oriented (Maslow, 1955). For example, in the Forest Service study, the need for security was positively related to commitment. Seeing the organization as a haven in which to maintain security may be dysfunctional for both the person and the organization.

Work-based commitment probably involves the fewest problems since it provides the most direct link between person, performance, and identification. However, when this form of attachment is operative, the organization must be alert to the need to provide challenging jobs. If the work-oriented and committed employee is moved to a stifling assignment, his organizational commitment would probably be correspondingly reduced.

Before adopting organizational commitment as a criterion of effectiveness, the organization must obviously ask whether this should be important to them. Commitment to the organization may be accepted too uncritically as important. It is probably most important to organizations with the following characteristics:

1. A policy of promotion from within and little lateral entry at middle and high levels.

2. Employees who need a long, costly training time to become effective in that organization's work. (There is a tendency for organizations to exaggerate the need and time required for training new people.)

3. Organizations in which work experience is more important to effectiveness than is current technical knowledge. (Where recent technical knowledge is required, *low* commitment and high turnover, especially among younger employees, may be the best for the organization.)

4. Commitment *per se* is important for some goal-relevant reason. An example here is research-and-development organizations, which are more effective if their professionals have accepted the company's financial goals (Hall & Lawler, 1970). As another example, for the Catholic Church, it is important that the personal style of its recruits fit with the celibate life style required of its priests.

NINE

Group Development and the Role of Action Researchers in an Authority-Based System

We have seen considerable evidence of unshared authority and psychological failure experienced by priests in the diocese studied. From these data we concluded that the diocese as a system tends to be more failure oriented than success oriented. We have seen that the state of the system now is such that its members may be so strongly affected by the organization's general authority and failure orientation that they may not be able to work collaboratively to deal effectively with specific organizational problems. Before any part of the system can become more effective at organizational problem solving and decision making, it must first experience development or growth.

The reader will notice that this chapter has a different "flavor" from that of earlier chapters. The reason is that here we are using a different method of collecting data—participant observation. We will be reporting on the events we experienced in our relationship with the personnel board, and the data will consist of critical events, feelings, problems, and developing processes, in contrast to the statistically based discussions of earlier chapters. As we said in Chapter Three, we hope that the multiple methods used will converge on the same conclusions, increasing their validity.

The personnel board, which initiated the study, was a group committed to solving, as well as identifying, organizational problems. It was also aware of the danger that it could be handicapped by the authority-based system in ways which the board members might not even be conscious of. Perhaps most important, the length of the board's existence, 2 years, gave it enough time to work on group development as well as its primary task. For these reasons, and after sharing their problems, we felt that the experiences of the personnel board may represent in microcosm the experiences of the larger organization as it attempts to solve its internal problems through the collaboration and participation of its members.

In addition to its value as a microcosm of the total system, the personnel board is also important when considered as a certain type of microcosm—a group. Because it is a group, it stands midway between a person and an organization in complexity as a unit of analysis. Both individual career issues and organization-level issues can be found in a group. And since this research is concerned with career development and organizational development, it is useful and efficient to study both processes in the same setting.

More generally, the history of the personnel board provides many clues about the process of development away from a closed, failure-oriented system. What would the theory of psychological success predict about the experiences of the personnel board as it attacked the organizational problems we have described in previous chapters? It is safe to assume that since the board was composed of members of a failure-oriented system, the members would tend to begin with rather low confidence in their ability to solve these system problems. Given this low self-esteem, the theory of psychological success would predict that they would pick goals which were either extremely difficult or extremely easy. Either strategy would tend to reduce the probability of failure rather than increase the odds for success, as extremely high goals make success so unlikely that failure is not too damaging, and very low goals almost insure success; in the first case, goal nonattainment may not produce strong psychological failure, while in the second, goal attainment will not produce strong psychological success.

When the personnel board began its work, it was in an extremely visible position, being created by popular interest, and all priests in the diocese were looking to it for important results. Therefore, of the two predictable options—excessively low or excessively high goals—it was most likely to choose the latter.

In our view, this is precisely what happened. Without unduly anticipating our data, it seemed to us that the board frequently chose extremely difficult goals for itself when it had the option of choosing easier ones. One example was their initial choice to sponsor an organization-wide study rather than to propose a new personnel system, as personnel boards in many other dioceses did.

Because of the selection of extremely difficult goals, one would expect a high anxiety about avoiding the failure which might occur. Further, because the members, as a group, were not accustomed to a system of shared authority, they would be unlikely to either attempt to achieve or experience competence in working collaboratively with the central authority of the organization.

As we worked with the personnel board, it seemed to us that all of these processes occurred—extremely high goals, anxiety about failure, and a tendency not to collaborate with formal authority. Since these processes can be logically predicted, we believe that they would occur in any group working in a system with such a strong tradition of unshared authority and psychological failure. If we thought these issues indicated some special idiosyncracies of the personnel board, we would certainly not describe them here.

What *is* remarkable about the personnel board is the fact that it was successful, despite the odds. It generated a creative set of proposals, presented by the entire board (there was no minority report), *and* these proposals are currently being implemented by the bishop. We want to emphasize the significance of their success since we will here be dealing more with the process of their labors than with the outcomes; our main interest is in the difficulties arising in development out of a failure orientation, and it may not always look as if the board was headed toward success.

Generally, what the personnel board found was that a system tends to act out its problems as it moves toward solving them. If the central system problems were authority and failure, many of the board's problems would center on those issues as well. In fact, the main theme which runs through the history of the personnel board seems to be the pervasive impact of the failure orientation of the total system of which they are a part. This chapter will show how this impact was felt in most of the major decisions they faced. We also hope to identify a number of developmental tasks which the personnel board encountered during its development. To do this we will first describe the major events in the life of the personnel board, concentrating on the data and keeping as far from interpretation as possible. Next we will interpret these experiences in terms of the issues and developmental tasks they seemed to represent. On the basis of these findings, we will look at the kinds of problems any system might encounter as it attempts to develop.

History of the Personnel Board

Preliminary Events

The personnel board met with the researchers on December 12, 1967, to discuss their needs and research areas of mutual interest. They had originally been thinking of engaging personnel consultants to establish a new personnel assignment system, and in the meeting the researchers raised the alternative possibility of an organizational diagnosis focusing on the career of the individual priest. This raised the issue of the primary task and identity of the board, in particular whether it was the appropriate body to conduct a broader study, focusing on broad classes of variables affecting the work of the priest, as opposed to the job-assignment procedure. Following this meeting, the personnel board decided to ask the Yale researchers to conduct an organizational diagnosis. We submitted a proposal to the board and the archbishop and the proposal was accepted.

The proposed period of research was from March 1, 1968 to March 1, 1969, with a final report to be sent to the chairman of the personnel board no later than March 1, 1969. On the basis of the findings and conclusions in the Yale study diagnosis, the personnel board would then develop and propose recommendations regarding personnel matters to the bishop.

The study was to be conducted in three phases. Phase I would consist of individual interviews with 90 priests, to be completed by June 1, 1968. Father Douglas Morrison, a member of the personnel board with skills in counseling, agreed to conduct one-third of the interviews. Father Morrison's collaboration was important not only because of our need for help in finishing the interviews before summer retreats and vacations but also because it would increase the involvement of the board in the ongoing research and provide a stronger link between the researchers and the client system. Phase II was the development and distribution of the questionnaire, which would be constructed on the basis of issues revealed in the individual interviews. Phase III would consist of meetings of small groups of priests to discuss the results of preliminary interview and questionnaire analyses. These meetings would also allow for additional data collection. It was planned that this phase would be completed by August 15. The remainder of the year would be spent analyzing the data and completing the organizational diagnosis and report due the following March.

The Wider Context in Which the Personnel Board Worked

To fully understand the experiences of the personnel board, it is important to be aware of the wider context, both within and outside the Church, created by the events of 1968 and 1969.

Within the diocese the bishop who created the personnel board and financed its work announced his resignation midway through the board's work but after all of the interview and questionnaire data had been collected. He was a popular bishop who maintained very personal, individual relationships with his priests. He was seen as a man who was always available for a priest with a problem. In the interviews many men had their own particular story of how the bishop helped them with warm support, confidence, or financial aid or in some other way at some critical time so that their lives were significantly affected by his assistance.

At the same time, he was seen as rather *laissez-faire* on organizational matters, with a tendency toward liberalism. Many priests had learned to experiment successfully with changes by either not informing the bishop or by informing him and then proceeding as long as there was no negative response. As a result of success with the latter tactic, many young priests came to cherish the "creative silence" of the bishop. This *laissez-faire* style was reinforced in later years by illness, which made him increasingly dependent upon his young chancery staff for advice.

The new bishop was a young, active man, reputed to be a conservative. Not a great deal was known about him aside from his reputation. He was appointed in the winter of late 1968 and was installed on March 19, 1969, just 19 days after our research report was due to the personnel board. Concerns about the transition to the new bishop, perhaps intensified by both his general reputation and the lack of more specific information about him, undoubtedly had a strong impact in the functioning of the personnel board.

In the Catholic Church there had been rising expectations of liberal reform since the second Vatican Council under Pope John XXIII. There was a great sense of hope and anticipation among young priests, apprehension and resignation among older ones. This trend was reversed, however, under Pope Paul. The first strong sign of this reversal took place in his encyclical on (opposition to) birth control issued in the fall of 1968. This reversal was reinforced by several later statements reasserting papal authority and the rigidity of the Church's stand on priestly celibacy.

On a societal level there was a growing awareness of the need for social change and the reform of many established social institutions, such as the political system, universities, and the draft. The Vietnam war and civil rights were the two best-focused issues, but the discontent appeared directed more generally at the total system of established authority.

However, a strong reaction against this reform movement was also forming, as the "silent [conservative] majority" began to be heard. Resistance to change stiffened, heightening the reformers' tendency to mistrust collaboration with established authority. A brief surge of the reformers' political type vanished with the defeat of Senator Eugene McCarthy in his bid for the presidency. There was increasing movement toward confrontation and organized use of the power of lower-level members of organizations (e.g., students, welfare recipients) as a means of forcing social change. The effectiveness of student and Black revolutionaries was closely watched by liberals and radicals in the priesthood.

The result of the liberal and conservative trends was a growing social division in the United States, reflected in the overuse of such terms as "generation gap," "backlash," and "confrontation." The nature of the social stress and the greater relative power of conservatives was illustrated by the main political events of 1968: the assassination of Dr. Martin Luther King, Jr.; the rise and fall of Eugene McCarthy, and the assassination of Senator Robert F. Kennedy, with the resulting disillusionment of many young people; the violent National Democratic Convention in Chicago; and the election of Richard M. Nixon and Spiro T. Agnew, with a strong third-party bid by George Wallace, a southern conservative.

All of these events, in the diocese, Church, and nation, appeared to represent the same trend—conservative reaction to and reversal of a trend toward liberal institutional reform. Perhaps these events further increased the personnel board's failure anxieties and mistrust of formal authority.

Work toward the Board's Final Report

Thus the study began officially on March 1, 1968. The first problem the personnel board faced was the fact that many priests expected their work to be completed in time to effect changes in personnel practices for that September's assignment changes. The fact that the board had to wait a full year prior to developing their recommendations might have been disturbing to priests wanting more rapid change. In view of this concern, the board sent a letter to all priests in the diocese describing the need for the organizational diagnosis as a source of valid information upon which to base change recommendations.

During most of April and early May the personnel board was relatively inactive, as the researchers and Father Morrison were extremely busy conducting the individual interviews. We conducted an average of three or four interviews per day, 2 days per week. It was for us an extremely busy period, characterized by much new learning about priests and the Church and the excitement of sharing impressions, ideas, and plans for the questionnaire. In contrast to this activity at Yale, the personnel board did not meet often, if at all, during this period.

May 23, 1968. We invited as many board members as could attend to a session to plan the questionnaire. Four members attended. We had prepared a preliminary draft, and we made substantial changes during the discussion. Later in May or early June we had a second such session to go over the revised form and produce a final version. After this session there seemed to be general satisfaction with the questionnaire. There seemed to be some concern, however, that specific diocesan and parish "structures" were not sufficiently covered.

Early June, 1968. The questionnaires were sent out to all active priests in the diocese.

June 25, 1968. The personnel board met. The Yale researchers were not present. The questionnaire planning session was discussed. It was generally agreed that specific structures were not sufficiently covered in the questionnaire and that a supplementary questionnaire might be considered. It was also suggested that all board members be notified in advance of the schedule of the group interviews so that they might be able to attend one or more of these meetings. The board also discussed possible recommendations it might make regarding personnel matters without jeopardizing the outcome of the Yale study.

A meeting was scheduled for July 2, to include the researchers and to consider the following:

1. Whether the questionnaire as sent would provide the needed information.

2. Feasibility of a supplementary questionnaire on "structures" and other items suggested by priests.

3. Whether the research team should issue an interim progress report.

4. Whether a representative sample of questionnaires had been returned.

5. Whether the board should make any preliminary recommendations before September.

6. Whether the chancery's views had been sufficiently considered.

7. What the board should be doing between then and March 1969.

Late June. A member of the personnel board phoned the researchers. During this conversation we discussed the seven points formulated at the June 25 meeting and some concerns of priests that had come to the attention of the personnel board. Two of these concerns had to do with the research team. The first was that we had no previous background in sociological studies of the Catholic Church. Another question related to the fact that neither of the researchers was a Catholic (one is an Episcopalian, one is Jewish); could non-Catholics really understand the Church and do the kind of job that a Catholic could do? The rate of return on the questionnaire, the possibility of progress reports, and the need for the researchers to meet periodically with the board were also discussed. The board members felt that all of these concerns could be summarized by the need for greater contact, for less distance between the researchers and the board.

July 2. A meeting of the personnel board and the researchers was held. The meeting began with a discussion by the researchers of how the research was progressing to date. Fifty-three percent of the questionnaires had been received so far, with many more arriving each day. Given the fact that they had only been out for two weeks, the researchers were pleased with the response rate. The researchers also presented a graph (Fig. 9.1) showing average responses to five questions describing the priests' evaluations of the study.

The data showed that on the average the reactions were positive. The most positive responses were on the questions "Is this study worth doing?" and "Will you learn something from this survey?" The lowest responses were on the question "What is the likelihood of improvements resulting from this survey?" There was considerable discussion about why priests were relatively pessimistic about the likelihood of change resulting from the survey.

We also discussed a supplementary questionnaire dealing with specific structures and possible changes that might be made. Several ideas were proposed, and several members favored a supplementary questionnaire, but no decision was made. There was also considerable interest in the group interviews, particularly in their planned composition. Some members felt homogeneous groupings (i.e., all pastors or all curates) should be used, while others wanted heterogeneous selections. The researchers felt the group should be randomly composed. It was also mentioned that some priests wanted to volunteer for the group interviews, and we agreed that priests should have this option.

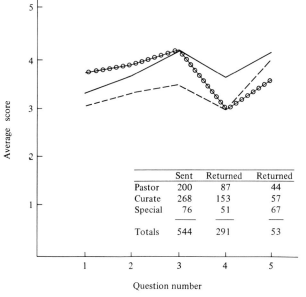

"Questions"

1. How valuable will survey be?
2. Are survey topics interesting?
3. Is study worth doing?
4. Likelihood of improvements resulting from survey?
5. Learn something from survey?

	Sent	Returned	Returned
Pastor	200	87	44
Curate	268	153	57
Special	76	51	67
Totals	544	291	53

Question number

Fig. 9.1. Opinions about this survey. Solid line, specials; dashed line, pastors; solid line with circles, curates.

Another topic generating considerable interest was the orientation and allegiance of the personnel board and the activities they should be performing until the Yale study was finished. Who were they? What was their identity? What was their function? What should they be doing? Since some members had been appointed by the senate and some by the bishop, there was disagreement about whom they should represent. One member described an attempt of 15 priests he knew to form a group to confront the bishop and demand changes. However, all they could agree upon was the strength of their dissatisfaction. They could not agree on the source of their discontent or on specific strategies. So they eventually disintegrated. The message was that the personnel board should work out its internal identity confusions before it attempted to work on particular diocesan problems.

Later there was a description of other dioceses in which structural changes were being tried. It was suggested that the personnel board might invite representatives of these dioceses, as well as outside consultants such as sociologist Father Andrew Greeley or psychologist Father Eugene Kennedy, to discuss present and possible changes in diocesan structures. This idea met with considerable enthusiasm, and it soon developed into a 2-day conference design, with the first day devoted to researchers such as Greeley or Kennedy and the second oriented toward the representatives from dioceses undergoing experimental change. Specific dates in the fall were proposed (September 11 and 12) as well as sources of funds for the conference.

July 9, 1968. The personnel board and reseachers met. The meeting began with more discussion about the symposium with outside consultants and diocesan representatives. It was decided to request funding from the priests' senate. In response to a proposal that the senate's Clergy Education Committee sponsor the symposium as an open educational session, most members felt it would be better if it were solely a personnel board function. They felt it was important for the board to do it alone to help provide a sense of accomplishment and identity.

The meeting then turned to a discussion of possible action recommendations which the board might make. One member said that if the pastor–curate relationship is "like the Spanish inquisition," perhaps they should "junk the whole thing." Another suggested that they should "junk" the system by having priests live in apartments and work in teams. When the researchers mentioned that there may be two sides to this relationship problem, suggesting that part of the problem may be due to a lack of initiative and responsibility on the part of the curate, some members felt that we were taking too much of a burden off "the system" and might be identified with the far right of the organization: "management representatives."

Much of the discussion took the form of questions directed at us. What exactly *was* our experience in other organizations? Had our previous research focused on problems similar to those of the diocese? What would we recommend? How likely was change? Why were priests so pessimistic about the chances for change?

We said that we would not make recommendations since that would be their job. We would, however, draw conclusions from our data, but we could not do that until all the data were analyzed. We stressed that the success of change would depend upon the commitment of the hierarchy and all priests in the diocese to the changes the board would recommend. Involving priests in this study would be one way of increasing this commitment. In particular, we felt that the success of change depended upon the commitment and strength of the personnel board since they were the leaders or levers for change in the system. We pointed out that they had already taken the first step toward change by calling in outside researchers to conduct the study and provide the data necessary for meaningful recommendations. We added that taking initiative would mean overcoming the tendency toward avoidance of conflict that we found in the individual interviews. The responses indicated that this assessment of the situation had made sense to them.

August 2, 1968. The personnel board and the researchers met. The initial discussion centered on the group interviews. Some priests in the diocese had been calling them "therapy" sessions because of the strong feelings that had been expressed in them. Another concern was that too much time was taken up by one or two members in these sessions. This led to a discussion of how interpersonal conflict is dealt with by priests as opposed to other occupational groups. We felt that conflict was strong but suppressed in the Church and were therefore pleased that people could experiment with more open conflict in the group interviews.

This in turn led to a discussion of how conflict was handled by the personnel board. Some members felt the board should strive for consensus, while others felt the members should live with their differences. From this discussion came a suggestion, made by the researchers, that the board meet in September to work on its own internal group processes and to postpone its meeting with the outside consultants and diocesan representatives. In this way the board could develop its internal identity and strength before it considered diocesan problems. After discussion this suggestion was accepted; it seemed to be an idea various members had themselves considered.

There was a discussion of how temporary or permanent the board should be. Was the task of the board to recommend new structures or to help create them? Who should implement the changes the board might recommend, the senate, bishop, or personnel board? Was the board a creature of the establishment (bishop) or the grass roots (senate)?

At this point a member made two recommendations which in retrospect were quite significant: (1) that the board become permanent and (2) that additional young curates be appointed to remedy a serious underrepresentation of this age group. (At the time there were 4 pastors, 4 specials, and 1 curate on the board.) After some discussion the first suggestion was modified to state that the board should remain permanent through the implementation of the results and that the board should be responsible for implementation. It was decided that the board would write to the bishop with three requests: (1) that the board work with the Yale researchers to develop joint recommendations, (2) that the board remain in existence long enough to deal with the implementation of personnel changes, and (3) that the bishop appoint 3 new members from a list of 6 young curates recommended by the board. The dates of September 17 and 18 were set aside for a 2-day session on internal process issues.

August 21, 1968. The bishop replied to the personnel board's requests. He approved the request for the personnel board to work with the Yale researchers after completion of the Yale study. He also indicated that he had written to "certain priests" asking them to serve on the augmented personnel board; these were three of the men proposed by the board.

On the subject of the tenure of the board, he said he had "no objections" to the board's serving for 6 months after the study's recommendations had been made, but he suggested that a final decision be reserved until it was certain that this would be in accord with the recommendations. He made no direct mention of the involvement of the board in implementing the recommendations.

Early September, 1968. The researchers had second thoughts after hearing of the bishop's reply. It seemed clear to us that the bishop did not feel it was appropriate to give the personnel board authority for executing changes until he knew what those changes might be. As we thought about what had happened at the August 2 meeting of the board, with the help of our colleague and consultant, Chris Argyris, we realized that we and the board had strayed from the original contract between the researchers, the board, and the bishop. In that agreement, the board was clearly a temporary body, formed only to recommend changes; now they were asking for authority to create changes. The Yale researchers were hired to conduct an organizational diagnosis, to provide feedback, and (if requested) to consult in making recommendations; however, in supporting the personnel board in its bid to become an implementer of change, we were becoming involved in the internal policy decisions of the diocese.

Incidentally, it was far clearer at the time to Argyris than to us that this was happening; while this was in large part due to his competence and experience in consulting relationships, it was probably also facilitated by his being in less immediate contact with the organization than we were. A less involved third party can be an objective source of valuable feedback, especially in a process as complex as organizational diagnosis and intervention.

As a result of these second thoughts, it seemed unfair and unethical for us to participate in the 2-day September session, which had been organized partly as a means of developing the board's internal strength to help it become a more effective implementer of change. The problem dealt more with the expectations of the board than with the value of examining its group processes. A process session could equally well help make the board a more effective proposer of change. However, this was not the stated purpose of the meeting, and for this reason we sent the following memo to the members of the board:

September 10, 1968

Memo To: Members of the Personnel Board

On the basis of recent developments and some rethinking on our part, we feel it would be better to meet for one full day next week rather than the previously scheduled two days.

The meeting will be at Father X's place, from 10:00 a.m. to 5:00 p.m. on Wednesday, September 18.

At this meeting we would like to discuss our role and the role of the Personnel Board in this study. We would also like to discuss some of the data that we have generated so far.

We are looking forward to seeing you then.

Sincerely,

Douglas T. Hall
Benjamin Schneider

September 18, 1968. The all-day meeting of personnel board and researchers was held. The meeting began with considerable dismay and puzzlement about the meaning of the bishop's letter and our reasons for changing the nature of the meeting. Some members felt that since the bishop had not specifically mentioned implementation of recommendations, he must have misunderstood the board's request. The researchers, however, thought that the bishop had understood the request perfectly and was sticking to the original contract regarding the personnel board's function. Further, the researchers indicated that they would accordingly stick to their contracted function as organizational diagnosticians and would not aid the board in becoming implementers of change. This position had a strong impact on many members of the board, being seen variously as withdrawing from involvement with the board, "selling out" to the chancery office, and betraying the board.

We felt that there was truth to these charges to the extent that we were withdrawing from a position we had erroneously assumed during the previous meeting. However, since the position we assumed previously was a withdrawal from the original terms of the research contract, we were not retreating but returning to what we saw as our rightful role. We stressed that we had clearly "goofed" at the July 9 meeting, we realized that they were disappointed and angry at us, and we owned up to our share of responsibility for the problem. After much heated discussion we all agreed that the Yale team would remain a data-gathering and interpreting agent and a *neutral* resource on organizational change, and the board would remain a recommendation-making agent. To help the board prepare for its task of making recommendations, the researchers would discuss preliminary findings with the board.

The board then began to consider other means to increase the chances of its recommendations being accepted. The researchers described general organization theory and research, indicating the importance of commitment from the top of a system for lasting change. Therefore, the board might meet occasionally with the bishop and develop the recommendations in collaboration with him. He would obviously feel greater commitment to the resulting proposals, which would be as much his as the board's.

Members of the board said that the bishop usually preferred to have diocesan committees complete their work on their own and present him with their recommendations in final form. There was also concern that if the recommendations were produced jointly with the bishop, it might not be possible to produce a unified report of the board. The basic question seemed to be: How much might the bishop influence the thinking of the board members?

As an alternative to a direct meeting between the board and the bishop, it was decided that the researchers would meet with him. In this meeting we would apprise him of the progress of the study and invite his participation in the board's meetings.

Late Fall, 1968. The bishop announced his resignation, effective immediately, citing poor health. He was appointed apostolic administrator of the diocese pending installation of the new bishop. All priests in the diocese were invited to propose candidates for the open position of bishop. There was much speculation about who the new bishop would be. Given the recent (conservative) papal encyclical on birth control and the recent activism among priests, the guesses were that the new man would be conservative. Shortly thereafter the new bishop was appointed, a young man reputed to be strong and conservative.

There was a feeling of bitterness that the appointment was made so shortly after the invitation to submit names of candidates. Since it takes so long for the Church hierarchy to go through all the steps necessary to select a new bishop, it was felt by many that the new man was already selected when the invitation was sent.

November 21, 1968. A meeting of the personnel board and the researchers was held. The meeting began with a clarification of the agreement on the use to be made of the data we gathered in the study. When we presented the data we had brought for the discussion, some priests said they had been wondering if we would in fact bring data, as we had said we would in the last meeting. They said they would have felt abandoned if we had brought no data. We then went on to discuss the meaning of the data.

There was another discussion of the best strategy for change, with some arguing for collaboration with the bishop and others arguing for collaboration with the local priests, through a series of mass meetings and discussions. These seemed to be seen as mutually exclusive alternatives.

Since the former bishop had retired, it was argued that there was no reason for the researchers to meet with him as originally planned. The question was raised of how to contact the new bishop. It was agreed that when the new man was appointed, the board and the researchers would meet with him to inform him of the study and to discuss the role he would play in it.

December 19, 1968. The personnel board and the researchers met. The meeting began with a discussion of the tapes made at meetings of the personnel board and whose property they were. It was decided that they were the property of the personnel board and would be made available to the Yale researchers.

One of the members had attended a regional meeting of personnel board representatives and presented a report of what boards in other dioceses were doing. Most other boards were working in the area of personnel assignment procedures and job descriptions. Following the presentation, the members generally felt that other boards were working on the more specific personnel issues that this board had decided against examining in favor of the organizational diagnosis. The remainder of the meeting was devoted to a rather detailed exploration of the general areas in which the board might want to develop recommendations. To the researchers, this seemed to be the first meeting where the board began to work hard at identifying and discussing different points of view on personnel problems.

January 13, 1969. The personnel board and the researchers met. Much of the meeting was spent discussing data from the study which showed graphically large differences in the climate of the assignments of pastors, specials, and curates, with the latter consistently the lowest.

It was decided to send a letter as a progress report to all priests in the diocese. This letter would also serve to remind priests that even though the Yale study would be completed by March 1, individual priests would not receive feedback until later, as the board's work would just be beginning on March 1.

January 26, 1969. The personnel board and the researchers met. The process of formulating recommendations was again discussed. With the naming of the new (reputedly conservative) bishop, there was now more support for involving all priests rather than the bishop. The most frequently cited reason for going to "the troops" was the help and ideas they would offer, but there was also awareness of the support and organizational power they could provide. There was increased reluctance to contact the new bishop regarding his participation. There was also uncertainty about whether the new bishop should get a copy of the Yale study at the same time as the board since he would not have been installed yet.

The board also discussed the progress report to be sent to the priests. Two members brought draft letters to the meeting. The final letter was a combination of the two, with two significant deletions: (1) an indication that the board's recommendations would deal with structural change and (2) an indication that the board, through its commitment to the principle of participation, would present a tentative draft of its proposals to all priests for consideration, modification, and approval.

January 28, 1969. The following letter was sent by the personnel board to all priests in the diocese:

PERSONNEL BOARD
c/o 125 Market Street
Hartford, Conn. 06103

January 28, 1969

Dear Father:

    The purpose of this letter is to bring you up to date on the activities of the preliminary Personnel Board and the progress of the Yale study.

    The procedure to be followed in the Yale study was outlined in a summary sent to you last March by the Bishop. As described, the data-collection process involved three phases: 1) personal interviews with individual priests; 2) questionnaires sent to every priest; 3) meetings with small groups of priests to discuss the information obtained in phases 1 and 2. The third phase was completed last fall. Since then the researchers have been engaged in detailed study and analysis of the data.

    You will be interested to know that over 400 priests, or about 75%, responded to the questionnaire. This percentage of response is considered quite good for sociological surveys of this kind, and offers a favorably broad base for the intended study. The Board wishes to express its deep appreciation for the cooperation shown by priests in all phases of the study.

    The Board members are: [names omitted here]. Because there was recognition of the need for more representation of assistants among its membership, the Board asked the Bishop to add three curates to the Board. From a list of suggested names, the Bishop last August appointed Fathers [names omitted here].

    The Personnel Board has been meeting regularly with Doctors Hall and Schneider. These discussions centered around the preliminary analyses of the responses to the questionnaire. The Yale report will be completed and submitted to the Chairman of the Personnel Board on March 1. The most important part of the Board's work then will be the development of recommendations suggested and supported by the report.

The Personnel Board is excited by the possibilities for creative growth that it sees in this study. The Board accepts its responsibility to investigate all possibilities and formulate recommendations according to its best judgment.

Sincerely yours,

Secretary, Preliminary
Personnel Board

February 17, 1969. The personnel board and the researchers met. With the researchers' report due on March 1, the board discussed a summary that could be sent to all priests in the diocese. It was not yet decided whether the bishop would receive a copy of the report or summary before the priests did. One suggestion was to clear the distribution of any summary with the outgoing bishop, even though it was thought he would defer any decision to the new bishop. Another view was that perhaps part of the board's "homework" was to involve the priests and get feedback before a final report could be sent to the bishop. In agreement with this idea, others felt it would be unfair to the bishop to give the Yale study to him before the board's final recommendations were available.

The researchers were asked if they would prepare a summary. For two reasons, we were hesitant to do this. First, we would have just finished the complete report by March 1 (a task we just barely completed on time), and the prospect of writing a summary, which would be short yet contain the most salient data, was not particularly attractive. Also, we felt that this task was within the board's competence and was more correctly their responsibility since they were going beyond the original plan by sending a summary to all priests.

The more important reason for reluctance on our part was our feeling that the summary was being sent to all priests as much to generate support for the board's ideas as it was to gather new data and ideas. This fear was reinforced by the board's reluctance to show the report to the bishop before the board had sent a summary to all priests and involved them in the recommendations. It seemed that the board was "using" the participation and collaboration of the priests to preclude the participation of the bishop.

For these reasons we were reluctant to provide a summary of our report. Some board members wondered if we were not getting too much involved in the board's decisions and responsibilities. Others emphasized that the uncertainty of the transition period and of the board's relationship to the two bishops made the proper procedures to follow less clear.

After much discussion, one member proposed that the board present the Yale study to the bishop along with a letter indicating the board's intention of and procedures for continuing to develop its recommendations. This proposal was accepted unanimously. The board also decided, after discussion, to submit its tentative proposals to all the priests for comments and suggestions.

The Board also voted that all future meetings should have time limits and that a quorum (7) be required for business. A motion that substantive issues require a two-thirds vote was deferred to the next meeting.

The researchers indicated that if the board received an active affirmative response from the bishop regarding its plans to send a summary to all priests, they (the researchers) would be willing to provide a summary. This would deal with our most serious objection to the summary idea.

March 1, 1969. The Yale study was completed and the report picked up by a member of the personnel board.

March 2, 1969. The personnel board met. The report was distributed and a letter to the bishop was discussed and agreed upon. One member felt that since the board should be completely open about its operation, it should send a copy of its letter to the bishop to all priests. The other members agreed on the importance of openness but did not feel that sending the letter was required.

March 3, 1969. The chairman of the personnel board met with the outgoing bishop, who agreed to the board's procedures for developing recommendations. The chairman contacted the researchers, who agreed to work on a summary, but added that this would be done better in collaboration with the board.

March 13, 1969. The personnel board and the researchers met. Procedures for distributing the report were discussed and agreed upon. A letter to all priests announcing receipt of the study and proposed procedures was approved.

Much time was devoted to discussing the type of summary to be used. The three most popular ideas were: (1) inclusion of all text, excluding appendices, graphs, and tables, (2) outline form, and (3) abridgment. It was finally agreed that one member would prepare a 20–40 page abridgment or condensation. Regional meetings with priests were also discussed.

March 31, 1969. The personnel board met. It was decided that the summary would be the text of the original report, deleting tables and appendixes. Certain graphs were to remain. The board identified four areas in which recommendations would be drafted: (1) exercise of authority, (2) assignment of priests, (3) development of skills and abilities, and (4) working conditions. Committees were assigned to work in each of these areas.

April 14, 1969. The personnel board and the researchers met. The relationship between the board and the researchers was discussed. It was acknowledged that the researchers' contract had been fulfilled and that they had given additional time and effort. Since the board was not then in a position to renegotiate its future relationship with the researchers, it was decided that in the interim they would not plan on attending future meetings of the board. The rest of the meeting dealt with discussions of the proposals, and some committee activities were discussed.

Since this marked the end of the researchers' formal association with the board, we will not describe further activities of the board in detail. We remained in frequent contact with particular board members and also received minutes of their meetings. Therefore, we will now present the highlights of the activities of the board after April, 1969.

As the board began to work on its proposals, the frequency of its meetings increased to every 1 or 2 weeks. As the work progressed, two factions, roughly based on age and liberalism/conservatism, seemed to emerge. All issues were decided by vote. As the issues became more clearly defined and as the board moved closer to the final version of its report, roll-call votes became more frequent.

A critical meeting occurred after the first committee report was submitted, containing what some members believed to be rather radical views. One of the more conservative members moved that the bishop receive a copy of the preliminary recommendations before the other priests. The motion was seconded by another of the more conservative members. This raised the issue of whether the board would be willing to modify the report, on the basis of the bishop's reactions, before sending it to all the priests. The sponsor of the motion argued that sending the report to the priests without the benefit of the bishop's reactions might create unreasonable expectations among the priests by stating an extreme position which the bishop might feel obliged to modify or reject. A younger priest proposed an amendment to the motion—that the same report be sent unchanged to the priests. The motion's sponsor opposed this, as he felt it gave the appearance of an ultimatum or challenge to the bishop. A younger member felt that sending the bishop a preliminary report might do him a discourtesy since it might make him feel obliged to react to it. If the unchanged report did create unrealistic expectations and turmoil, he continued, this would be turmoil that already exists (as shown in the Yale study) and would be healthier brought out into the open. If the board had certain ideas and recommendations it could not in good conscience suppress them; what was good for the diocese was good for the bishop, he argued. By a roll-call vote, the motion was rejected 6–5.

Next, another conservative member proposed that, beginning with that meeting, all minutes of the board's meetings be sent to the bishop to keep him informed on the activities and differences of opinion on the board. The motion was seconded by another conservative. In the discussion it was noted that the board had not sent minutes to the former bishop and had already offered to discuss its activities with the new bishop. Also, the possibility of a minority report was always open. Supporters of the motion felt that openness required it; others felt that openness was not contradicted by following present practice and that the only alternative was to send minutes to all priests as well as to the bishop. By a roll-call vote (requested by the motion's sponsor) the motion was defeated 7–4.

The changes recommended in the report of the committee basically involved experimental team parishes in two deaneries. Pastors would be asked to resign as pastors and assume a copastor status with their (former) curates. There was a long discussion of particular phrasings and conditions in this report as well as concern about whether such a large-scale organizational structural change could or should be achieved in such a short time. Some felt that this would severely limit the freedom of choice of priests in the experimental deaneries who did not wish to participate in the experiment.

After several meetings of hard work, an apparent impasse was overcome and the board was able to evolve an experimental plan that appeared to maximize the choices for both those who did and those who did not want to join the experiment: Those who did not want to join could be transferred to other deaneries. This solution was not reached easily because some members felt a certain amount of pressure was required in order for priests to try a change in working relationships. Generally, the votes were split on the basis of age, with the older members opposed to the experiment and the younger ones in favor of it.

When the tentative proposals were completed, three open meetings for priests were scheduled. The report was sent to all priests, along with a questionnaire asking for reactions to each section of the report plus questions about the respondent's desire to be on a team, his date of ordination, position and town, and signature.

The board's deadline, September 1, was approaching rapidly. On August 10, 1969, the board decided to write to the bishop explaining the difficulty of completing its work by then and indicating its intention of sending the final report later in September.

Also on August 10, the board considered but decided against a meeting with the bishop to get his views of the report. It was noted that their original offer to meet with him remained open and that he appeared to prefer to remain uninvolved at that stage of the board's work and to await their final report.

The board also considered but decided against meeting with the Yale researchers. It was felt that they would prefer not to comment on specific proposals. The board also decided against a suggestion that they meet with outside consultants such as Fathers Eugene Kennedy, Andrew Greeley, and Joseph Fichter. The board would, however, send them copies of the tentative report along with a request for their comments.

Also considered and rejected was a proposal to meet with the senate's committee on parishes or with a representative group of laymen. It was judged that too little time remained; the board did not feel that it was in a position to do widespread consultations and to take new directions in the shape of its report.

One hundred ten priests attended the three open meetings held by the board (36 pastors and 74 curates and specials). One hundred nineteen returned questionnaires, 83 pro, 26 con, 10 doubtful. There was a long discussion at the August 10 meeting of how to use the questionnaire. Some members wanted to incorporate these ideas into the final report. Others felt that this was unnecessary since the responses showed a predictable difference of opinion and board members would be led to repeat earlier debates and decisions. It was added that the final responsibility for recommendations was to rest with the board. It was decided to divide up the questionnaires and draw up a list of potentially useful suggestions for discussion later.

In August, 1969, the researchers received a letter from the board requesting comments on their tentative report. We sent the following reply:

August 20, 1969

Reverend ———
Secretary, Personnel Board
Archdiocese of Hartford
125 Market Street
Hartford, Connecticut 06103

Dear ———:

Thanks for your note. We appreciate the copies of your report and the minutes that you have been sending us. It sounds as if the Board has been very busy in the last few months. Regarding your request, we feel ourselves unable to make meaningful comments on the *substance* or *content* of the report. We hope you understand that since we don't really know about all the ideas and issues in writing the report and in deciding what to include and not include, it is difficult for us to pass judgments on what you have concluded and on the recommendations you have made.

On the other hand, we feel very comfortable in expressing our feelings about the general *style* of your report. Both of us were pleased in the way the Board used the portions of our report you considered most relevant and in the way it was integrated with your own thinking and the comments and proposals of others. Our report was used as one of many inputs into your list of recommendations, and we think this is as it should be. We also very much liked the organization and easy readability of the report.

Incidentally, we would be pleased to meet informally with the Board and discuss in more detail the background and content of your report. This would afford us the opportunity to more fully understand the process of your conclusions.

Sincerely,

Douglas T. Hall
Benjamin Schneider

BS:
DTH:dn

We received no reply from the board.

In September the board worked on modifications and additions to the preliminary report. On September 23 the final changes were made, and plans were made to distribute it to the former and present bishop, their auxiliary bishops, and the priests of the diocese. In the last part of this chapter, we examine portions of this report and some outcomes of the changes that have occurred.

Developmental Tasks of the Personnel Board

During the personnel board's existence it faced a series of problems it had to resolve at a particular time before it could move on to other activities. By "resolve" we do not necessarily mean "solve" in the sense of being finished with the problem once and for all. In fact, general problems seem to recur in different forms over the history of any group. In this section we will examine these general problems as *developmental tasks*, problems whose solutions contain the potential for group growth and effectiveness. These recurring tasks were *identity, authority, internal integration*, and *work competence*. We will now reexamine the history of the board in terms of these issues.

The initial *identity* issue arose during our first encounter with the board in December 1967, when it had to choose between a personnel study and an organizational diagnosis. By hiring us, the board chose a broader identity than they had originally conceived.

Identity also arose as a problem in April and May of 1968, when the researchers were conducting the individual interviews. The board members began to wonder just what their role should be as the researchers conducted their study. Nothing really was required of them for another year, yet they were feeling internal and external pressure to "do something" about the reassignments coming in September.

The resolution of this problem involved two other issues, *authority* and *work*. The board's response to the problem was to establish more frequent contact with the researchers and to collaborate with us in the ongoing process of the study and interpretation of the data. They also became highly interested in sponsoring a 2-day symposium with well-known outside experts. In this way they defined work for themselves, and their anxiety over their lack of activity decreased.

Another source of the board's anxiety over the researchers' high activity and their low activity was due to their uncertainty about the competence and commitment of the researchers, an *authority* issue. This problem was gradually resolved through a process of testing during the summer and fall of 1968. References to our competence were made in many ways—what other organizations had we studied? How were the questionnaire responses coming? Why were priests rather pessimistic about the prospects for change resulting from the study? Could non-Catholics really understand the problems of priests? Were the group interviews becoming "therapy" sessions? How about Yale submitting interim reports? Was it really possible to study the priest, a spiritual person, as a working man? These concerns were resolved through discussion of the specific questions and the underlying anxieties and uncertainties as well as through the presentation of specific data about and from the questionnaire responses. This resolution occurred at two levels: We had "good" answers to all the specific questions, and we were able to discuss the general issue.

The second area of the board's uncertainty dealt with our orientation, commitment, and the probable conclusions from our study. The questions (about us) seemed to be, "Who would Yale support—the Establishment or those who want change?" "Does Yale's commitment and loyalty lie with the board or the bishop?" The question about our data was "Will the results of the study support proposals for significant changes?"

The question of our loyalty emerged strongly when we first supported and then withdrew from supporting the board's bid to become implementers of the changes resulting from their proposals. This issue was dealt with in the September 1968 meeting, which we had converted from a 2-day internal process session to a 1-day discussion of our role and that of the board. The outcome was a decision that the researchers would be loyal to neither the board nor the bishop; we would provide data and be neutral regarding the internal decisions and policies of the diocese. In retrospect our feeling is that we just barely avoided being "seduced" into becoming an ally of the personnel board. It is not clear if they saw the process in that way; in their anxiety over being effective in their task they may have been unaware of how they were using the outside authorities to support their bid for wider powers.

The issue of the seduction of the outside change agent and authority figure is a classic one in the therapy and organizational change literature. Patients falling in love with therapists and organizations offering jobs to consultants are two common means of incorporating the change agent into the ongoing system as a means of increasing the system's control over him.

Concerns about the thrust of our report were reduced as we began to share the methods we used and some of our preliminary data with the personnel board. Data which we brought to the next meeting after the September clarification of our role showed clear differences in work climate and satisfaction for pastors and specials, on the one hand, and for curates, on the other. (As one member said in that meeting, our bringing data also reaffirmed our commitment to continue collaborating with the board, allaying a fear that we might withdraw completely after the September meeting.) Subsequent data made it very clear that the results would support proposals for change.

During the period of the summer and fall of 1968 our feelings before and during these meetings also supported the idea that there was a problem involving our relationship with the board. We sometimes felt that the board could take virtually any issue—be it the weather, the Papal encyclical, or the fate of the Red Sox—and convert it to a serious concern about "Yale's" activities! We often felt trapped in the role of the universal scapegoat.

After the problem of our relationship to the board was resolved, it became clearer why we might have been put in this role. With March 1 drawing closer, the board clearly saw that it had its own work to do—with a new bishop being appointed, it had to decide how to deal with the new man and proceed with the recommendations. This would take some ingenuity since legally its existence would terminate with the resignation of the outgoing bishop. Therefore, it had to find a means of continuing its work under a new man who had not formally granted it permission to continue.

As the board began to perform work that was uniquely its own, as contrasted to collaborating with the researchers, clear divisions within the board quickly emerged. Generally, these were political differences between those who wanted to collaborate with the bishop (proauthority) and those who wanted to collaborate with the priests and implicitly "work around" the bishop (counterauthority). Thus the board had to deal with *integration, work,* and organizational *authority* issues.

Some degree of integration had to be achieved first, though, before the other work could get under way. Given the strong divisions within the board, it was clear that its problems with us had helped keep it from confronting these issues. With us no longer involved as focal figures, the board had to turn to its own internal differences.

Before the new bishop was appointed there was division among the younger members as to whether the board should attempt to involve the bishop in the board's work. After the new bishop was named, however, the sentiment switched away from collaborating with the bishop and toward the involvement of all priests. There was a strong assumption held by many board members and often discussed explicitly that the new bishop was a controlling person who could not be trusted to collaborate. The problem then became how the board could continue operating with the new bishop in office. In our view, the board chose to "work around" the bishop, although this interpretation was not accepted by the board.

This second authority problem was resolved to a degree when the board decided to go to the outgoing bishop for approval of its plan to involve all priests in formulating recommendations. This was done about 2 weeks before the new bishop was to be installed, and it was generally expected that the outgoing bishop would defer to the incoming man. To the board's surprise and delight, the older man approved their plan, and a major authority obstacle was removed.

One way to interpret this action is as an indication of the board's underestimation of the extent to which a bishop would be willing to cooperate with it. Much of its behaviors and attitudes vis-à-vis either bishop were based on untested assumptions about his attitudes or probable responses. When we pointed out the importance of these assumptions in determining its actions and the fact that they were untested, board members generally replied that the risks involved in testing them would be too great; e.g., if, as they feared, the new bishop did want to control their activities, once they approached him, he might take advantage of the opportunity and assume control.

It is easy to get caught up in the failure of the board to consult with the bishop and to seek support from the priests. At the conclusion of the chapter we will detail some theoretical ideas in explanation of this phenomenon. At this junction it is sufficient to indicate that the board was apparently engrossed in its own obvious development and did not feel ready to encounter an authority which had the power to negate the progress which had been made. This progress concerned the attempt to deal with its internal mechanisms so that the actual assigned task, development of recommendations, could be accomplished.

With the procedural issues somewhat resolved, the board was able to turn to the *work* of preparing its recommendations. In the process of doing this, the young–old split became strongly felt. At this time a voting procedure was adopted which gave the board a mechanism for operating without consensus. However, at one point they appeared to be at an impasse over the kind of experimentation to advocate. Finally, this was resolved by a compromise which increased the options available for pastors and made it possible for some more conservative members to vote in favor of a motion.

Completing the tentative report had been a highly significant success experience for the group. In a system badly split between liberals and conservatives, a representative group of priests had been able to agree on specific and innovative action recommendations. This agreement required months of effort and was obviously hard won. The feedback they received was decidedly positive. It is probably safe to say that no other diocese had ever produced such a plan for change through such a thorough and democratic process. Plaudits were received from a number of prominent priest–social-scientists as well as priests in the diocese. In addition, copies of the board's recommendations were sent to the bishop of each diocese in the United States.

In the view of the researchers, at this point the board saw its main task as winning support for its report rather than changing it. Three meetings were held with priests and a questionnaire was sent to all priests; the majority of the respondents were in favor of the report, but it is not clear to us that the priests' comments and suggestions markedly affected the final report. For various reasons the board chose not to obtain feedback from the bishop, the researchers, laymen, the senate committee on parishes, or outside consultants. They had already terminated the ongoing relationship with the researchers, and they had explicitly decided not to send their minutes to the bishop. As was stated in regard to the questionnaire inputs, considering these other inputs might have endangered the hard-won agreement on the preliminary report and opened all the old debates all over again. It seemed to us that the closer they came to filing their final report, the more closed they became about it. We further felt that this closedness was necessary to preserve the resolutions they had achieved to their problems of identity, authority, integration, and work competence.

The Process of Self-Directed Change in Failure-Oriented Systems

On the basis of the experiences of the personnel board and the theory of psychological success, it is possible to derive some propositions about the processes which may occur as members of a failure-oriented system attempt to change the system without the involvement of the chief executive in the system.

1. *Because of the members' history of failure in dealing with authority in the system, they will tend to overestimate the likelihood of failure in any particular future encounter with authority.* This process clearly occurred in the personnel board's assumptions about how the bishop would respond to its attempts to cooperate with him.

2. *This expected failure in cooperation with authority leads to an orientation of either avoidance or competition vis-à-vis authority.* In a situation in which the members are forced to deal with the authority in some way (i.e., flight is impossible), the only alternative open is competition. For the personnel board, though, there were long periods in which they were able to avoid all contact with the bishop and operate independently. However, even the process they used to avoid him reflected the perception of him as adversary rather than ally.

3. *As a result of the competitive orientation, the members tend to become closed to new information about the authority which might reduce the sense of competition.* A climate of competition is self-reinforcing, creating stereotypes and perceptual closedness which feed on the original negative evaluations of the other. This closedness is described by Schein (1965, p. 81) as a common outcome of intergroup competition:

> (a) Each group begins to see the other group as the enemy, rather than merely a neutral object.
>
> (b) Each group begins to experience distortions of perception—it tends to perceive only the best parts of itself, denying its weaknesses, and to perceive only the worst parts of the other group, denying its strengths; each group is likely to develop a negative stereotype of the other.
>
> (c) Hostility toward the other group increases while interaction and communication with the other group decreases; thus it becomes easier to maintain negative stereotypes and more difficult to correct perceptual distortions.
>
> (d) If the groups are forced into interaction . . . , group members tend to listen only for that which supports their own position and stereotype.

4. *When the members achieve a success, there is a tendency to preserve that success rather than to attempt further risks in order to achieve other successes.* This principle comes from Lewin's research, in which he found that

individuals with a history of failure (i.e., low self-esteem) tend to quit following success, whereas people accustomed to success are more likely to raise their aspiration levels and continue. As we have said, the personnel board achieved a significant success in reaching agreement on a bold plan, and it appeared reluctant to attempt to modify (and perhaps improve) its proposals. Successful members in failure-oriented systems thus show the characteristics of winning groups in intergroup competition (Schein, 1965, p. 82):

(a) Winner retains its cohesion and may become even more cohesive.

(b) Winner tends to release tension, lose its fighting spirit, become complacent, casual, and playful (the "fat and happy" state).

(c) Winner tends toward high intragroup cooperation and concern for members' needs, and low concern for work and task accomplishment.

(d) Winner tends to be complacent and to feel that winning has confirmed the positive stereotype of itself and the negative stereotype of the "enemy" group; there is little basis for re-evaluating perceptions, or re-examining group operations in order to learn how to improve them.

5. *As a means of preserving the sense of competence following success, the members tend to close themselves off from sources of information which might provide some negative feedback calling for an alteration of the successful end product.* This closing process appeared as the personnel board neared its deadline and appeared unwilling to disrupt the agreement it had achieved on the preliminary report.

6. *As a result of processes 1–5, success experiences in failure-oriented systems will tend to be isolated, nonreinforcing events. Either outside intervention or positive action from the top management indicating a change in the system state would be necessary to produce continuing success.* In the psychological success theory presented in Chapter One, we mentioned that two aspects of the organizational environment were critical in attaining psychological success: (1) the environment must be benign and facilitative of success and (2) the individual must develop confidence in the benignness of the environment. If the organization is not benign, as is the case with a failure-oriented system, the individual will not be able to develop confidence in that system. One way that movement toward a success orientation can occur is if the top members of the system decide to use their power to make the system more benign toward individual success. If lower-level members attempt to change the system without the collaboration of the top members, it will be difficult for them to be open to changes in the attitude of higher authority, even if the change effort is successful and authority does become more benign. Outside third parties may be necessary to help higher- and lower-level members become aware of their respective changes of attitude.

The Failure-Oriented Environment
as a Truncator of Group Development

Using Mills' (1967) theory of stages in group development, it is possible to show from a somewhat different perspective how the closedness resulting from a failure orientation inhibits a self-reinforcing cycle of success and growth. Building from the work of Deutsch (1963), Mills classifies the formation and operation of groups into five orders: (1) immediate gratification, (2) development of a structure defining itself as a group (which would then permit sustained gratification), (3) pursuit of a collective goal, (4) self-determination, and (5) growth. The orders are cumulative, and each depends upon the achievement of the preceding ones. In other words, before a group can work toward a collective goal it must demonstrate the capacity to gratify its members' needs and develop a structure defining itself as a group.

Corresponding to each order of development is a critical issue (or, in our terms, developmental task) which must be successfully resolved before the group can move on to the next level. Order 1, need gratification, requires the generation of *commitment* of members to participate in the group's activities. Order 2, development of group structure, requires the development of a system of group *authority*. Pursuing a common goal requires the management of affect in relationships—intragroup conflicts and loyalties, group beliefs and values—which develop through joint effort. Order 4, group self-determination, requires the development of self-awareness and the ability to change goals while maintaining the group's integrity. Because of resistance to group self-awareness, this stage raises "issues which are likely to discourage even the most able and confident" (Mills, 1967, p. 110). Mills states that

> . . . groups, quite beyond their conscious intentions and in the service of cohesion, resist "too much" self-knowledge. . . . Groups, like the villagers who stone the prophet, burn the philosopher, and crucify the messiah, turn against their fellows who hold a mirror to them.

As we have suggested, even following success, a group in a failure-oriented system tends to be closed to feedback about itself in relation to other parts of the system. Thus it may be difficult for such a group to completely resolve the issue at the fourth order of development.

The fifth order, growth, involves the creation of new possibilities, widening the group's awareness of possible goals, structures, and ways of behaving. Mills (1967, pp. 111–112) describes the requirements for group growth as follows:

[Growth] requires the crossing of traditional boundaries separating insiders from outsiders, one's own group from other groups. It means an expanding network of outside relations: a readiness to contact "foreigners"; to take into the group their ideas, languages, and products; and to send out (or give up) to foreigners one's own ideas, products, and even personnel. . . . It means, in short, the progressive permeation of those boundaries which ordinarily define and secure one's group, the reformation of relations with other groups, and the formation of new groups. . . . The problem of maintaining system integrity while boundaries are being permeated and the group is becoming interdependent with other groups we call the issue of *interchange*. How is it possible for the group to increase its receptivity to new information, to expand its network of intergroup contacts, to increase the volume and variety of its imports and exports, without suffering the loss of its capabilities, its identity, and its autonomy? The issue is critical for the executive, for, if unresolved, not only will the group lose what it might have gained through contact, but it runs the danger of either dissolving into other groups, or becoming increasingly closed off from others and, as a result, becoming increasingly ethnocentric.

From the theory of psychological success and failure it seems clear that the person or group accustomed to failure would not be likely to accept the risk of opening itself to this interchange of new information and possibilities. Not accustomed to the security of success, it (he) would tend to preserve what it has attained rather than set out into unexplored areas. This, then, is a second way in which the background of a failure orientation can inhibit group development.

The development of the personnel board fits well with the Mills paradigm and with the theoretical impact of the failure orientation. Need gratification was probably apparent when the members were invited to serve on the board, as they anticipated the rewards of helping to solve an important organizational problem. Group structure was imposed by the bishop's definition of the board's purpose and the appointment of a chairman. It achieved its first work success, after a fashion, in searching for outside consultants to help it conduct the study. It entered the area of self-determination when it broadened its mission and hired us to conduct an organizational diagnosis. It accomplished more in this area when it attempted to become a change-implementing group as well as proposers of change. A level of growth was achieved, by Mills' criteria, when the board decided to add new members to make it more representative of all the views in the diocese.

Because the board was part of a basically closed system, however, it had difficulty in being open either to its own internal processes or to groups and people beyond its boundaries. The process feedback provided by the researchers was often resisted, and very little internal feedback was provided after the researchers left. This made the self-determination task more difficult.

The closedness to outside people and groups—the bishop, laymen, a senate committee, feedback from priests, and the researchers—severely hampered group growth. The interchange process described by Mills was little in evidence after the board agreed on its preliminary report, as we have indicated previously. The board tended to solidify its boundaries and lost the benefit of potentially useful outside feedback.

Parallels between Group and Individual Growth

Throughout this chapter we have been discussing group and individual psychological success and growth in roughly equivalent terms. The predictions regarding probable outcomes of success in failure-oriented systems were stated in terms of "members," which could be either people or groups.

To reinforce this connection between system (group or organization) growth and individual growth, we will now present Maslow's (1954) model of individual human development and show how strikingly similar it is to the Mills group paradigm just described. Maslow posits five basic categories of human needs—physiological needs, safety, belongingness and love, achievement and autonomy, and self-actualization or growth. Like Mills, he proposes a process of prepotency, or cumulative development: Before a need at a given level becomes salient, all needs at lower levels must be generally satisfied.

What is striking about the Mills and Maslow models is the similarity of their five categories and the hierarchical relationship among the levels. In the physiological category, Maslow places the satisfaction of basic body or tissue needs such as thirst and hunger. These needs relate to the satisfaction of various component parts of the human body. Under order 1, immediate need gratification, Mills places the gratification of particular component parts of the group, individual members; safety to Maslow means developing a sense of long-range security, freedom from threat to one's existence. Order 2, development of group structure, involves developing conditions to sustain the group's existence over time. Belongingness and love involve developing close affective relationships with others and becoming integrated in groups; to Mills pursuing a collective goal involves intimacy and work, managing rewarding and effective relationships around a task. Group self-determination involves autonomy and self-awareness, which comes quite close to Maslow's fourth level of ego needs, autonomy and achievement. The fifth level is the same in both systems—growth, the development of new possibilities as to what the person or group is capable of becoming. These two sets of categories are listed side by side in Table 9.1 to further describe the similarities in the models.

TABLE 9.1

Comparison of the Stages of Group and Individual Development

Group Development			Individual Development		
(Mills, 1967)			(Maslow, 1954)		
Level	Description	Issue	Description	Issue
1.	Immediate grati- fication	Need satisfac- tion of individ- ual members (component parts) of group. Not relevant to group as entity.	Physiological needs	Satisfaction of tissue needs (hunger, thirst). Gratifica- tion of component parts of human body. Not relevant to total person.
2.	Group structure	To sustain condi- tions for long- term gratifica- tion and exist- ence as a group.	Safety	Elimination of threat to one's existence. Development of sense of safety.
3.	Collective goal	Resolution of issues dealing with interper- sonal intimacy and group ties in regard to work.	Belongingness and love	Development of sat- isfying affective interpersonal rela- tionships. Sense of belonging in group relationships.
4.	Group Self- determination	Capacity for self- awareness and changing of goals	Ego Needs: autonomy and achievement	Development of sense of identity, self-esteem and self-control
5.	Growth	Development of new possibilities, new ways of existing.	Self-actualization or Growth	Development of po- tential aspects of self; new ways of existing.

Very simply, this similarity between group and individual development permits us to combine all the insights provided by the individual interviews and questionnaires, group interviews, and the personnel board. We will then be in a position to revise the model of psychological success as a descriptor of individual and organizational growth in the light of the findings from all of these sources of data.

TEN
Personal and Organizational Influences on Psychological Success and Failure

In the preceding chapters we have examined the priest's personal characteristics, assignment characteristics, and career outcomes. These analyses have taken the form of average amounts or levels of various factors experienced by men in each of the three positions and by men with varying degrees of seniority. It has been shown that personal qualities, perceived assignment characteristics, and career outcomes do, in fact, vary primarily with position but also with tenure. In this chapter the focus will be more on how career outcomes in addition to commitment are related to the man's personal and assignment characteristics. If the relative lack of psychological success for assistant pastors arose through the cycles described in the theoretical model presented earlier, it should be possible to pin success outcomes down to particular features of the work environment, such as the amount of challenge experienced in the work, and to particular personal qualities, such as the values attached to various work activities. Our purpose here, then, will be to bring together the three levels of analysis which have been described separately to this point, and to show how personal and situational influences interact to shape the course of a man's career outcomes.

A Framework for Analysis

The framework for analysis which we will use as a basis for examining these relationships is the result of three considerations: (1) our original model of psychological success in organizations, (2) a theoretical statement by Schneider (1973) on people's perceptions of organizational contexts, and (3) the use of the professional specialists as a criterion group against which patterns of relationships for pastors and curates may be compared.

Our basic model of psychological success in organizations suggests that a person's values and the conditions under which he works jointly determine his chances for experiencing psychological success. The model indicates that people must (1) have autonomy in their work, (2) have the opportunity to perform meaningful, challenging tasks, and (3) take advantage of the opportunities in the environment if they are to experience psychological success. Specifying these conditions and outcomes allows for a general test of the model by examining groups of individuals who work under different environmental success conditions and then comparing these groups on the outcomes they experience in their assignments.

We have already shown that specials, who work under conditions more conducive to the psychological success experience, do indeed report more positive career experiences than curates, who have fewer opportunities. Therefore, specials will serve as an important criterion group as we probe the mechanism of success. Similarly, assistant pastors will serve as a criterion group as we attempt to understand the correlates of psychological failure.

As stated earlier (in Chapter One), it may be that the process of failure is simply not the obverse of the success process. Perhaps different factors and different relationships among factors are involved in the two different experiences. We may find that two different models are required, one for the failure experience and the other for the success experience. By examining career processes separately for the groups under extreme degrees of success (specials) and failure (curates), we hope to learn more about how these experiences occur and whether they do in fact require different models.

In our data we will analyze the hypothesized links between (1) *personal qualities* (self-image, organizational values, and task values, in increasing order of situational relevance), (2) *personal behavior* (task performance), (3) *assessment of assignment characteristics* (challenge and autonomy), and (4) the resulting *evaluation of the behavior-in-context* (feelings of skill utilization and work satisfaction). We will be looking for a hierarchy of variables with the personal qualities preceding the behavior and the behavior preceding the evaluation of the situation.

Prior to proceeding with a detailed analysis of the variables included in this study, it is important that we inform the reader regarding some of the steps which preceded the decision to finalize the presentation. We spent a great deal of time simply poring over the correlation matrices. We outlined correlations in various age groups and examined changing patterns of relationships; those of significance will be presented, although we found that most of the patterns were fairly consistent within the three positions. Another approach to the correlations was to follow a rule (Schneider, 1973) which yields, given the inclusion of variables measured at different levels of generality, a hierarchy with more specific variables (say task values and the amount of different activities) preceding the more general or more inclusive constructs (say work satisfaction). Thus the hypothesis is that individuals perceive and process a great deal of information prior to drawing general conclusions about the nature of their satisfaction.

This hierarchical analytic scheme was particularly useful in the present study because of the levels of variables measured to test the psychological success model. Measures were taken of individual values, individual behavior, situational conditions, and evaluations the person reached about the outcomes of his behavior in the environment. We will show the hierarchical arrangements of these variables for each of the positional roles and for the entire sample of priests. These presentations will be a matter of empirical determination.

In presenting these data we will focus on the specials as the role in the priesthood which most clearly exemplifies how these measures would be related to each other under conditions of psychological success. The curates will serve as a useful frame of reference for the patterns of relationships to be expected for a group of organizational employees working under conditions which might lead to psychological failure experiences.

Perhaps, we reasoned, the model which most accurately reflects the situation for the largest proportion of employees is a representation of how all priests in the diocese we studied see themselves and their work world. Deviations from the general picture that we might expect for curates and specials would be indications of where the general analysis fails to account for specific work groups. The general analytic scheme presented in Fig. 10.1 and based on the total sample is probably representative of the conditions existing in organizations where the individual must work through organizational constraints to invest his identity in his work.

The Best-Fit Model

The model of relationships which best fits the data according to Schneider's criteria, the psychological success model, the total sample, and priests on special assignment is presented in Fig. 10.1. Recall that this figure is the result of data analyses which have already been accomplished. In subsequent figures we will present information useful to the reader who wishes to see how we arrived at our conclusions. In any case we now proceed through this figure, referencing the numbers to give some preliminary explanation regarding each variable's inclusion in this model.

To simplify the analysis, only the most critical variables studied were considered. They are listed as follows, with the reasons why they were deemed critical:[39]

1. *Work satisfaction.* We have chosen this criterion variable as the most global evaluation of the person in the situation. It is his assessment of the extent to which his career work is rewarding to him as a person. In this chapter we have dropped the other measures from the JDI, for they are not central to our theoretical position. The intercorrelation of work and the other satisfactions presented in Chapter Six indicate the basic similarity in relationships for pastors and curates. Specials show some deviations, predominantly the negative correlation between work and supervision satisfaction. It is clear, however, that in all these matrices work satisfaction is the central concept. (See Table 6.5.)

2. *Use of skills and abilities.* The feeling that one is utilizing his important skills and abilities is seen as a central part of the more global concept of work satisfaction. For professionals we would expect a generally high relationship between a feeling of skill utilization and work satisfaction, but as Dubin (1970) has shown, not all workers who are satisfied with their work feel actualized in their work. This was shown to be true in Chapter Six where the correlation of work satisfaction and skill utilization is higher for specials and curates than the correlation of use of skills with any other variable. For this relationship, however, it was the

---

[39]Organizational commitment is included neither in this list nor in Fig. 10.1 because data on this variable were only available on the sample that was interviewed. At the end of the chapter commitment will be reintroduced.

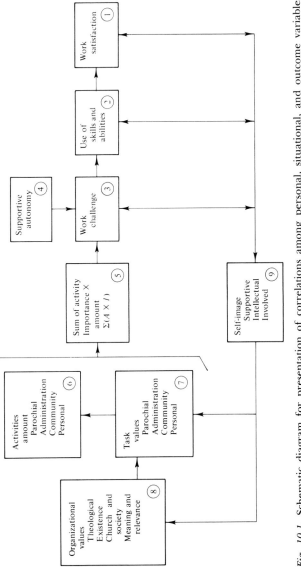

Fig. 10.1. Schematic diagram for presentation of correlations among personal, situational, and outcome variables.

pastors who seemed to be most influenced by the superior, with superior satisfaction and the subordinate subidentity correlating more highly with use of skills than work satisfaction. The differences, however, were nonsignificant, and we accept the satisfaction–skill-utilization link with the caution to examine the impact of authority on this relationship.

3. *Work challenge and meaning.* A central concept in specifying the conditions necessary for psychological success is that the individual be presented with work that he finds meaningful and challenging. Again, in most professional careers this is relatively commonplace (Glaser, 1968). However, we know that differences between the three positions exist in the extent to which this is true. We will show that these differences are attributable to the relative impact of the superior. Thus we include number 4, supportive autonomy.

4. *Supportive autonomy.* This second aspect of climate has been included because of our feeling that differences in the three roles are in large measure a function of differences in the immediate impact of authority. Authority, we feel, is the organizational condition which comes between a person seeing the challenge in his work a product of himself (an investment of his person and values directly into his work) and his assessment of the work world as being strongly tied to the impact of others. Indeed, we will show that specials, who as a group are high on challenge and autonomy, have their self-image and their organizational values more immediately related to their assessment of work challenge and meaning than do pastors and curates. Superior effectiveness was not retained for this analysis for two reasons: (1) It tends to be highly correlated with supportive autonomy (see Chapter Six) and thus adds little understanding to our analysis. (2) Theoretically, the notion of autonomy at work, the opportunity to establish goals and the means for achieving them, is more relevant. It should be noted that other kinds of interpersonal relationships (peer relationships, e.g.) are probably important to include in organizations where coercive authority is not as central as in the Church (Argyris, 1965). In Chapter Nine we have examined the impact of authority on *group* development and have shown the cumulative effects authority can have on a system.

5. *Sum of amount of activities times importance of activities.* This index [sometimes called $\Sigma(A \times I)$] was developed for this analysis as a way of summarizing the extent to which individuals are performing career-related tasks which they value. The measure is simply the sum of the products of the four activities: Σ(activity × importance). The reason for developing this index was that over time there are considerable changes in the specific activities performed (e.g., a change from emphasis on community involvement to an emphasis on administration) and the

specific activities most valued. By summing across the products of amount times importance the changes in specific activities are nullified and a global index of how much a person is doing what he values is obtained. $\Sigma(A \times I)$ is the one truly direct person–environment interaction measure employed in our analyses. It is similar in concept to the interaction in analysis of variance. This interaction implies that the effects of the two components taken together is equivalent to more than the simple sum of the impact of each alone. We will show that assessing the work as challenging and meaningful is strongly related to doing what is valued.

6. *The amount of activities.* This measure of how much of each activity priests say they accomplish is a necessary variable for a number of reasons. First, the contribution of amount of activities to $\Sigma(A \times I)$ should indicate the extent to which "keeping busy" at an activity is the major contributor or if it is the *value* of doing the activity that is more important. Thus a person may be relatively high on the $\Sigma(A \times I)$ index because he is high on A (amount) and low on I (importance), vice versa, or moderate on both. The clarification of this index is necessary for detailed inter- and intrarole comparisons.

The second reason for its inclusion is that the amount of each specific activity is seen as the most direct connection between the person's value system and his eventual work satisfaction. This is the level at which priests implement their values through their work. We already know, for example, that for specials the correlation between activities and importance of activities tends to be higher than for pastors, and in turn pastors are higher than curates. Our framework permits specification of which activities are most important—it allows for specification of the details which make up the more global assessments and conclusions about the work, work world, and outcomes.

7. *Task values.* The level of these data indicate the transfer of the individual's more permanent personality and belief system into work-related values. Task values (importance of activities) are included for the same reasons as the amount of activities: (a) They change quantitatively over time and, therefore, may indicate specific qualitative relationships of interest in the study of priests. These relationships may in turn suggest more general qualitative trends in the task values of professionals in organizations. For example, one may ask whether the importance of activities related to systems maintenance (administration) are more strongly related to challenge early or late in the career? (b) Also of more immediate interest is the contribution of work values to the $\Sigma(A \times I)$ measure, as is (c) the way in which task values are related to more general measures of self-image and organizational values. When

viewing task values as flowing from more general values, these correlations are important data.

One last comment on the usefulness of the measures of activities is necessary. We were fortunate to develop four work activities dimensions which are statistically independent of each other (see Chapter Six). This statistical independence is useful when attempting to use information of one kind (like different activities) to predict information of another kind (like perceived work challenge). Given that two activities are highly related to challenge but not related to each other, we know more about the experience of challenge than when using one global measure of activities.

9. *Organizational values.* These are the responses to the question "What should the goals of the Roman Catholic Church be?" They are, in a sense, a reflection of where the individual thinks his larger organizational world should be going. The connection between these values and the work values indicates the extent to which his general organizational values can be implemented by doing particular kinds of work he values.

10. *General self-image.* Of all the concepts which we are employing, this seems the one most usefully viewed as both a personal measure and an outcome measure. Since it does not change greatly over time, it is viewed as a general identity each priest brings with him into the priesthood. But all priests clearly do not have the same identity. This variability in the way priests see themselves allows examination of how the self-image is related to other aspects of the person as well as to how he perceives the characteristics of his work and the outcomes he experiences from his work as a priest in the Roman Catholic Church.

We will show that it is under conditions of high autonomy that the general self-image is most strongly related to task values and to the challenge and meaning found in the work. As we present the data for various groups of priests and the total sample, two important issues related to the career model will be considered in each analysis. The first concerns the most important inputs to perceived work challenge. Specifically, does the priest experience more challenge in response to conditions in the work environment (e.g., supportive autonomy from the pastor)? Or does the challenge experienced depend more upon his own personal characteristics, values, and self-image? In other words, to what extent is he dependent upon the work environment or proactive with regard to experiencing challenge in his assignment?

A second critical issue concerns the role of the person's self-image in his work experiences. On the input side (related to the first issue), is the person able to perform activities and find challenges congruent with his self-image, or is the job so highly externally defined that he is unable to "put his fingerprint" on the assignment? On the output side, is he sufficiently involved in his job so that his self-image is related to his work satisfaction? Or is he alienated, with his self-image detached from the satisfactions and frustrations of his assignment?

Results

The Data for the Total Sample

Figure 10.2 presents the analyses for the total sample of priests. The correlations in this figure are probably representative of those one might find in organizations in which contextual constraints over the professional members is relatively high.

Of course, this figure does not represent the complete table of inter-correlations of the measures on which it is based; it is an abstract of that matrix. The same will be true for subsequent presentations. Suffice it to say at this point that the variables closer to each other tend to be more highly correlated with each other than they are with any other variable. For example, "Work challenge" is more strongly related to $\Sigma(A \times I)$ than to any *single* activity; in turn, a general self-image high on the dimension involved is more strongly related to engaging in a high amount of community activity; amount of community activity is more highly related to $\Sigma(A \times I)$ than it is related to any other variable in the matrix. Also, the amounts of various activities performed are generally more strongly related to work challenge than they are to a feeling of using one's skills and so on.

Since the framework in the figure was determined as the best fit in terms of multiple criteria, it does not fit perfectly with each of the correlations. Not all variables are as hierarchically arranged as the form of the figure would suggest. For example, the importance attached to administration as an activity is overrepresented at all levels. However, as we present the same information by position rather than across all positions, there will be changes in correlation between administration-relevant measures and the other variables. Thus the correlations presented in Fig. 10.2 are a rough estimate of the patterns of relationships to be expected in any one subgroup of priests.

In a sense then, we will be looking, in the subgroup analyses, at position in the diocese as a moderator of the hierarchically ordered relationships (Dunnette, 1966; Tyler, 1965). Simply stated, we feel that the correlations on the total sample obscure important issues that are related to position and tenure in the diocese.

Prior to proceeding to the specials, we will mention a few relation-

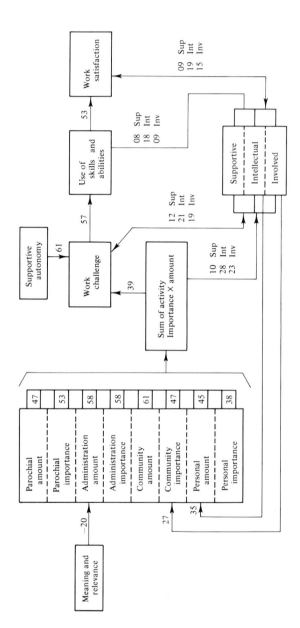

Fig. 10.2. Relationships between personal, situational, and outcome variables for the total sample.

ships of note in the total sample as shown in Fig. 10.2. Self-image is strongly related to community and personal development activities, while administration and community activities tend to be more strongly related to $\Sigma(A \times I)$ and work challenge.

Self-image is significantly but not strongly related to work challenge ($\bar{r} = .17, p < .01$), while supportive autonomy is highly related to challenge ($\bar{r} = .61, p < .01$). For activities, in three cases (all but parochial) the *value* of the activity is less strongly related to work challenge than is the amount of the activity.[40] This suggests that the value attached to an activity may determine the amount of that activity which the person chooses to perform. The amount performed in turn affects [through $\Sigma(A \times I)$] the challenge the person experiences. This reasoning is consistent with a conscious-intention–based model of work behavior (Locke, 1970; Ryan, 1970).

Causality could work the other way, of course, with the activities performed influencing the perceived value of those activities through a dissonance-reducing process. Some support for this view is found in Chapter Seven, which shows that the importance assigned to the performance of different activities changes more over time within position than does the amount of activities actually performed as reported by the priest. Thus we observe the anticipatory socialization effect, especially for the importance assigned to the performance of administration-type activities.

However, both the Schneider (1973) theoretical hierarchical model of personal characteristics leading to behaviors and behaviors leading to outcomes and the empirical best-fit model shown in Fig. 10.2 support the intentional view of causality with values shaping behavior.

Specials

Figure 10.3 presents data for the specials, whose jobs provide the highest autonomy and challenge. Note that supportive autonomy is not related to work challenge ($\bar{r} = .04$) but that an organizational value, feeling that the Church should emphasize Church and society, is directly related to challenge ($\bar{r} = .32, p < .05$), as are the three self-image measures ($\bar{r} = .44$). A complex set of individual-level measures are related to community involvement, suggesting the personal investment the priest

---

[40]Methodologically, some readers may suggest that the relation between the value of activities and the amount of activities is to be expected since the data are collected from the same position of the questionnaire, with the same factors and the same items. While this is true, and some of the value × amount correlation may be attributable to these methodological issues, the fact that the amount of activities is more strongly related to challenge than is the value of activities is theoretically meaningful.

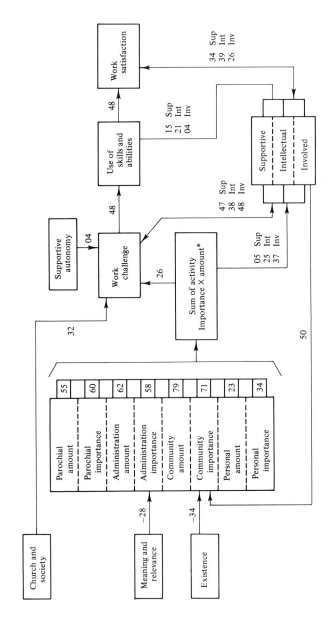

Fig. 10.3. Relationships between personal, situational, and outcome variables for specials.

on special assignment has in community work. Community involvement is strongly represented in $\Sigma(A \times I)$ (correlation of .84). In each case (except administration) the value of the activity is more strongly related to work challenge than is the amount of the activity performed. Three of the four Church values are represented in this analysis, all but theological.

The relatively low relationship between $\Sigma(A \times I)$ and work challenge was not expected. For specials, perceived challenge is due more to personal than job variables. Thus, because of the relatively low intercorrelations among self-image, the organizational value, Church and society, and $\Sigma(A \times I)$, and because they correlate with challenge, it follows that challenge for specials has multiple independent determinants. We will show later that for pastors and curates the superior–subordinate relationship is related more strongly to perceived challenge than are these personal variables.

Curates

The choice of presenting the data for curates after the specials was not coincidental; on the average, curates are close in age to the specials (average age of specials is 40, of curates 36, of pastors 56) and they have the same self-image scores and the same organizational values. Differences between them, however, are very strong in the conditions for psychological success in their work. At this point in the text, contrast between the two positions will be on the *patterns* of relationships rather than the level distinctions we have previously examined. These data for curates are presented in Fig. 10.4

Supportive autonomy is highly related to work challenge ($\bar{r} = .64$), suggesting the strong impact of the pastor on the curate's work. However, the self-image measures are not strongly related to challenge for curates ($\bar{r} = .18$, as compared to $\bar{r} = .44$ for specials). This may indicate the relatively low impact of the curate himself in defining his own challenges. No organizational value is directly related to challenge. In addition, for specials the value of the activity tends to be more strongly related to challenge than the amount; for curates the reverse is true. In all cases, but especially for community involvement ($r = .42$), the amount of activity is most highly related to work challenge. *One general pattern for curates seems to be the low impact of personal factors on the challenge and meaning of their work.*

An unexpected finding, but one consistent with the low level of personal definition of challenge for curates, is that self-image is more highly related to $\Sigma(A \times I)$ ($\bar{r} = .27$) than it is to challenge ($\bar{r} = .18$). This

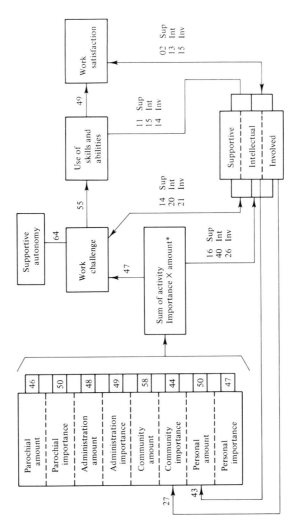

Fig. 10.4. Relationships between personal, situational, and outcome variables for curates.

suggests to us that curates are identifying more with keeping busy per se than with challenge in their work.

As with specials, we find that curates who perceive themselves as involved are, in fact, involved in, and value, community activity.

Challenge for curates, then, seems to be composed of $\Sigma(A \times I)$ and autonomy, with neither organizational values nor self-image playing an important role. The challenge a curate finds in his work is more organizationally than individually determined. Remember in this context that challenge for curates is related to the amount, not the importance of the activities performed.

Pastors

Figure 10.5 indicates that pastors are between specials and curates in patterns of relationships as well as in absolute levels of variables. Supportive autonomy is correlated with challenge at .38 (.64 for curates, .04 for specials), and $\Sigma(A \times I)$ is more strongly related to amount than importance of activities, but the magnitude of the difference is not as great as it is for curates. Again, we see self-perceived involvement and Church and society values represented in community involvement.

Pastors differ from the younger priests in the following ways: Self-image is most strongly related to work satisfaction [while for specials self-image relates most strongly to work challenge and for curates, $\Sigma(A \times I)$]; parochial, personal, and administrative $A \times I$ are more strongly related to challenge for pastors than is community involvement; and the single highest activity correlate of challenge is the importance of personal activities at .32. For specials this same valued activity is the highest, while for curates the amount of community involvement is the strongest correlate of perceived challenge.

Changes Over Time

Curates

In view of the great changes in values, identification, and satisfaction which occur during the curate years, it seemed reasonable that the impact of specific job activities might also change. To test this, we correlated the amount and importance of each type of activity with the overall measure, $\Sigma(A \times I)$, in the four curate tenure groups. We also correlated perceived challenge with $\Sigma(A \times I)$ to see if the impact of the summary measure remained constant. These correlations are shown in Table 10.1.

The correlations reveal a change in the activities which contribute to $\Sigma(A \times I)$ and thus to perceived challenge. During the early curate

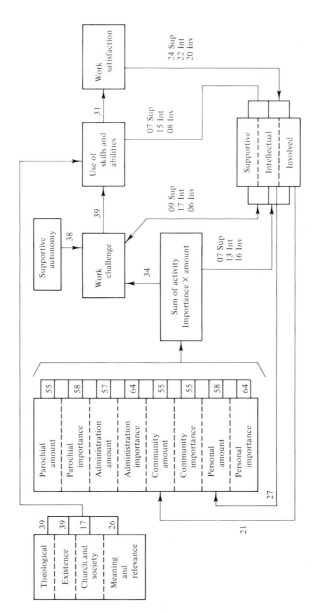

Fig. 10.5. Relationships between personal, situational, and outcome variables for pastors.

TABLE 10.1

Changing Correlates of $\Sigma (A \times I)$ for Curates[a]

| | | $\Sigma (A \times I)$ vs: | | | | | | | |
| | | Parochial | | Administration | | Community | | Personal | |
Tenure group	Work challenge	Amount	Importance	Amount	Importance	Amount	Importance	Amount	Importance
0–5 (N = 58)	51	60	43	37	37	66	54	54	34
6–10 (N = 48)	53	23	41	14	23	73	71	47	55
11–16 (N = 56)	42	34	48	67	68	52	35	44	46
17–22 (N = 34)	43	69	70	52	50	55	39	50	61

[a] Sample sizes reported may not be the same as those involved in each of the correlations reported. However, the most important sample size differences are between the 17- to 22-year group and the other three tenure groups. Decimals have been omitted.

TABLE 10.2

Work Challenge, Σ (A X I), and Work Satisfaction as Correlates
of Self-Image over Time (Pastors and Curates)

Years since ordination	Self-image dimension	Work challenge	Σ (Amount X importance	Work satisfaction
0–5 (N = 58)	Supportive	−30*	03	−35*
	Intellectual	15	36**	−37**
	Involved	17	20	02
6–10 (N = 48)	Supportive	41**	16	21
	Intellectual	17	48**	15
	Involved	30*	29*	25
11–16 (N = 56)	Supportive	11	25**	03
	Intellectual	18	37	17
	Involved	08	18	11
17–22 (N = 34)	Supportive	22	18	49**
	Intellectual	35*	38*	21
	Involved	34*	47**	24
22–25 (N ≐ 20)	Supportive	12	11	26
	Intellectual	21	27	37
	Involved	02	24	28
26–30 (N = 35)	Supportive	20	04	21
	Intellectual	37*	11	−0−
	Involved	24	20	−06−
31–35 (N = 24)	Supportive	24	04	26
	Intellectual	07	24	37
	Involved	17	07	43*
36–40 (N = 21)	Supportive	−19	01	−0−
	Intellectual	15	13	17
	Involved	−38	13	13

*$p < .05$, two tail.
**$p < .01$, two tail.

years (0–5) community work, followed closely by parochial duties, relate most strongly to the summary measure. In the 6- to 10-year period, community activities alone are clearly most important. Between the eleventh and sixteenth years, administrative work contributes most heavily to $\Sigma(A \times I)$. In the prepastor years (17–22), parochial work again comes to the fore. To generalize roughly, as one goes from the first half of the curacy (0–10 years) to the latter half (11–22), the importance of community work decreases, and the role of administrative work increases. The early value of community work is consistent with the "new-breed" characteristic of the younger curates. The increasing role of administration is consistent with the evidence of increasing organizational identification among older curates reported earlier. This increased concern with administration over time is also found in the careers of other professional groups (Hall *et al.*, 1970).

Thus the correlations reported in Fig. 10.4 between activities and $\Sigma(A \times I)$ are *not* representative of all curates. However, the relationships between $\Sigma(A \times I)$ and challenge do not change very much over time ($r = .51, .53, .42$, and $.43$, respectively), so the logic of using $\Sigma(A \times I)$ as a summary measure is substantiated.

The relationship between the self-image and job perceptions and attitudes among a group of workers may be viewed as an index of how ego involved they are in various aspects of their work (Schneider *et al.*, 1971). Since we know that organizational involvement increases over time for curates, we wondered if this correlational index of work involvement changed as well. Therefore, correlations of self-image with work challenge, $\Sigma(A \times I)$, and work satisfaction are presented for various tenure groups in Table 10.2

The correlations of self-image with $\Sigma(A \times I)$, challenge, and work satisfaction do change over time, more for challenge than for $\Sigma(A \times I)$. These data are shown in Table 10.2 for pastors as well as curates. The negative correlation between a supportive self-image and challenge suggests that in the early years of the priest's career, if he has high self-esteem, he may not find his work challenging and meaningful. Generally speaking, the correlations between self-image and the other measures suggest two peak periods during the curate years—6–10 and 17–22. In these periods, curates with high self-esteem tend to view their work positively. Generally, then, the correlations presented in Fig. 10.4 seem to be fairly accurate reflections of the correlations over time. We will comment on the same relationships for pastors in the section after specials.

Specials

Since the total number of specials was only 55, any correlational findings on subsamples of them might be in error due to sampling errors which arise as a result of small samples. Keeping this caution in mind, we split the sample into three subgroups: 0–10 ($N = 15$); 11–16 ($N = 20$), and 17–22 ($N = 12$). Our data for these subgroups presented in Table 10.3 indicate that the relationship between $\Sigma(A \times I)$ and challenge is stronger in the youngest group ($r = .56$) than in the older two groups, where $r = .24$ and $.32$, respectively. This finding will assume importance toward the end of the chapter, where it will be shown that there are two paths to a sense of challenge in one's work, the value

TABLE 10.3

Changing Correlates of Σ $(A \times I)$ for Specials[a]

| | | Σ $(A \times I)$ vs. | | | | | | | |
| | | Parochial | | Administration | | Community | | Personal | |
Tenure group	Work challenge	Amount	Importance	Amount	Importance	Amount	Importance	Amount	Importance
0–10 (N = 15)	56	68	46	62	64	91	83	41	22
11–16 (N = 20)	24	45	44	71	72	72	59	17	49
17–22 (N = 12)	32	65	94	27	25	85	81	−07	59

[a] Other correlations appeared to remain relatively constant over the three age groups.

or personal path and the activity path. For parish priests it seems to take much longer to get to the value path than for priests on special assignment.

In addition to the drop in relationship over time between $\Sigma(A \times I)$ and challenge, the impact of the particular activities on challenge varies over time. Thus while community involvement remains fairly strong over time, administration drops precipitously in the 17–22 age group, and the importance of parochial activities rises sharply in the 17–22 age group [correlates .94 with $\Sigma(A \times I)$]. A comparison of these data with those for curates suggests some similarities, with community-related activities being strongest early in the career, administration-related activities in middle nonpastor years, and parochial activities just prior to the pastorate.

Pastors

Throughout this book we have tended to emphasize differences between curates and the priests in other positions. It was when we examined the correlations over time for pastors that we realized this group of priests is not as homogeneous as we might have thought. We became aware of considerations such as the fact that all pastors have the same supervisor, yet the bishop is described in widely different ways; that pastors ordained more than 30–35 years are over 60 years old (the average age of our pastors was 56); and that pastors are given their first official parish responsibility after they have turned 45, an age of midcareer crisis in many occupations (D. J. Levinson, 1968; H. Levinson, 1969).

We expected to find some changes in patterns of relationships over time but were surprised at (1) the severity of changes and (2) the level at which the changes occurred. Table 10.4 presents some of these data over time for pastors. The table indicates good stability but consistently low relationships for pastors between use of skills and work satisfaction ($\bar{r}$ = .21, .31, .20, and .17, respectively). The correlations between challenge and use of skills, however, continually drop over time: $\bar{r}$ = .71, .50, .09, and .01, respectively. The relationships between self-image and challenge (presented in Table 10.2) become negative in the 36–40 age group, and the correlation between self-image and work satisfaction in that period is essentially zero. Indeed, if one examines the relationships between the average of the self-image measures and utilization of skill over the length of a priest's career, it follows an almost perfect inverted U, moving from negative in 0–5 ($\bar{r}$ = −.17) to 6–10 ($\bar{r}$ = .16) to 11–16 ($\bar{r}$ = .27) to 17–22 ($\bar{r}$ = .30) to 22–25 ($\bar{r}$ = .27) to 26–30 ($\bar{r}$ = .14)

TABLE 10.4

The Changing Nature of the Correlations in the Links
between Σ (A $\times$ I), Work Challenge, Use of Skills,
Work Satisfaction, and Self-Image[a]

	Use of skills with work satisfaction	Work challenge with use of skills	Use of skills with average self-image	Work challenge with Σ (A $\times$ I)
0–5	42**	57**	−17	51**
6–10	58**	48**	16	53**
11–16	60**	70**	27*	42**
17–22	44**	55**	30	43**
22–25	21	71**	27	41
26–30	31	50**	14	47**
31–36	20	09	07	64**
36–40	17	01	02	−48*

[a] See Table 10.2 for sample size.
* $p < .05$
** $p < .01$

to 31–36 ($\bar{r} = .07$) to 36–40 where $\bar{r} = .02$. Apparently, the self-image becomes tied to different aspects of the priesthood and perhaps later in the priesthood to the organization itself.

Early in the priesthood we have shown the self-image to be related to work-related variables. One wonders what the self-image becomes related to later in the priest's career. Our data reveal three factors: (1) The fewer the number of pastor assignments a priest has had, the higher is his self-image; (2) the fewer curates he has had, the higher is his self image; and (3) the more positively he describes his first assignment, the higher is his self-image.

It may be that as the priest gets older, the *work* of the priesthood becomes less an object of identification than it is early in the career. Data supporting this concept have been presented, for if we accept the hierarchical nature of $\Sigma(A \times I) \rightarrow$ challenge $\rightarrow$ work satisfaction, we have shown that a curate's self-image is related to specific activities, a special's to the characteristics of the work (work challenge), and a pastor's to the more global evaluation of the work (work satisfaction).

Another possibility is that pastors just get tired of the same work routines they have been engaged in for 30 or more years. One piece of data supporting this idea is the drop in the relationship between $\Sigma(A \times I)$ and challenge, as shown in Table 10.4; for age groups 22–35 inclusive, $\bar{\bar{r}} = .53$, while for 36–40 it is −.48. The Church as a one-career organization also provides a dead-end career. As a curate, there is always the pastorate to look forward to. As a pastor though, there is only retirement ahead; some priests, about to retire, referred to themselves as "retarded" priests.

Fichter (1968) has suggested, as we have elsewhere (Schneider & Hall, 1970), that a good assignment for a pastor is a rich parish with many curates. This may be an oversimplification or at best it is true only for the young pastor. The older pastor seems to be the forgotten man; even with all of the data we have collected, we have little to offer in understanding these abrupt changes in patterns of relationships.

Discussion

Clearly, there are differences in the patterns of relationships between personal, situational, and outcome experiences, both inter- and intrarole. Priests' careers are characterized by changes in relationships between variables as well as by absolute changes in the levels of measures. Sorting out which of these changes are due to the impact of the person, forces within the organization, or aging is not possible, but we may speculate.

Changes in the curate years in the valued activities and their relationships to challenge can probably be attributed to socialization. The fact that pastors and specials show more direct relationships between task and organizational values and work challenge is attributable to differences in the levels of authority experienced by the three role incumbents. The tendency for the self-image to be more strongly related to community and personal activities seems to be a function of the person. That work challenge for specials and pastors, but especially for specials, is determined by both personal and value–task components, while curates' challenge is more organizationally determined, also seems to be a result of authority conditions.

On balance, in this system it appears that the situation is overdeterminant of assignment experiences. This is in contrast to the extent to which self-employed professionals are free to invest themselves in their careers. We recall from the interviews that curates our age (late twenties, early thirties) compared our freedom to their "servitude." We note the loss of work as a correlate of self-image for pastors and wonder what organizations can provide as a source of identification as the career draws to a close. Our data suggest that these are important questions.

What may we conclude? Beginning with our "ultimate" criterion, work satisfaction, we suggest that this criterion may not be relevant to actual work performed late in a priest's career; other factors having more global organizational rather than work relevance may be more useful indexes. Work challenge, of course, follows a similar argument, but it is a more "work itself" concept than is work satisfaction. We view challenge and autonomy as being highly related when challenge and self-image are not related. Thus work challenge may be viewed as created either by the organization or the individual. In the final analysis, then, there is a basic strain between the individual's and the organization's effect on the person's work. Early in the priest's career most of the influence comes from the organization, as represented by the superior. Later in the career, more impact comes from the individual himself. In Bakke's (1950) terms, it appears as though the young man is socialized by his work, while the older man tends to personalize his career experiences. This idea is also consistent with Schein's (personal communication) idea that early in one's career the person is socialized by the organization, while later, after he acquires age, status, and power, he is more likely to cause innovations in the organization. The direction of influence in the person–organization relationship may reverse in favor of the individual later in the career.

ELEVEN
Conclusion: Work Climate and Organizational Careers

Up to this point, we have examined many specific relationships regarding the original model of psychological success in organizational careers. In this chapter we will attempt to draw together the central findings of this research. To do this, we will first test the original model and present a revised model, based on our data. Then we will briefly summarize the most important conclusions.

Summary Analysis of the Priestly Career:
The Impact of Organizational Authority[41]

In this study we have found a strong tendency for satisfactions, challenge, and utilization of skills to be consistently higher among pastors than curates. However, these are average figures we are talking about, and some curates scored high on satisfaction and self-perception. Generally, these were the curates whose pastors were effective, who provided

[41]In this discussion we draw heavily on our initial report (Hall & Schneider, 1969) and a summary of the longer report (Schneider & Hall, 1970).

both support and autonomy to their curates, and who assigned meaningful and challenging work.

It appears, then, that there are two different pervasive impacts which authority has on the career experiences of priests. The first, *authority level*, refers to the position in the formal hierarchy which the particular priest occupies (bishop, pastor, etc.). The second, *authority relationship*, refers to the nature of the interpersonal interactions between the priest and his superior. The nature of the authority relationship is dependent on the two individuals—the occupants of the positions. One way of viewing authority is to look at the level of the position as a variable related to particular outcomes. A second way of viewing authority is to consider the relationship between superior and subordinate as a correlate of these outcomes. Our data clearly show that both of these aspects are important. In analyzing data by position, consistent and significant differences are found. Similarly, when correlational analyses are computed, the manner in which the position authority is used seems to be strongly related to our indexes of psychological success. A review of how the use or misuse of authority hinders the opportunities for positive career experiences can be accomplished with reference to the earlier conceptual framework.

Priest Career Patterns

Earlier in the psychological success model we considered how people might potentially develop self-esteem and competence in their careers; let us examine how members of an ideal bureaucracy, priests, actually *do* experience the process of their careers.

In the individual interviews we had a sense that the most critical career experiences tended to be the same from one priest to the next: seminary, ordination, first assignment, later assignments, and pastorate. The striking characteristic of these experiences is that they are all standard, *institutional* events; they occur in the career paths of all priests in a regularized progression. Anselm Strauss (1959) uses the term *regularized status passage* to describe this sort of institutionalized process, which occurs in a variety of organizations.

We also found that three-quarters of our priests responding to a question on career selection had chosen the priesthood by the end of high school; two-fifths had chosen by the end of the eighth grade. This seems to be a very early age range to be making such an important commitment to a total style of life. Indeed, according to Ginzberg (1952), this is normally the age of tentative career choices for most people. We wonder how mature and active such an early choice can be.

Along this same line we also found that in describing why they entered the priesthood, 75% of the respondents indicated influences other than themselves, their own interests, and their desire to serve others. Their family, a particular priest, or the general influence of the Church tended to be the most important factors in their career selections.

The problem with this sort of career path is that there is little evidence of active choosing on the part of the priest, and little evidence of the system offering any opportunity to choose. The important events in a priest's career (the assignments he has, the promotions he receives, the place he lives) are usually not of his own choosing. The priest has little control over his own life's development in the priesthood. Seeing institutionalized events as critical in one's own career is not a problem per se, but when these events completely overshadow events of one's own making, the likelihood of psychological success is extremely low. This type of career pattern leads to a person's being influenced much more by his environment than by himself. We would predict that for some individuals this would result in a person's inability to make independent choices and in dependence on the organization.

We conceive the general dependence of priests on the system to be the result of two interacting factors: (1) a tendency for some immature decision makers who are passive, nonchoosing individuals to enter the system and (2) the tendency for the organization to create and reinforce acquiescence and nonchoosing. The combination of some individuals with a tendency toward passivity and a system rewarding passivity creates a potent climate inhibiting psychological success. Indeed, in examining the work experience of the parish priests (not the specials) in this system, one is hard pressed to think of extant occupational systems of professional personnel with fewer structural opportunities for psychological success and growth.

Organizational Blocks to Psychological Success

These are strong statements to make about the lack of career growth opportunities for the parish priest. There are almost an unlimited number of factors in the organization which may be employed to block the priest's career development; to reduce the opportunities of the parish priest to experience psychological success.

Considering the first condition of psychological success, what opportunities does a parish assistant have to *actively choose challenging goals for himself?* This condition actually has two aspects—active choice and challenging goals—neither of which is met in most curate assignments. The data presented on activities performed and on the climate variable of work challenge and meaning demonstrate the relative lack of challenge experienced by the curate. Pastors and specials both score significantly higher on these measures of work challenge.

In the area of *choice*, there again is little opportunity provided for the curate. First, he has no choice over the type or location of assignment he is to receive. Furthermore, once he is in an assignment, he has little choice about what duties he will perform and how he will perform them. The specific duties of the curate are generally assigned by the pastor. A third area of nonchoice is the curate's living environment; he is required to live in a particular place—the parish rectory—and is thus deprived of the opportunity to make a multitude of choices about the management of his personal life.

It should be added that there are variations in choice among the different types of priests. Pastors do have more control than curates over the location of assignments, and certainly more control within their assignments. Specials generally have a fair amount of choice within their assignments, but not as much choice in the type or location of their work. All three groups typically have little choice of living environment.

Considering the second condition for psychological success, *the opportunity to work autonomously on one's own tasks*, we again note that curates rank much lower here than pastors and specials. Often the pastor has his own ideas about how a certain activity should be performed (e.g., training altar boys, running the school), and the curate frequently feels that his work is closely controlled by his superior or, as some priests described it, he feels like a glorified altar boy.

However, a large number of curates have complete autonomy to work in their own way; their pastors give them their assignments and then rarely intervene. The problem here, as we indicated before, is that this nonintervention is often viewed as noninterest or nonsupport (financial as well as psychological). There seems to be little opportunity to have autonomy *and* assistance or support from the pastor. Supportive autonomy from the superior ranked very low for curates, yet this variable was correlated highly with two of our criteria—satisfaction and use of skills. Thus the curate's independent work tends to be either nonexistent or hindered by a lack of support from the pastor. Pastors, too, seem to suffer from a lack of supportive autonomy from their superior. Only the specials seem to find this combination of support and freedom in their work, and their immediate superior is as likely to be outside the diocesan authority structure as in it. Thus on the questionnaire all but 10 curates indicated that their pastor was their immediate superior, 98 pastors indicated the bishop was their immediate superior, and 16 said "others," while 28 specials said bishop and 28 said "others."

Related to the lack of support in one's work is a lack of training and preparation. In the interviews, curates reported that they generally feel unprepared by the seminary for the first parish assignment; pastors often reported feelng overwhelmed by the first pastor assignment; and specials frequently receive no professional training for their specialized duties. Like support from one's superior, training and preparation are also vital—and often missing—elements in facilitating the priest's feelings of effectiveness and success in his work.

The third condition is also violated by the work of many curates; *the activities they perform are often ones which are not those of most importance to them*. For example, assistants tend to see community involvement and personal development as being very important, yet they see themselves as performing less of these activities than do the other two groups. The average discrepancy between the importance of such activities and the amount of these activities performed is greater for the curates than for either of the other two groups.

Another way of determining the fit between the importance attached to performing certain activities and the amount performed is to correlate these two variables, importance and amount performed. The correlation between the importance of activities and the amount of activities performed was lower for the curates than for specials or pastors. Thus the curates tend to be doing work which appears less relevant to them than other activities; in cases where the actual duties the priest performs are unimportant to him personally, he could not experience psychological success in them regardless of how objectively effective he was.

In this light, another element necessary to help the person improve the quality of his work is *feedback* on his performance. Most parish priests—curates and pastors—report the difficulties caused by a lack of feedback. Performance in the priesthood is hard to define and even harder to measure. It seems that the specials would have more opportunities for feedback than the parish priest.

This feedback is also necessary to meet the fourth condition—*attaining the person's work goal*. Without some form of information about one's performance, it is difficult to determine if one has in fact achieved his goal. Thus the priest may often be successful or unsuccessful without ever realizing it. This lack of awareness of results can be a strong block to the cycle of work success.

For all of these reasons, then, we conclude that the conditions necessary for successful career experiences through psychological success are generally lacking for assistant pastors in this diocese, although certain of these conditions are present in varying amounts for pastors and specials. This means that for the largest segment of priests in this diocese a vast quantity of human resource potential remains untapped.

A Revised Model of Organizational Career Development

To determine more precisely how causality is operating in the career processes we have been studying, a statistical technique proposed by Blalock (1964, 1969) will be employed. Basically, the Blalock approach consists of (a) identifying rival models which could also exist to explain the relationships found and (b) comparing through the use of partial correlation analysis the explanatory power of the original model vs. the alternative models. The analysis was conducted with the total sample, $n = 373$.

Because the number of possible combinations of partial correlations increases sharply with the number of variables studied, Blalock proposes reducing the number of variables to only those most central. By this criterion the following variables were retained:

1. Self-image (average of correlations for all three separate dimensions).
2. $\Sigma(A \times I)$.
3. Work challenge.
4. Supportive autonomy.
5. Work satisfaction.

The main deletions were organizational values and organizational commitment. Values were omitted because there were so many separate value dimensions, and their statistical independence made it impossible to combine them into one global measure, as we did with the three self-image factors. Organizational commitment was highly related to work satisfaction, and data were available only from the smaller interview-plus-questionnaire sample ($n = 72$), which makes strict comparison of correlation coefficients risky.

To simplify this discussion, we will simply present the original version and the model as revised by the correlations for the total sample in Chapter Ten (Fig. 11.1). The revised feature of the model is that, for all groups combined, self-image acts not as a feedback variable to $\Sigma(A \times I)$, but rather as a direct contributor to perceived work challenge. Support for this version of the model is provided in a set of partial correlations to follow. The condition for an arrow to be drawn between two variables in Fig. 11.1 is that the correlation between those variables must remain strong, even after other possible intervening variables have been held constant (i.e., "partialed out"), and the rival partials must be much lower, near zero. For example, it is possible that the relationship between challenge (variable 3) and satisfaction (variable 5) might be an artifact of the relationship of supportive autonomy (variable 4) with each. In order for the direct challenge–satisfaction relationship to hold,

Partial	Should be	Actual	Partial	Should be	Actual
$r_{13.2}$	Positive	+.401	$r_{25.3}$	Near zero	+.167
$r_{23.1}$	Positive	+.343	$r_{12.3}$	Near zero	+.034
$r_{24.3}$	Near zero	−.066	$r_{35.4}$	Positive	+.414
$r_{14.3}$	Near zero	−.166	$r_{35.2}$	Positive	+.470
$r_{45.3}$	Near zero	+.091	$r_{35.1}$	Positive	+.538
$r_{15.3}$	Near zero	−.129			

$r_{35.4}$[42] should be strongly positive, while $r_{45.3}$ should be near zero. Therefore, in order for the revised model to be the best fit for the present data, a complete set of necessary partial correlations may be listed, along with the actual partials obtained, as listed above.[43] (The variable numbers refer to the variables in Fig. 11.1):

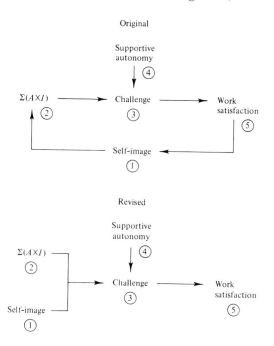

Fig. 11.1. Original theoretical model and revised version. Based on total sample, $n = 373$. Numbers below variable names are for reference purposes only.

[42]$r_{35.4}$ may be read, "the correlation between variables 3 and 5, holding variable 4 constant."

[43]Partial correlation analyses within each of the three positions are presented in Appendix B.

The revision in the model was a change in the role of the priest's self-image in his career experiences. Considering men in all three positions combined, a priest's self-image is not generally related to the kind of satisfaction he derives from his work. Similarly, his image of himself does not influence his constellation of activities $\left[\Sigma(A \times I)\right]$ as much as it does the amount of challenge he experiences in performing these activities. Thus self-image seems to act as an "input" to perceived challenge, but it does not serve as a feedback variable connecting satisfaction outcomes and activity or satisfaction input. [Under conditions of success, however (i.e., for specials), self-image is related to both satisfaction and challenge.]

The other relationships in the model seem to occur as expected. $\Sigma(A \times I)$ and supportive autonomy both act as inputs to perceived work challenge, which in turn is the main factor influencing work satisfaction. It is interesting to note that perceived challenge is a function jointly of the individual (self-image), the work environment (supportive autonomy), and the interaction between the person and his environment $\left[\Sigma(A \times I)\right]$.

The role of the person's self-image in his career process is therefore dependent upon whether he is working under conditions for success or failure. Our original model was not sufficiently differentiated to point this out. Apparently, the important change regarding self-image which occurs under success conditions (as for specials) is not that self-image is on the average greater than under failure conditions; rather the important change is in what self-image becomes related to. Under success conditions, the self-image is strongly and increasingly related to or invested in work satisfaction. Under failure conditions (as for curates) the person's adaptations and defense mechanisms seem to function to keep his self-image insulated or alienated from his work outcomes so that his self-image is not eroded by his impoverished job. When the conditions for success are available to the person, however, it may be emotionally safer for him to become more involved in his work. In time, probably after many cycles of success and failures (but more successes than failures), he develops enough confidence and trust in the work and his work world that he may risk letting his self-esteem be enhanced through successes and satisfaction—and possibly reduced through failures. This risk of failure in work involvement is probably why attaining personal involvement is a more complex and emotional matter than simply providing enlarged jobs, as McGregor (1960) has pointed out. Apparently, the defenses of the curate are effective enough so that his self-image does not appear lower than the specialist's and is not affected by increases or decreases in his work satisfaction. Specialists, however, have let their work become more personally central to their lives, and within this group for whom success conditions are available, those who actually do experience success have more positive self-image than those who do not.

Another reason for the greater connection between work satisfaction and self-image under success is that success entails self-relevant *feedback* from the environment on one's performance. In the priesthood, the pastor can see the results of his efforts in new schools, increased attendance, and healthy balance sheets, and the specialist receives feedback through his professional achievements, e.g., a respected newspaper or a well-run school. The assistant pastor, however, is personally responsible for very few specific projects, and there is little opportunity for him to receive feedback on his performance. This is a structural characteristic of his work which further tends to insulate his self-concept from his work outcomes. Therefore, this lack of performance feedback seems in part responsible for the lack of a personal feedback loop in the assistant's career development process (see Appendix C).

Summary and Conclusions

Taking into account the revised model and the more specific positional relationships presented earlier, we conclude with the following points:

1. Of all the conditions for psychological success, the *key factor* is perceived challenge in the work itself. The other factors—autonomy regarding goals and means and the personal importance of one's work activities—all feed into challenge, which in turn feeds into the experience of psychological success.

2. Where autonomy tends to be low (e.g., curates), the main factor affecting the degree of perceived challenge in the work assignment is the amount of supportive autonomy provided by the superior. In terms of the specific pastor behaviors in supportive autonomy, those curates most likely to experience challenge and, therefore, psychological success are those whose pastors encourage them to express their ideas and to exercise initiative, discuss work and nonwork matters with their curates, treat curates as equals and are willing to accept their ideas and establish a congenial climate in the rectory. Where autonomy is higher (e.g., specials), work challenge is more a function of one's personal characteristics (self-image).

3. The person's self-image may affect the challenge he experiences in his work; thus, under conditions of high challenge (specials) he has

some control over the amount of success he will experience by permitting him to more easily invest his self-image in his work.

4. Given challenging work, the individual has a necessary condition for experiencing psychological success, leading to a feeling of satisfaction with work.

5. Work satisfaction has the potential for becoming tied to the person's self-image and his commitment to the organization. This is most likely to happen when the work climate provides for psychological success (e.g., for specials).

6. The person's increased organizational commitment will be related in turn to his organizational and task values, and the amount of certain activities performed.

7. Under failure conditions the psychological success cycle may become "short circuited," the individual never or only rarely achieving the psychological success experience. Thus psychological failure may be not just the reverse of the success process, but represented by an abbreviated form of the success cycle. For example, the data presented for curates showed that the major feedback loop did not proceed further than $\Sigma(A \times I)$.

8. The structural characteristics of a given position, particularly the amount of autonomy it provides, can greatly affect the operation of the career-development cycle. To the extent that autonomy is low and the individual does not perceive work satisfaction to be his own responsibility, the feedback loop through self-image may not develop; i.e., the person may not change his self-perceptions even if he experiences work satisfaction.

9. It appears that if a person is deprived of opportunities for psychological success in an organization over many years, he may lose much of his desire to utilize conditions for psychological success through challenging work when they are finally made available to him.

This is in marked contrast to data obtained in another system similar to the Church in many respects—the United States Forest Service. One important difference between the two organizations is the amount of challenge and autonomy available to the Forest Service's members through their entire careers. In this organization the impact of work challenge on career outcomes remains strong among older members (Schneider et al., 1971).

10. The differences between specialists and parish priests suggest that there may be a variety of different types of commitment which may grow out of a person's work experiences. Over time parish priests develop greater organizational commitment—the locals (Gouldner,

1958a,b). Specialists probably develop greater professional commitment—the cosmopolitans. Some may become committed to both of these entities—the local–cosmopolitan group (Glaser, 1964). Other objects of commitment may be to the job [i.e., job involvement (Lodahl & Kejner, 1965)] or the work group or parish. It is not clear whether commitment to one's career exists distinct from these other types of attachment. Alternative objects of commitment which should be studied to better understand the interaction of human lives and work are the family, community, avocation, and nonoccupational organizations.

In the course of this book several other findings relevant to general career processes have been identified. These are summarized as follows:

11. A person's first assignment in an organization appears to have a lasting impact upon his later career satisfactions and commitment. In fact, his organizational commitment appears to be more affected by the characteristics of his first assignment than by those in his present position. This finding is consistent with previous research (Berlew & Hall, 1966; Peres, 1966) on the continuing impact of the first job in other types of organizations. If the person's career is seen as a cumulative collection of work-related experiences, the initial experiences, when the person's "organizational life space" is relatively undifferentiated, will logically have exceptional impact. Thus the initial job and the first year of employment represent a critical period in the person's organizational career.

12. It appears that many of the organizational factors in the career-development model change over the years for priests in general—perceptions of work challenge and supportive autonomy increase and self-esteem vis-à-vis the superior becomes more positive. Also the amount of administrative activity they perform increases. However, these increases appear to be due more to moving into a higher position over time than to the effect of time per se. Previous research has also found evidence for more positive work perceptions (Porter, 1961) and increases in administrative activity (Rubin, Stedry, & Willits, 1965) as people move into higher levels in the organization.

13. There is considerable change over time in the person's values related to organizational goals and work activities. Generally, these reflect an increasing agreement with the formal or generally sanctioned goals of the organization and a movement away from more reform-oriented views. This tendency for individuals to become increasingly congruent with the organization's goals has been well documented in the socialization literature (Hall, 1971). Similarly, the person's identification with the organization increases over time (and this change is due more to

time than position). Perhaps related to this increased congruence between person and organization, job satisfaction and perceived utilization of skills generally increase over time. Again this general increase, with perhaps a decrease in the first few years, seems to be a general phenomenon in organizational careers (Smith *et al.*, 1969).

14. As was noted earlier, self-image remains fairly stable for the population in general over the years, although there do appear to be transient increases or decreases during important transitional periods. For example, among academics there appears to be an increase in self-image during professional training (Hall, 1968), followed by a decrease in the first year of teaching (Walberg, 1968).

The conclusions presented here deal with experiences of the individual as a result of his career in the organization. We have also presented data regarding some of the processes which seem to underlie the development of groups in organizational settings. What can we say about how the organization develops as its individual members strive for psychological success?

15. The career development of individual members cannot be divorced from the development of the organization. Because organizational factors such as work challenge and autonomy and supervisory behavior bear so directly upon the career-development process, any attempt to stimulate personal development would entail changing and improving these organizational factors. The writers know of at least one organization whose career development program entailed enriching initial jobs, in line with the findings mentioned earlier. However, the organization quickly found that jobs could not be enriched without training the supervisors in the initial jobs. It later found that there was great dissatisfaction when new people moved from enriched initial jobs to less challenging second jobs. Finally, the organization launched a broader program of supervisory training and job enrichment at several levels in the organization. Similarly, the changes implemented in the organization studied here entail new experimental parish structures rather than programs for individual priests (as detailed in Chapter Twelve).

16. There appear to be strong parallels between individual career development and the development of groups within the organization. If the group operates as a microcosm of the total system, the development of a particular group may similarly be analogous to the development of the organization.

17. As a specific analogue between personal and group development, our relations with the diocese's personnel board showed a process of initial mistrust and low self-esteem, leading to expectations of failure in achieving change regarding the organization. This initial attitude led

it to behave competitively rather than collaboratively, which in turn led it to become closed to new information about the authority which might reduce the competition and help achieve its goals. When a success did occur, the group tended to preserve it rather than attempt further success. It avoided further information regardng its performance as a means of success preservation. Thus there was no feedback loop, no chance for success to breed further success. This process results in isolated achievements and retards ongoing, continuous organizational development.

This group experience seems to parallel that of the parish curate, where the important factor in the assistant's self-image was activity rather than challenge or success, perhaps because of the strong impact of authority in his job. The curate, too, has no feedback mechanism from success in his work so that the opportunities to grow as a result of success are reduced.

18. As the experiences of the personnel board show, development, whether it is personal, group, or organizational, is largely an emotion-based process. In the board's case, it had to deal with emotional issues of integration, work, and authority before it could finish its task. The developmental tasks of various systems may differ, but it is clear that any interventionist must be prepared and competent to look for and deal with the emotional as well as the substantive dimensions of these initial tasks (Argyris, 1970).

These, then are the main conclusions we can draw about career development in organizations on the basis of the present study. Although the study was conducted in the Catholic Church, our focus has been on general organizational concepts and factors (genotypes) rather than particular aspects of the priesthood (phenotypes). The extreme features of the Church present forms of organizational control generally unheard of outside of a laboratory experiment. The existence of professional specialists, who seem to operate virtually outside of the Church bureaucratic system, presented an important opportunity to contrast the impact on the person of a professional and a bureaucratic work environment with many other important personal characteristics essentially held constant (i.e., both specialists and assistants are priests). Therefore, because we (1) focused on genotypic organizational and work characteristics and (2) examined two radically different types of work environments within the same organization and for basically similar types of people, it seems reasonable to apply the findings to organizations in general.

If nothing else, we hope this research has conveyed three messages to the reader. First, careers continue to develop as a result of personal experiences in organizations, long after the initial choice of the career has been made. Second, individuals in organizations have a past history and a planned future as well as a present state. This research has shown that the impact of organizational factors on an individual depends not only on the nature of those factors but also upon the degree of development or deprivation in the person's career to that point. Similarly, in deciding how to respond to particular organizational stimuli, the person will refer to his future plans and expectations. At a gross level, this implies that a person's age is an important factor in determining the impact of such activities as organizational development, job enrichment, or career development programs. More precisely, his previous history of success or failure and anticipated future rewards would give even better predictions of his responses.

Third, and related to the importance of the individual career history, the compounding nature of successes and failures indicates that the impact of poor or good organizational conditions can have an important time dimension. Unchallenging jobs can be upgraded, but the lack of challenge that did exist may continue to have an impact on the careers of the incumbents, especially those people who held them early in their careers. Job enlargement, if done well, will enrich not only the job and performance but also the performer—both his present performance and his future performance. As in most complex systems, the system-wide effects of organizational activities damp out very slowly. When we begin to broaden the process of organizational behavior and view it as influencing not only present performance and attitudes but also people and their future lives, the need for organizational renewal becomes more urgent.

TWELVE
Epilogue: Diocesan Events
Following the Study

By now the reader may be curious about what has happened in the diocese since the research was completed. At the time of this writing 2 years have passed since the "Yale Study" was submitted to the personnel board and 8 months since the personnel board's report was presented to the bishop. Although organizational change is always a continuing and unpredictable process, enough events have occurred to provide some sense of the directions in which the diocese might move.

National Attention on the Diocese Studied

In September 1969 the researchers presented a paper on the study of priests at a symposium of the American Psychological Association's annual convention in Washington, D.C. By agreement with the diocese, this was to be the first presentation of the data to the public. Prior to September, we had been contacted by the media since discontent among priests was big news then, but we deferred all requests for infor-

233

mation to the September presentation. It was also mutually agreed that the diocese would remain anonymous. We remained silent so that the board could prepare its recommendations without outside influence.

A few weeks after the convention a Catholic news service ran a story on the research, and it was printed in numerous Catholic newspapers across the country. These papers printed the story "straight" off the wire, maintaining the anonymity of the diocese. However, one large city newspaper ran its own story, in which it identified the diocese and the bishop initiating the study.

At this point the researchers and the diocese agreed to confirm the identity of the diocese. In fact, we were pleased to see the diocese receive the recognition it deserved for initiating such a comprehensive study and guaranteeing publication rights in advance. To do these things when the report was virtually certain to contain information that would be somewhat negative deserved recognition in its own right. This was the first time a Roman Catholic diocese had ever permitted independent, outside researchers to conduct such a survey, and we felt that this openness and courage should be recognized.

As a result of both the naming of the diocese and the uniqueness of the study, articles continued to appear nationwide in both the secular and Catholic press. These articles focused attention on the diocese studied and created strong expectations of significant changes, as illustrated by headlines such as the following:

A DIOCESE UNDERGOES SURVEY: PERSONNEL POLICIES TO CHANGE
(*The National Register*, Sunday, September 28, 1969)

At that time, however, the personnel board had just recently submitted its report to the bishop and there was, of course, no basis for predicting whether changes would or would not occur.

This national interest in the diocese that fall was made strikingly evident to the researchers when they spoke about the study at a conference held at the University of Notre Dame. Our talk was to describe the study and main findings. To our dismay, though, we found that many of the attendees knew about both the study and the personnel board's report; what they wanted to hear was: What is the bishop going to do?

The Personnel Board's Report

Before getting too far ahead of ourselves, though, let us consider the report of the personnel board, which was the main reason for conducting the research in the first place.

In our view the most significant change proposed by the personnel board (1969, p. 21) was a set of recommendations aimed at implementing the following policy:

EVERY PRIEST, BY THE NATURE OF HIS OFFICE, SHOULD HAVE THE OPPORTUNITY FOR A DIRECT SHARE IN PASTORAL LEADERSHIP AND THE PASTOR–CURATE RELATIONSHIP AS WE HAVE KNOWN IT SHOULD THEREFORE BE ABOLISHED, SINCE IT IS SOCIOLOGICALLY, PSYCHOLOGICALLY, AND THEOLOGICALLY UNSOUND.

(This policy was printed in all capitals in the original and was the only part of the personnel board's report so presented.)

This policy would be implemented through the creation of the following new structures:

1. *Team parishes*—Where the team members are brought together by mutual consent and also determine by mutual consent their areas of responsibility within the parish.

2. *Co-pastorates*—Where the co-pastors have autonomous pastoral responsibility over a geographical segment of an existing parish territory, while sharing central parish facilities (rectory, church, school, hall, etc.) with other co-pastors.

3. *Pastor–curate parishes*—Where the relationship appears largely similar to the present one, with the significant difference that it exists by mutual consent.

4. *Other experimental communities*—In which people share a community of interests based on their profession, job, vocation, or common background; parallel communities of worship and service.

These changes would be coordinated by a "Vicar for the Clergy" (a new position) who would be responsible for vocations for seminarians and diocesan priests, their salaries, education, retreats, grievances, retirements, excardination,[44] incardination,[45] appointments, and resignations. He would work with an advisory board of priests and would serve for a term of 5 years. With a list of priests nominated by all the priests in the diocese, an election would be held, and the top three vote-getters' names would go to the bishop, who would select one to serve as the vicar for the clergy. The report also proposed an entire system of vicars (for planning and research, community affairs, financial affairs, education, etc.), the option for priests to live outside the rectory, and opportunities for continuing education.

After the bishop received the board's report, he told the press that he would have no comment at that time about either the research study

[44]Transfer out of the diocese into another.
[45]Transfer into the diocese from another.

or the board's report. He thanked the personnel board for the work and indicated that they had quite evidently performed a monumental task. He also said that he planned to meet with the board to discuss their report and that he hoped their work would be helpful to other dioceses. Hopefully, he said, it would lead to fruitful outcomes for the people and the priests in his diocese.

Although many priests were skeptical about the prospects for change, we were encouraged by the bishop's reference to other dioceses. We felt that he was aware of the attention and expectations of other dioceses and that this outside interest might produce additional pressure for change. Also, the bishop might be interested in having his diocese be a leader in instituting changes which might alleviate some of the discontent among the clergy.

Consistent with the considerable social and political polarity among the clergy at the national level, division became evident in the diocese, especially on the issue of the board's recommendations. In one of the deaneries proposed by the board for experimental team parishes (following the resignation of all pastors), an association of pastors was formed to oppose the board's report. This group held well-attended meetings and obtained a consultant on canon law.

In the winter of 1969 the bishop met with the personnel board to discuss their report. In the view of most members of the board, the meeting was conducted in a cordial and positive vein with the bishop raising questions which indicated understanding of the recommendations and a serious interest in exploring them further.

Near the end of the meeting, the bishop suggested that they get on with the necessary action and pick a committee to supervise the election of a vicar for clergy. This had been the first step recommended in the board's report. After he selected 5 board members to serve in this capacity, he was asked if this meant he accepted the rest of the report. His reply was that the changes should be taken one step at a time.

Upon leaving the meeting, as they later reported, the board members were "stunned" by the bishop's warm response and action. Even the most radical, pessimistic members found it difficult to believe that he had been so encouraging.

After the election committee had begun to solicit and receive names for the new position, the bishop sent a questionnaire to all priests. In it he requested their opinions on each of the separate recommendations of the personnel board. He indicated that he had come to no conclusions on any part of the report and would withhold any action pending consultation with all priests through the questionnaire.

The election committee was shocked with and bitter over this action. They had understood that the bishop's decision to form a nominating committee had shown commitment to the position of vicar for clergy, as described in their recommendations. In a letter to the bishop they said they felt they now lacked the necessary authority to proceed, and they therewith resigned.

The responses to the bishop's questionnaire were strongly bimodal, indicating a strong division of opinion on the board's recommendations. At this point, after the election committee resigned, there was a general feeling in the diocese that the recommendations would not be implemented.

However, in April the bishop met again with the election committee, and a working relationship was restored. The committee had strongly wanted the bishop's commitment to a concrete job description for the proposed vicar, and they were all able to agree with the bishop on one. The following letter and job description describe the outcome of that meeting:

ELECTION COMMITTEE

May 8, 1969

Dear Father:

In a meeting with the Election Committee on April 17, the bishop outlined the duties of the Vicar for Priests to whom he had referred in his letter of March 26 to all priests, and requested that the election for the Vicar be conducted as soon as possible. The description of the Vicar's duties as approved by the Archbishop is enclosed.

The election procedure will be as outlined in the report of the Preliminary Personnel Board with one exception—the number of nominees for the second ballot will be limited to six.

Each priest is asked to nominate two priests on the enclosed card. The list of the six nominees who receive the largest number of votes and who accept nomination will be distributed to all priests for a final vote.

Please mail the enclosed card with the names of your two nominees on or before May 22.

Sincerely yours,

THE ELECTION COMMITTEE

The Creation of Experimental Team Ministries

In June 1969 the bishop announced the formation of experimental team ministries in six parishes. In one of the parishes, the pastor resigned so that a team ministry with three copastors could be formed in his

parish, with him as one of the copastors. In the other parishes, the
pastor's position had become open either through death or retirement.

This significant change was announced in the front page headlines
of the diocesan newspaper.

In Archdiocese 6 Parishes Given Team Ministries

Hartford—The establishment of "team ministry" co-pastorates in six parishes of
the Archdiocese of Hartford, the appointment of one priest to a traditional pastorate,
the assignment of chaplains to three institutions, the transfer of 19 assistant pastors
and the appointment of 10 newly ordained priests as assistant pastors were
announced today by Archbishop John F. Whealon. All appointments will be effective
June 12.

The team ministry represents a new approach to pastoral authority involving
the voluntary association, mutual cooperation and shared responsibility of each
co-pastor in the total pastoral care of the parish.

Approval of the team ministry concept on an experimental basis in the archdiocese was originally announced by Archbishop Whealon last March in response
to proposals made to him by the Preliminary Personnel Board of the archdiocese,
a study commission established in 1967 following a recommendation of the Senate
of Priests. In his Transcript column last week, the Archbishop described the new
approach of the team ministry as follows:

"Our people are accustomed to having a pastor who is assisted by one or
more assistant pastors. In the team ministry the assignment is of the group rather
than of individuals, so that all will function as co-pastors. Of this group one will
be appointed as administrator to fulfill the requirements of civil law and to assure
individual and ultimate responsibility to the Archbishop for pastoral care of the
parish; however, each priest on the team will have his own area of responsibility
and there will be the added responsibility of keeping the other members of the
team informed so that this will be truly a combined and coordinated effort."

The reaction to these team ministries varied widely. Moderates were
encouraged that steady, if slow, progress was being made. More radical
priests felt that this was only a token change, representing the least
the bishop could do in light of the national interest in his diocese. There
were criticisms of what was seen as negative wording in his announcement
and concerns that the men chosen were not committed to the team
concept.

In addition, in cases where parishes have become vacant but team
ministries were not appointed, the bishop has appointed administrators,
not pastors. The assignment process has also apparently received attention. Curates are now consulted about their assignments and are given
2 weeks, rather than the previous three days, to move from the old
to the new parish.

Perhaps the most important long-term change the bishop has made
is to carefully assign newly ordained priests to the "better" pastors. He
is doing this without the interim summer assignment.

The Researchers' Assessment of Diocesan Changes

The researchers see the proposed changes as significant ones. Although it is difficult to understand why the bishop appeared to undermine the charter of the election committee, his idea of soliciting the opinions of all priests before acting was a useful means of consulting with them. That he publicized the results was a degree of openness often not present in the workings of the Church. His attitude of experimentation with a limited number of parishes also makes sense to us, pragmatic empiricists that we are.

The main problem we see so far, however, is that there is as yet no formal program for evaluating the success of these experiments so that objective data will be available for continual updating and change. One of the dilemmas of change is that the process, once begun, probably must continue. The benefits of an attitude of experimentation can be easily offset by a lack of valid data with which to judge the experiments and thus propose new methods and procedures.

Current Issues in the Church

In Chapter Eleven we concluded that authority (and its counterpart, individual freedom) was the central issue in the results of our study. The freedom of the parish priest to have a say in decisions affecting his life and career and to define his own challenging work goals and the means of achieving them—all of which are now in the hands of his superiors—seems to be the central concern of the priests in our survey. Further, we would submit that authority and freedom are also the core issues behind the main contemporary issues in the Church today—birth control, priestly celibacy, and organizational renewal.

In a sense, birth control and celibacy are red herrings, false issues which detract our attention from the core problem of authority. Although celibacy was not included specifically in our interview schedule, we were interested to see if priests would bring up the subject themselves. A glance at the interview schedule will show that in several places where we asked open-ended questions to probe the priest's own most important concerns, celibacy would have been quite appropriate to mention. Few priests did.

Some of the priests who mentioned celibacy explained its current importance in the following way (and we agree with them): All priests know when they enter the seminary that being a priest involves the sacrifice of foregoing marriage and a family of one's own. Because of the attractiveness and high expectations of the planned priestly career, the young man is prepared to make this sacrifice. As one young curate put it, "I loved my girl, but I love Christ more." The opportunity to serve, to do Christ's work, is worth the sacrifice, including the celibate life, because of the great challenge and involvement required.

Then the man is ordained, is placed in his first parish, and encounters the reality shock of the curate's work and life. He wonders where all the anticipated challenge, service, and involvement are. As he realizes how dissatisfied he is with his priestly work and with his lack of freedom to change it, he may begin to rethink his sacrifice: "I gave up marriage for *this?*"

Work frustration may stimulate new thinking about celibacy in other ways as well. The lack of meaning and challenge in his assignment may leave him feeling like less than a whole person, whereas marriage might provide the additional fulfillment and enrichment required. Further, frustrations with the assignment often lead to feelings of depression and a need for warmth and support. The priest may find this in a relationship with a woman and mistake it for love. Indeed, there is anecdotal evidence that some priests who have left the Church to marry have been separated or divorced soon after they made the successful transition to another occupation.

We would argue, then, that celibacy is not as central to the priest's life as the meaning and freedom he experiences in his work. This idea is supported by a recent survey of priests who left the priesthood. The results showed that work dissatisfaction was mentioned as a contributing factor far more than the desire to marry (Schallert, 1970). This is consistent with findings in the present study that lack of work challenge and dissatisfaction with the superior were two of the most important differences between priests who left and those who stayed.

Subsequent confirmation of these conclusions is found in the results of two comprehensive parallel studies of the priesthood, one psychological and the other sociological. These studies were described by John Cardinal Krol, chairman of the national committee of bishops which commissioned them as "the most massive single examination of the priesthood" (*Catholic Transcript*, April 23, 1971, p. 1). The sociological study, directed by Father Andrew Greeley of NORC, found that "authority" was the most frequently mentioned problem of the priesthood." Loneliness ranked second, followed by celibacy.

When probed on celibacy in the sociological study, the majority of priests were in favor of optional celibacy, the *freedom* to marry, while at the same time the "overwhelming majority" see celibacy as an asset in their ministry and would not exercise the option to marry. This finding was confirmed by the psychological study, which concluded that the core issue is freedom:

> This suggests that the real psychological issue, even when it is not identified psychologically as such, is greater freedom rather than the question of celibacy itself (quoted in *The Catholic Transcript*, April 23, 1971, p. 3).

The studies also found that the majority of priests do not support Pope Paul's 1968 encyclical against artificial birth control. However, in our opinion, the authority implications of *Humanae Vitae* are not as "hot" for most priests as those of the celibacy issue because birth control represents an area where priests have a great deal of de facto freedom. Birth control is an issue which need go no further than the confessional, and there each priest is free to treat the issue in his own way. In fact, the Pope has little actual power over priests in this area, and our impression is that many priests see him as being out of step with the realities of the Church.

Celibacy, however, is an ideal issue on which to fight the battle over authority because of its greater visibility and susceptibility to Church control. The celibacy rule is simply very difficult to disobey privately, and it affects the life of every priest in the most profound way. Because priests want the freedom to marry, but not necessarily marriage itself, the rule seems to possess great symbolic potential.

In the national sociological study we also found that as a way to increase the freedom of priests, many priests favor considerable decentralization of decision making—sharing of the bishops' power—within the dioceses. Since the bishops do not seem greatly dissatisfied with the way decisions are made, the report suggests that "serious conflict" may lie ahead over matters of power and decision making.

We would agree with the forecast of greater conflict, but we would add that this conflict may actually *increase* if the bishops agree to the need for change and take action to decentralize. Research on individual and group development shows that as a system (person or group) moves from a state of dependence to independence, it generally must move through a period of counterdependence—a time of great hostility and general opposition to established authority. The rebelliousness of the adolescent years is a good example of a counterdependent stage. In national development it is known as the "revolution of rising expectations." It is a perfectly normal part of the maturing process, involving a suspicion and rejection of everything authority figures propose (even in the most collaborative way) so that the person (or group) can find his (or its) own way. Following a number of emotional encounters with authority, the person can establish his own autonomy and will then be able to collaborate with authority without fear of being overcontrolled or manipulated. However, there is no way of knowing how many such encounters may take place or how violent they may be. They will be prolonged, however, if the response of authority is repressive, limiting the newfound freedom.

We have seen evidence of this conflict and tension in the personnel board's development toward autonomy. Many complex emotional issues in organizational process arose during our collaboration with the board, and it was important to be able to talk about them as well as about our primary task. If the client system were the entire diocese of the Church or the Church as a whole rather than a small group, the conflicts would be enormously compounded. Therefore, we feel it would be terribly important for the Church to devote at least as much time and energy to the *process* of change as it devotes to the *content* of the changes. What is needed is a well-planned overall strategy for implementing organizational change rather than a piecemeal acceptance of discrete recommendations. In short, if it is to escape the fate of bureaucracy described by Bennis (1969), the Church needs a long-range program for organizational development.

A - 1

APPENDIX A

ASSIGNMENT AND WORK EXPERIENCES QUESTIONNAIRE

DOUGLAS T. HALL, Ph.D.   BENJAMIN SCHNEIDER, Ph.D.

In Collaboration With

CHRIS ARGYRIS, Ph.D.

DEPARTMENT OF ADMINISTRATIVE SCIENCES

YALE UNIVERSITY

This questionnaire is designed to help the research team and subsequently the Archdiocese as a whole understand some of the issues of importance to you as a priest.

The questionnaire represents a systematic attempt to gather ideas from all the priests in the Archdiocese about their work experiences and their impact on the growth and development of priests.

The majority of the ideas and items in this questionnaire have come from interviews conducted with 95 of your fellow priests. This does not mean that all of the issues of relevance to you personally have been covered; throughout the questionnaire we hope you will take advantage of the opportunity to contribute your own thoughts. In addition, at the end of the questionnaire is a blank page for any comments you may have. If additional pages are necessary, please feel free to add them.

All data utilized in this study will be treated with the strictest professional confidence by the Yale University research team. Statistical analyses will be conducted on an aggregate basis, insuring that no individual will be identified. All data--both questionnaires and interview tapes--will remain the property of Yale and will not be available to the Archdiocese of Hartford.

Please try to answer the questions as candidly and conscientiously as possible since without answers of this type the research cannot be successful.

It will be useful later to collect supplementary data, such as the group interviews this summer. It will be important to be able to link these data up with the information collected with this questionnaire. For this reason, it will be helpful if you would put your name on your questionnaire.

We would like to thank you in advance for your cooperation. We will be in touch with you all again next spring with a complete summary of the results of this study.
_____

NAME_____ LOCATION_____ _____

TODAY'S DATE_____ YOUR AGE_____ _____

POSITION TITLE_____

WERE YOU INTERVIEWED AT YALE IN CONNECTION WITH THIS SURVEY? ____YES ____NO

    IF ANSWER ABOVE IS "YES", BY WHOM WERE YOU INTERVIEWED?

        ____DR. BENJAMIN SCHNEIDER   ____DR. DOUGLAS T. HALL
               ____FR. DOUGLAS A. MORRISON

    HOW OPEN AND FRANK DID YOU FEEL YOU COULD BE IN THE INTERVIEW? (Please circle one number below.)

        5   4   3   2   1
        /   /   /   /   /
        Extremely   Not at all
        open and frank   open and frank

Please go on to the next page.

SECTION ONE

A - 3

HISTORY OF ASSIGNMENTS

Please list below the assignments you have had since you were ordained

Year of ordination_____

Position Title	Name of Parish or Organization	Location	From (Year)	To (Year)	*

*If you requested to be moved from any of these assignments, please put a check mark (√) in the right-hand column next to that assignment.

Please indicate below the reason(s) for the request to be moved.

Please go on to the next page.

SECTION TWO

ACTIVITIES

Listed below are a number of duties connected with the work life of a priest. Please indicate with a check mark (✓) in the appropriate column (1) The amount of each activity you perform and (2) How important it is to you that you perform the activity.

In the third set of columns:

If you are a pastor please indicate how important you think it is to your curate(s) that this activity be performed.

If you are a curate please indicate how important you think it is to your pastor that this activity be performed.

(Leave the third set of columns blank if they do not apply to your type of assignment.)

NOTE: Not all possible duties can be included in one common list, especially for people in non-parish work. Please list under "Other" those activities you perform which are not included in this list.

DUTIES	Amount Performed by you			Importance to you to perform			Importance to Pastor or Curate (Circle Title)		
	Above avg.	Avg.	Below avg.	Above avg.	Avg.	Below avg.	Above avg.	Avg.	Below avg.
Visiting the sick.....									
Home visitation.......									
Preaching.............									
Hearing confessions...									
Being on duty in the rectory.............									
Being on call outside the rectory.........									
Saying Mass in church.									
Saying Mass in homes..									
Attending Deanery meetings.............									

Please go on to the next page.

SECTION TWO (Continued)   A - 5

DUTIES	Amount Performed by you			Importance to you to perform			Importance to Pastor or Curate (Circle Title)		
	Above avg.	Avg.	Below avg.	Above avg.	Avg.	Below avg.	Above avg.	Avg.	Below avg.
School administration									
Administering diocesan affairs									
Baptisms									
Teaching religion in school									
Teaching other courses in school									
C.C.D.									
Marriages									
Funerals									
Parish organization meetings									
Community meetings									
Ecumenical work									
Inner-city work									
Motivating the laity to become more active Catholics									
Reading									
Private prayer									
Supervising lay employees									
Supervising priests and/or Sisters									
Preparation for duties									
Training (self-improvement)									

Please go on to the next page.

SECTION TWO (Continued)

A - 6

DUTIES	Amount Performed by you			Importance to you to perform			Importance to Pastor or Curate (Circle Title)		
	Above avg.	Avg.	Below avg.	Above avg.	Avg.	Below avg.	Above avg.	Avg.	Below avg.
Answering telephones and/or doors.......									
Giving religious instructions.......									
Parish administration.									
Raising funds........									
Attending workshops and conferences....									
Marriage counseling...									
Other counseling (please specify) _____									
Other (please list below) _____									
_____									
_____									
_____									
_____									
_____									
_____									

Please go on to the next page.

SECTION THREE

CHARACTERISTICS OF FIRST ASSIGNMENT

In the interviews that we conducted some men felt that a priest's first permanent (i.e., non-summer) assignment is more important in his development than are subsequent assignments.

To what extent do you agree or disagree with this idea? (Circle the number on the scale which most closely reflects your opinion.)

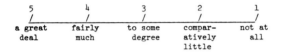

5	4	3	2	1
a great deal	fairly much	to some degree	compar- atively little	not at all

Please think back to your own first permanent (non-summer) assignment. In comparison to the first assignments of other priests you have known, how would you describe the following? (Please indicate your choice by placing a check mark (✓) in the appropriate column.)

Above Average	Average	Below Average	
....	....	....	The amount of responsibility in your work.
....	....	....	The amount of challenge in your duties.
....	....	....	The opportunity to express ideas to your pastor or other immediate superior.
....	....	....	The willingness of your pastor or other immediate superior to accept your ideas.
....	....	....	The feeling of contributing to decision-making.
....	....	....	The administrative effectiveness of your pastor or other immediate superior.
....	....	....	The pastoral effectiveness of your pastor or other superior.
....	....	....	The amount of discussion of your work with your pastor or immediate superior.
....	....	....	The amount of friendship between you and your pastor or immediate superior.
....	....	....	Your respect for your pastor or immediate superior as a person.

Please go on to the next page.

SECTION THREE (Continued)

Above Average	Average	Below Average	
....	....	....	The congeniality of life in the rectory.
....	....	....	The amount of authoritarian control exercised over you by your pastor or immediate superior.
....	....	....	The amount of personal interest in you shown by your pastor or immediate superior.
....	....	....	The amount of constructive criticisms provided by your pastor or immediate superior.
....	....	....	The feeling of being treated as an equal by your pastor or immediate superior.
....	....	....	The amount of priestly meaning in your work.
....	....	....	The amount of discussion between you and your pastor or immediate superior on issues of importance aside from your work.
....	....	....	The opportunity to exercise initiative.
....	....	....	The encouragement to exercise initiative.
....	....	....	The amount of initiative actually exercised by you.
....	....	....	The amount of housekeeper interference.
....	....	....	Opportunity to get to know the people in your parish.
....	....	....	Recognition of your accomplishments by your pastor or immediate superior.
....	....	....	The amount of direction provided by your pastor or immediate superior.
....	....	....	Your workload as a priest.
....	....	....	Feeling of contentment in your work.
....	....	....	The amount of guidance provided by your pastor or immediate superior.
....	....	....	Feeling of confidence in your work.
....	....	....	Feeling of being accepted by other priests in the rectory.

Please go on to the next page.

A - 9

SECTION THREE (Continued)

Above Average	Average	Below Average	
....	....	....	Amount of <u>constructive leadership</u> provided by your pastor or immediate superior.
....	....	....	Feeling of being <u>accepted by the laity as a priest</u>.
....	....	....	Feeling of being <u>accepted by the laity as a person</u>.
....	....	....	<u>Adequacy of seminary training</u> for your assignment.
....	....	....	The amount of <u>assistance</u> given to you by fellow curates in the parish.
....	....	....	The amount of <u>task structure</u> provided by the pastor or immediate superior.
....	....	....	Other (please specify)_____
....	....	....	Other (please specify)__ _____

Now please think about <u>your present assignment</u>. In comparison to other priests about your same <u>age</u> in the priesthood, please go back and rate the characteristics on the preceding pages again. Indicate your choice by placing a P (for Present assignment) in the appropriate column for each characteristic. The P may appear in the same box as the check mark.

Some of the preceding characteristics refer to "your pastor or other immediate superior." Please indicate here who your present immediate superior is. _____

Please go on to the next page.

SECTION FOUR

SELF-PERCEPTIONS IN THREE KINDS OF RELATIONSHIPS

Different situations or types of relationships bring out different
aspects of an individual's personal characteristics. In this section we are
interested in learning how priests in the Archdiocese of Hartford perceive
themselves in three types of relationships. We realize that you have
relationships with many different types of people, but here we are asking
you to think of three kinds of relationships: (1) your relationship with
your immediate superior; (2) your relationships with close friends; and
(3) your relationships with your parishioners (or with the Catholic laity,
if you are in non-parish work). We will be asking for your perceptions of
yourself in each of these different relationships.

The adjective pairs contained in the next few pages have been found to
be used by many people in describing themselves. Probably not all persons
use all of these characteristics to describe themselves in all relationships.
If you find that some of these characteristics are not a part of your present
picture of yourself in a particular relationship, please indicate that by
writing "NR" (not relevant) on the small line in the left-hand margin.

Each characteristic is represented graphically by a scale. Please
indicate the location on the scale where you picture yourself in the given
type of relationship by a check (✓).

Do not restrict yourself to a particular range on the scale; feel free to
place your responses anywhere on the scale. The only requirement is that you
be honest with yourself. Please do not be concerned with the way your
answers would be judged by others; this is completely irrelevant here.

Please feel free to make any comments you like on the margins.

The scale runs continuously from one labeled extreme to the other with
varying degrees being indicated by lines. Please place your check marks over
the lines, not over the colons.

Example:

____ FORMAL   ____:____:____:____:____: ✓ :____ INFORMAL

If you see yourself in a particular relationship as being relatively
informal, you might place a check mark as above. On the other hand, if the
Formal-Informal dimension is not relevant to the particular type of
relationship under consideration, you would write "NR" on the line to the left
of the word Formal, as below:

_NR_ FORMAL   ____:____:____:____:____:____ INFORMAL

Please go on to the next page.

SECTION FOUR (Continued)   A - 11

On this page, please describe <u>yourself</u> as <u>you relate to your immediate superior</u> (i.e., the way you perceive yourself to be as you are interacting with your immediate superior.)

____ ENTHUSIASTIC	___:___:___:___:___:___:___	UNENTHUSIASTIC
____ INSINCERE	___:___:___:___:___:___:___	SINCERE
____ UNCREATIVE	___:___:___:___:___:___:___	CREATIVE
____ KIND	___:___:___:___:___:___:___	UNKIND
____ PASSIVE	___:___:___:___:___:___:___	ACTIVE
____ INFORMAL	___:___:___:___:___:___:___	FORMAL
____ NOT HELPFUL	___:___:___:___:___:___:___	HELPFUL
____ SENSITIVE	___:___:___:___:___:___:___	INSENSITIVE
____ UNAGGRESSIVE	___:___:___:___:___:___:___	AGGRESSIVE
____ TRUSTING	___:___:___:___:___:___:___	SUSPICIOUS
____ NOT OBEDIENT	___:___:___:___:___:___:___	OBEDIENT
____ INTELLECTUAL	___:___:___:___:___:___:___	NOT INTELLECTUAL
____ MUDDLED THINKING	___:___:___:___:___:___:___	CLEAR THINKING
____ FRIENDLY	___:___:___:___:___:___:___	UNFRIENDLY
____ BRIGHT	___:___:___:___:___:___:___	DULL
____ NOT WILLING TO CHANGE	___:___:___:___:___:___:___	WILLING TO CHANGE
____ WARM	___:___:___:___:___:___:___	COLD
____ NOT CONCERNED ABOUT PEOPLE	___:___:___:___:___:___:___	CONCERNED ABOUT PEOPLE
____ KNOWLEDGEABLE	___:___:___:___:___:___:___	UNINFORMED
____ COOPERATIVE	___:___:___:___:___:___:___	UNCOOPERATIVE
____ PRIESTLY	___:___:___:___:___:___:___	UNPRIESTLY
____ INDUSTRIOUS	___:___:___:___:___:___:___	LAZY
____ APPROACHABLE	___:___:___:___:___:___:___	UNAPPROACHABLE
____ CONSIDERATE	___:___:___:___:___:___:___	INCONSIDERATE
____ AVAILABLE	___:___:___:___:___:___:___	UNAVAILABLE
____ COMMITTED	___:___:___:___:___:___:___	UNCOMMITTED
____ DEDICATED	___:___:___:___:___:___:___	NOT DEDICATED
____ INVOLVED	___:___:___:___:___:___:___	UNINVOLVED
____ EXPRESSES EMOTIONS	___:___:___:___:___:___:___	DOES NOT EXPRESS EMOTIONS

Please go on to the next page.

SECTION FOUR (Continued)

On this page please describe <u>yourself</u> <u>as</u> <u>you</u> <u>relate</u> <u>to</u> <u>your</u> <u>close</u> <u>friends</u>.

____ ENTHUSIASTIC	___:___:___:___:___:___:___	UNENTHUSIASTIC
____ INSINCERE	___:___:___:___:___:___:___	SINCERE
____ UNCREATIVE	___:___:___:___:___:___:___	CREATIVE
____ KIND	___:___:___:___:___:___:___	UNKIND
____ PASSIVE	___:___:___:___:___:___:___	ACTIVE
____ INFORMAL	___:___:___:___:___:___:___	FORMAL
____ NOT HELPFUL	___:___:___:___:___:___:___	HELPFUL
____ SENSITIVE	___:___:___:___:___:___:___	INSENSITIVE
____ UNAGGRESSIVE	___:___:___:___:___:___:___	AGGRESSIVE
____ TRUSTING	___:___:___:___:___:___:___	SUSPICIOUS
____ NOT OBEDIENT	___:___:___:___:___:___:___	OBEDIENT
____ INTELLECTUAL	___:___:___:___:___:___:___	NOT INTELLECTUAL
____ MUDDLED THINKING	___:___:___:___:___:___:___	CLEAR THINKING
____ FRIENDLY	___:___:___:___:___:___:___	UNFRIENDLY
____ BRIGHT	___:___:___:___:___:___:___	DULL
____ NOT WILLING TO CHANGE	___:___:___:___:___:___:___	WILLING TO CHANGE
____ WARM	___:___:___:___:___:___:___	COLD
____ NOT CONCERNED ABOUT PEOPLE	___:___:___:___:___:___:___	CONCERNED ABOUT PEOPLE
____ KNOWLEDGEABLE	___:___:___:___:___:___:___	UNINFORMED
____ COOPERATIVE	___:___:___:___:___:___:___	UNCOOPERATIVE
____ PRIESTLY	___:___:___:___:___:___:___	UNPRIESTLY
____ INDUSTRIOUS	___:___:___:___:___:___:___	LAZY
____ APPROACHABLE	___:___:___:___:___:___:___	UNAPPROACHABLE
____ CONSIDERATE	___:___:___:___:___:___:___	INCONSIDERATE
____ AVAILABLE	___:___:___:___:___:___:___	UNAVAILABLE
____ COMMITTED	___:___:___:___:___:___:___	UNCOMMITTED
____ DEDICATED	___:___:___:___:___:___:___	NOT DEDICATED
____ INVOLVED	___:___:___:___:___:___:___	UNINVOLVED
____ EXPRESSES EMOTIONS	___:___:___:___:___:___:___	DOES NOT EXPRESS EMOTIONS

Please go on to the next page.

SECTION FOUR (Continued)   A - 13

On this page please describe <u>yourself</u> <u>as</u> <u>you</u> <u>relate</u> <u>to</u> <u>your</u> <u>parishioners</u> in general (or, if you are not in a parish, yourself as you relate to the Catholic laity with whom you work).

_____ ENTHUSIASTIC	____:____:____:____:____:____:____	UNENTHUSIASTIC
_____ INSINCERE	____:____:____:____:____:____:____	SINCERE
_____ UNCREATIVE	____:____:____:____:____:____:____	CREATIVE
_____ KIND	____:____:____:____:____:____:____	UNKIND
_____ PASSIVE	____:____:____:____:____:____:____	ACTIVE
_____ INFORMAL	____:____:____:____:____:____:____	FORMAL
_____ NOT HELPFUL	____:____:____:____:____:____:____	HELPFUL
_____ SENSITIVE	____:____:____:____:____:____:____	INSENSITIVE
_____ UNAGGRESSIVE	____:____:____:____:____:____:____	AGGRESSIVE
_____ TRUSTING	____:____:____:____:____:____:____	SUSPICIOUS
_____ NOT OBEDIENT	____:____:____:____:____:____:____	OBEDIENT
_____ INTELLECTUAL	____:____:____:____:____:____:____	NOT INTELLECTUAL
_____ MUDDLED THINKING	____:____:____:____:____:____:____	CLEAR THINKING
_____ FRIENDLY	____:____:____:____:____:____:____	UNFRIENDLY
_____ BRIGHT	____:____:____:____:____:____:____	DULL
_____ NOT WILLING TO CHANGE	____:____:____:____:____:____:____	WILLING TO CHANGE
_____ WARM	____:____:____:____:____:____:____	COLD
_____ NOT CONCERNED ABOUT PEOPLE	____:____:____:____:____:____:____	CONCERNED ABOUT PEOPLE
_____ KNOWLEDGEABLE	____:____:____:____:____:____:____	UNINFORMED
_____ COOPERATIVE	____:____:____:____:____:____:____	UNCOOPERATIVE
_____ PRIESTLY	____:____:____:____:____:____:____	UNPRIESTLY
_____ INDUSTRIOUS	____:____:____:____:____:____:____	LAZY
_____ APPROACHABLE	____:____:____:____:____:____:____	UNAPPROACHABLE
_____ CONSIDERATE	____:____:____:____:____:____:____	INCONSIDERATE
_____ AVAILABLE	____:____:____:____:____:____:____	UNAVAILABLE
_____ COMMITTED	____:____:____:____:____:____:____	UNCOMMITTED
_____ DEDICATED	____:____:____:____:____:____:____	NOT DEDICATED
_____ INVOLVED	____:____:____:____:____:____:____	UNINVOLVED
_____ EXPRESSES EMOTIONS	____:____:____:____:____:____:____	DOES NOT EXPRESS EMOTIONS

Please go on to the next page.

SECTION FIVE

GENERAL SELF-PERCEPTION

    On this page, we are interested in the way you perceive yourself most generally--not in any particular type of relationship. This, then, would be your description of yourself as a total person.

____ ENTHUSIASTIC	____:____:____:____:____:____:____	UNENTHUSIASTIC
____ INSINCERE	____:____:____:____:____:____:____	SINCERE
____ UNCREATIVE	____:____:____:____:____:____:____	CREATIVE
____ KIND	____:____:____:____:____:____:____	UNKIND
____ PASSIVE	____:____:____:____:____:____:____	ACTIVE
____ INFORMAL	____:____:____:____:____:____:____	FORMAL
____ NOT HELPFUL	____:____:____:____:____:____:____	HELPFUL
____ SENSITIVE	____:____:____:____:____:____:____	INSENSITIVE
____ UNAGGRESSIVE	____:____:____:____:____:____:____	AGGRESSIVE
____ TRUSTING	____:____:____:____:____:____:____	SUSPICIOUS
____ NOT OBEDIENT	____:____:____:____:____:____:____	OBEDIENT
____ INTELLECTUAL	____:____:____:____:____:____:____	NOT INTELLECTUAL
____ MUDDLED THINKING	____:____:____:____:____:____:____	CLEAR THINKING
____ FRIENDLY	____:____:____:____:____:____:____	UNFRIENDLY
____ BRIGHT	____:____:____:____:____:____:____	DULL
____ NOT WILLING TO CHANGE	____:____:____:____:____:____:____	WILLING TO CHANGE
____ WARM	____:____:____:____:____:____:____	COLD
____ NOT CONCERNED ABOUT PEOPLE	____:____:____:____:____:____:____	CONCERNED ABOUT PEOPLE
____ KNOWLEDGEABLE	____:____:____:____:____:____:____	UNINFORMED
____ COOPERATIVE	____:____:____:____:____:____:____	UNCOOPERATIVE
____ PRIESTLY	____:____:____:____:____:____:____	UNPRIESTLY
____ INDUSTRIOUS	____:____:____:____:____:____:____	LAZY
____ APPROACHABLE	____:____:____:____:____:____:____	UNAPPROACHABLE
____ CONSIDERATE	____:____:____:____:____:____:____	INCONSIDERATE
____ AVAILABLE	____:____:____:____:____:____:____	UNAVAILABLE
____ COMMITTED	____:____:____:____:____:____:____	UNCOMMITTED
____ DEDICATED	____:____:____:____:____:____:____	NOT DEDICATED
____ INVOLVED	____:____:____:____:____:____:____	UNINVOLVED
____ EXPRESSES EMOTIONS	____:____:____:____:____:____:____	DOES NOT EXPRESS EMOTIONS

Please look back over the above and circle the five (5) characteristics you feel are most important in your conception of the ideal priest.

Please go on to the next page

SECTION SIX

ENVIRONMENTAL CHARACTERISTICS OF PRESENT ASSIGNMENT

In this section of the questionnaire, we are interested in your describing (1) some of the characteristics of your assignment as it is NOW; and (2) characteristics of your assignment you would PREFER. For each category, place a check mark (✓) in the NOW column if the item describes your present assignment. If the item describes how you would PREFER your assignment to be, place a check mark (✓) in the PREFER column. You may check one or both of the columns.

NOW	PREFER		NOW	PREFER	
....	....	Large parish	....	....	Transient (mobile) parishioners
....	....	Medium parish	....	....	Settled parishioners
....	....	Small parish	....	....	Generally younger parishioners
....	....	National parish	....	....	Generally older parishioners
....	....	Territorial parish	....	....	Private bath in rectory
....	....	Inner city parish	....	....	No private bath in rectory
....	....	Urban assignment	....	....	One room to yourself in rectory
....	....	Suburban assignment	....	....	Suite of rooms to yourself in rectory
....	....	Rural assignment			
....	....	Special assignment	....	....	Rectory near church
....	....	Parish assignment	....	....	Rectory away from church
....	....	Lower class laity	....	....	Live in rectory
....	....	Lower-middle class laity	....	....	Live outside rectory
....	....	Middle class laity	....	....	Full-time housekeeper in rectory
....	....	Upper-middle class laity	....	....	Part-time housekeeper in rectory
			....	....	Full-time secretary in rectory
....	....	Upper class laity	....	....	Part-time secretary in rectory
....	....	Mixed population	....	....	Telephone answering service in rectory
			....	....	Adequate telephone facilities

Please go on to the next page.

SECTION SIX (Continued)

	P R E F E R			P R E F E R	
N O W			N O W		
		Number of Curates	....	....	Other (please specify)_____
....	....	.... None			_____
			....	....	Other (please specify)_____
....	....	.... One			_____
....	....	.... Two	....	....	Other (please specify)_____
					_____
....	....	.... Three or more (please specify)	....	....	Other (please specify)_____
		Number of priest co-workers (if special assignment)			_____
....	....	.... None			
....	....	.... One			
....	....	.... Two			
....	....	.... Three or more (please specify)			

To what extent do you feel you are utilizing your important skills and abilities in your present assignment? (Circle the number on the scale which most clearly reflects your opinion.)

5	4	3	2	1
/	/	/	/	/
a great deal	fairly much	to some degree	compar- atively little	not at all

To the degree that you consider your response to be at the negative end of the scale, what changes could be made in your present assignment to increase the utilization of your important skills and abilities?

Please go on to the next page.

SECTION SEVEN   A - 17

OPINIONS ON THE WAY ASSIGNMENTS SHOULD BE MADE

In this section of the questionnaire we are interested in how you would
like to see assignments made for work or special training. Listed below are
a number of statements that have come out of the interviews regarding
assignments; we would like to know the extent to which you agree with the
statement as a policy for making assignments. Please use the five-point
scale below as a frame of reference for your responses. Thus, if you
definitely agree with the statement, you would put the number "5" on the line
to the left of the statement; on the other hand, if you definitely disagree
with the statement, you would put a "1" on the line to the left of the
statement.

5	4	3	2	1
Definitely	Agree	Uncertain	Disagree	Definitely
Agree				Disagree

NOTE: You may find it useful to preface each of the following statements
      with the words "Assignments should be made..." :

____with consultation of priest involved.

____with consideration of (taking into account) interests and abilities of
    the priest involved:

    ____based upon psychological testing.

    ____based upon professional guidance.

    ____based upon an interview with the priests.

    ____based upon performance in previous assignments.

    ____based upon a survey of all priests' interests and talents.

____with the opportunity for special training where necessary.

____as at present.

____by a new committee of priests whose main function is the development and
    assignment of priests.

____based on the needs of the Archdiocese.

____based on the needs of particular parishes or other Archdiocesan functions.

____with routine periodic evaluation of each priest's performance.

____with routine periodic evaluation of each priest's suitability for his
    assignment.

____with evaluation of a priest's suitability for an assignment only at the
    priest's request.

____based on the interests and personal characteristics of the pastor in the
    new assignment.

Please go on to the next page.

SECTION SEVEN (Continued)   A - 18

```
    5           4           3           2           1
   /           /           /           /           /
  /           /           /           /           /
Definitely    Agree    Uncertain   Disagree   Definitely
 Agree                                         Disagree
```

Assignments should be made...:

_____ based on the interests and personal characteristics of the other assistant(s) in the new assignment.

_____ with the opportunity for special training or further education where necessary.

_____ with the guarantee that reasons for not granting requests for a certain assignment or special training would be discussed with the priest involved.

_____ taking into account the specialized training (and/or lack thereof) of the priest involved.

_____ with a _maximum_ time allowed in the assignment. (If you indicated Agree or Definitely Agree, please specify time desired: _____years.)

_____ with a _minimum_ time allowed in the assignment. (If you indicated Agree or Definitely Agree, please specify time desired: _____years.)

_____ with the opportunity to refuse reassignment without prejudice.

_____ with the opportunity to express a desire for a particular assignment.

_____ based on consultation with the laity.

_____ based partially on seniority.

_____ based solely on seniority.

_____ based partially on merit.

_____ based solely on merit.

        How and by whom should merit be judged? Please
        list criteria in order of importance.

_____ (other; please specify)_____

_____ (other; please specify)_____

_____ (other; please specify)_____

_____ (other; please specify)_____
                         use back of page for more opinions if necessary

                              Please go on to the next page.

SECTION EIGHT

PERCEIVED MEANING OF THREE TYPES OF ASSIGNMENTS

In this section of the questionnaire, we are interested in learning what important associations you have regarding the three types of assignments available: Pastor, Curate, Special work. In the columns below please indicate which of the following characteristics you feel are important aspects of each type of work in general. If you tend to associate a certain characteristic with a certain type of work, put a check mark (✓) in the appropriate column next to that characteristic. The columns are labelled as follows: P for Pastor, C for Curate, and S for Special work.

We are interested here in your strongest (most salient) associations with each type of work. Thus, for example, if you feel that "having assistants" is one of the more important aspects of being a pastor, you would put a check mark (✓) in the "P" column next to "having assistants". If this is not an important aspect of the pastorate, to you, you would leave the column blank. You may, of course, put a check in more than one column, for any given characteristic.

P	C	S	
			Not enough prior training
			Being a "real" priest
			Having control over one's life
			Comes too late; after one's energy wanes
			A new parish to be established
			Having more say in one's assignments
			Reduced pastoral activities
			Being close to the Archbishop
			Increase in salary
			Status in eyes of the parishioners
			Detracts from on one's own spiritual life
			More problems
			Helping younger priests

P	C	S	
			Overwhelming
			Increase in own wealth
			Security
			Too much work
			Running one's own house
			Better opportunity to use talents
			Being able to exercise authority
			Challenge
			Opportunity to make changes
			Creativity
			Worth looking forward to
			Not worth looking forward to
			More opportunity to help people

Please go on to the next page.

SECTION EIGHT (Continued)

P	C	S	
....	....	....	Effecting social change
....	....	....	Dependence
....	....	....	Having assistants
....	....	....	Independence
....	....	....	Responsibility
....	....	....	More leisure
....	....	....	Long time coming
....	....	....	Administration
....	....	....	Financial work
....	....	....	Loneliness
....	....	....	Stability
....	....	....	Not enough work
....	....	....	Other_____
....	....	....	Other_____
....	....	....	Other_____

Please go on to the next page.

SECTION NINE

GENERAL ISSUES

Listed below are some general issues which arose in the interviews. Since not every issue was mentioned by every priest interviewed, we would like to use this opportunity to obtain a better representation of opinions on these issues.

1. How important to you is the issue of salaries?

```
        5            4            3            2            1
        /            /            /            /            /
      very                                              not at all
    important                                           important
```

2. How adequate do you feel your present salary is?

```
        5            4            3            2            1
        /            /            /            /            /
      very                                              not at all
    adequate                                            adequate
```

3. Do you feel the present stipend system should be retained?   YES___ NO___

4. Without the present stipend system, how much do you feel your present monthly salary should be increased? $_____

5. Do you feel the parish should accept stole fees for:

    (a) Weddings?   YES___ NO___

    (b) Baptisms?   YES___ NO___

    (c) Funerals?   YES___ NO___

6. How important is the issue of time off to you?

```
        5            4            3            2            1
        /            /            /            /            /
      very                                              not at all
    important                                           important
```

7. How much time off do you have each week?   _____

8. How much time do you feel you should have off each week?   _____

9. Counting yourself, how many children were there in your family?_____

    How many older brothers did you have?_____
    How many younger brothers did you have?_____
    How many older sisters did you have?_____
    How many younger sisters did you have?_____

10. Please state briefly how and when you decided to enter the priesthood. (Please use reverse side if necessary).

Please go on to the next page.

A - 22

SECTION TEN

CHURCH GOALS

(Please read both questions on this page first before answering either one. The first question asks <u>what</u> <u>exists</u> <u>now</u>, and the second asks <u>what</u> <u>should</u> <u>exist</u>.)

What would you say is (are) the most important goal(s) of the Roman Catholic Church today? (If listing more than one goal, please list them <u>in</u> <u>order</u> <u>of</u> <u>importance</u>.)

What would you say <u>should</u> <u>be</u> the most important goal(s) of the Roman Catholic Church today? (If listing more than one goal, please list them <u>in</u> <u>order</u> <u>of</u> <u>importance</u>.)

Please go on to the next page.

SECTION ELEVEN   A - 23

Picture yourself in a decision making meeting conducting, in your
opinion, important business. Please complete the following sentences,
keeping the type of meeting in mind:

(1) In a decision making meeting an effective leader is one who.....

(2) The most effective members tend to.....

(3) When disagreement erupts into personal antagonisms and hostile
    feelings, the best thing for a leader to do is.....

(4) How much members trust each other is usually shown by.....

(5) In your experience the most serious blocks to group progress
    in a meeting are.....

Please go on to the next page.

A - 24

SECTION TWELVE

DESCRIPTION OF PRESENT ASSIGNMENT

Copyright 1962
Patricia C. Smith
Bowling Green University

Think of your present work. What is it like most of the time?
In the blank beside each word given below, write

<u>y</u> for "Yes" if it describes your work

<u>n</u> for "No" if it does NOT describe it

<u>?</u> if you cannot decide

....

WORK ON PRESENT ASSIGNMENT

_____Fascinating

_____Routine

_____Satisfying

_____Boring

_____Good

_____Creative

_____Respected

_____Hot

_____Pleasant

_____Useful

_____Tiresome

_____Healthful

_____Challenging

_____On your feet

_____Frustrating

_____Simple

_____Endless

_____Gives sense of accomplishment

Please go on to the next page.

A - 25

SECTION TWELVE (Continued)

Think of the pay you get now. How well does each of the following words describe your present pay? In the blank beside each word, put

_y_ if it describes your pay

_n_ if it does NOT describe it

_?_ if you cannot decide

....

PRESENT PAY

Income adequate for normal expenses _____

Barely live on income _____

Bad _____

Income provides luxuries _____

Less than I deserve _____

Highly paid _____

Underpaid _____

Please go on to the next page.

SECTION TWELVE (Continued)

Think of the opportunities for promotion that you have now. How well does each of the following words describe these? In the blank beside each word, put

<u>y</u> for "Yes" if it describes your opportunities for promotion

<u>n</u> for "No" if it does NOT describe them

<u>?</u> if you cannot decide

....

OPPORTUNITIES FOR PROMOTION

_____Good opportunity for advancement

_____Opportunity somewhat limited

_____Promotion on ability

_____Dead-end assignment

_____Good chance for promotion

_____Unfair promotion policy

_____Infrequent promotions

_____Regular promotions

_____Fairly good chance for promotion

Please go on to the next page.

A - 27

SECTION TWELVE (Continued)

Think of the kind of supervision that you get on your job. How well
does each of the following words describe this supervision? In the
blank beside each word below, put

 y if it describes the supervision you get on your job

 n if it does NOT describe it

 ? if you cannot decide

....

SUPERVISION ON PRESENT ASSIGNMENT

Asks my advice_____

Hard to please_____

Impolite_____

Praises good work _____

Tactful _____

Influential_____

Up-to-date_____

Doesn't supervise enough_____

Quick-tempered_____

Tells me where I stand_____

Annoying_____

Stubborn_____

Knows job well_____

Bad_____

Intelligent_____

Leaves me on my own_____

Around when needed_____

Lazy_____

Please go on to the next page.

A - 2 8

SECTION TWELVE (Continued)

Think of the majority of the people that you work with now or the people
you meet in connection with your work. How well does each of the
following words describe these people? In the blank beside each word
below, put

_y_ if it describes the people you work with

_n_ if it does NOT describe them

_?_ if you cannot decide

....

PEOPLE ON YOUR PRESENT ASSIGNMENT

Stimulating_____

Boring_____

Slow_____

Ambitious_____

Stupid_____

Responsible_____

Fast_____

Intelligent_____

Easy to make enemies_____

Talk too much_____

Smart_____

Lazy_____

Unpleasant_____

No privacy_____

Active_____

Narrow Interests_____

Loyal_____

Hard to meet_____

Please go on to the next page.

A - 29

SECTION THIRTEEN

OPINIONS ABOUT THIS SURVEY

(Please circle the appropriate number below each question.)

1. How valuable do you feel this survey will be?

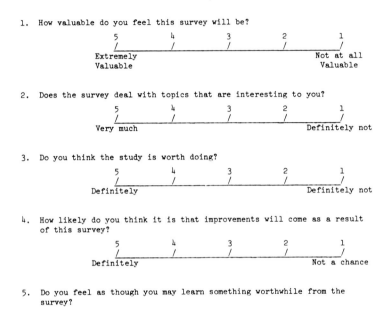

2. Does the survey deal with topics that are interesting to you?

3. Do you think the study is worth doing?

4. How likely do you think it is that improvements will come as a result of this survey?

5. Do you feel as though you may learn something worthwhile from the survey?

Please go on to the next page.

SECTION FOURTEEN

OTHER ISSUES OF IMPORTANCE

Are there any other important issues which we have not covered? If so, would you describe them here?

What are your views on these issues?

APPENDIX B
Partial Correlation Analyses of Career Variables within Position

In Chapter Eleven we presented a partial correlation analysis of the five most central variables in the career-development model. Since we have argued that pastors and specials work under conditions most favorable to psychological success, one would expect the partial correlation analyses to provide greater support for the career model among these two groups than among curates.

The revised model is as follows:

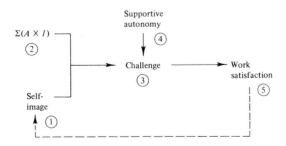

TABLE B.1

Data for Partial Correlation Analyses within Position

Partial[a]	Should be	Actual: specials (n = 55)		Actual: pastors (n = 120)		Actual: curates (n = 198)	
12	Near zero	.22	(✓)	.12	(✓)	.26	(X)
13.2	Positive	.40	(✓)	.07	(X)	.07	(X)
23.1	Positive	.17	(X)	.32	(✓)	.43	(✓)
24.1	Near zero	−.05	(✓)	.07	(✓)	−.05	(✓)
14.3	Near zero	−.18	(✓)	.11	(✓)	−.21	(X)
45.3	Near zero	.00	(✓)	.16	(X)	.02	(✓)
15.3	Positive	.18	(X)	.20	(✓)	.00	(X)
25.3	Near zero	.04	(✓)	.17	(X)	.15	(X)
12.3	Near zero	.12	(✓)	.08	(✓)	.20	(X)
35.4	Positive	.41	(✓)	.14	(X)	.41	(✓)
35.2	Positive	.39	(✓)	.15	(✓)	.42	(✓)
35.1	Positive	.31	(✓)	.20	(✓)	.51	(✓)
15.32	Positive	.17	(X)	.19	(✓)	−.02	(X)
14.32	Near zero	−.18	(✓)	.11	(✓)	−.21	(X)

Zero-order intercorrelations

	Pastors				Specials				Curates			
	1	2	3	4	1	2	3	4	1	2	3	4
1. Self-image	—				—				—			
2. Σ (A × I)	.12	—			.22	—			.26	—		
3. Challenge	.11	.33	—		.44	.25	—		.18	.46	—	
4. Supportive autonomy	.15	.19	.38	—	−.15	−.04	−.04	—	−.05	.26	.64	—
5. Work satisfaction	.22	.23	.22	.23	.33	.14	.41	.01	.10	.36	.52	.35

[a] See model in text for labeling of reference numbers.

The testing of the model was conducted with techniques proposed by Blalock (1964, 1969), as described in Chapter Eleven.

Partial correlation data for the three positions are presented in Table B-1. As expected, the partials for specials and pastors fit the model better than those for assistant pastors, although the fit is not perfect for any group. The strongest chain of relationships for specials was self-image → challenge → satisfaction. Perceived challenge is related more to the self-image of the specialist than to his particular activities or to the amount of supportive autonomy in his work environment. The feedback relationship between work satisfaction and self-image is weakened when challenge is held constant.

For the pastors a similarly large number of the theoretical relationships are supported by the actual data (11 for specials, 10 for pastors).

However, for pastors there are some different relationships that match the theoretical model. For example, satisfaction is related to self-image independent of challenge and activities. Activities and supportive autonomy relate more strongly to perceived challenge than does self-image.

In many respects, the data for curates do not fit the model. Self-image is not related to perceived challenge independent of $\Sigma(A \times I)$. $\Sigma(A \times I)$ and supportive autonomy far overshadow self-image as contributors to perceived challenge, again showing the small degree of personal causation experienced by curates. Further, there is no feedback from satisfaction to self-image, with or without holding challenge constant. However, activities are significantly related to satisfaction, even with challenge held constant, showing the primacy of activity per se over the challenge and meaning experienced in that activity for curates.

Interestingly, when challenge [or challenge and $\Sigma(A \times I)$] is held constant, there is a significant *negative* relationship between the curates's self-image and the supportive autonomy his pastor provides. Normally, a supportive pastor also provides challenge ($r = .64$), but when he does not, the curate's self-image suffers. Further, with challenge held constant, the link between supportive autonomy and work satisfaction disappears. Therefore, work challenge is the critical factor in the psychological success of the curate, and supportive autonomy is only important as a means of providing challenge. In fact, supportive autonomy alone from a pastor (without challenge) is probably the equivalent of what Blake & Mouton (1964) would call pure relationship-oriented, or 1, 9, management. Supportive autonomy plus challenge would be a combination of concern for relationship and concern for production, or 9, 9 team management.

APPENDIX C
Intercorrelation Matrices, Outcome Measures, for Pastors, Curates and Specials

The intercorrelation matrices contain all the variables initially considered to be criterion variables. The triangles presented on each matrix highlight the intercorrelations for the scales within a particular global construct; climate, self-image and so forth. These triangles show, for example, that the three traits measured by the self-image semantic differential tend to be interrelated at about .60 within each subidentity relationship (friends, laity), and in the general self-image description.

In addition to the triangles, we have highlighted the trait X subidentity diagonals. These diagonals reflect the extent to which the trait being measured is independent of the subidentity relationship in which the priest responded. For example, in every case, the trait "supportive" is more highly related to supportive in other subidentities and in general than it is related to any other trait in any other subidentity. However, the particular subidentity in which the priest was responding did have an impact. This can be seen by noting that the intercorrelations of the

276

three traits within a subidentity tend to be higher than any trait is related to the same trait in another subidentity.

Thus the trait "supportive," for example, has similar meaning regardless of the subidentity under consideration; on the other hand the subidentity has meaning regardless of the trait under consideration. One might speak of trait and subidentity variance in a modification of the Campbell and Fiske (1959) terminology. In these matrices, both types of variances are clearly represented.

Intercorrelations of Criterion Measures for Pastors[1]

	1	2	3	4	5	6	7	8	9	10	11	12	13	14	15	16	17	18
1. Use of skills and abilities																		
2. Work satisfaction	31																	
3. Pay satisfaction	-03	16																
4. Promotion satisfaction	01	27	09															
5. Supervision satisfaction	35	35	16	33														
6. Co-worker satisfaction	25	61	03	16	52													
7. Supportive (superior)	32	39	15	17	39	35												
8. Intellectual	22	33	11	29	41	33	66											
9. Involved	38	37	17	35	25	27	54	68										
10. Supportive (friends)	13	20	05	-07	09	15	69	84	29									
11. Intellectual	05	18	-07	02	01	08	34	35	27	58								
12. Involved	10	14	-03	05	04	07	35	35	52	53	64							
13. Supportive (laity)	06	19	10	07	10	16	60	31	26	76	56	49						
14. Intellectual	14	25	-01	10	10	18	51	51	37	60	74	67	69					
15. Involved	09	22	09	10	08	13	40	39	58	54	57	84	62	73				
16. Supportive (general)	07	24	13	11	15	20	65	37	28	80	56	49	89	69	61			
17. Intellectual	15	22	-01	02	14	14	46	57	31	50	67	55	58	85	56	67		
18. Involved	08	20	06	09	-03	15	31	33	52	45	52	83	55	67	89	58	59	

[1]Decimals have been omitted. Sample size is approximately 120 although it varies due to incomplete information on some measures.

Intercorrelations of Criterion Measures for Curates[1]

	1	2	3	4	5	6	7	8	9	10	11	12	13	14	15	16	17
1. Use of skills and abilities	49																
2. Work satisfaction	14	15															
3. Pay satisfaction	17	26	09														
4. Promotion satisfaction	27	34	08	16													
5. Supervision satisfaction	28	42	13	17	33												
6. Co-worker satisfaction	30	30	-0-	15	50	23											
7. Supportive (superior)	30	34	-11	18	24	08	52										
8. Intellectual	28	31	-08	18	18	12	51	68									
9. Involved	09	-03	-17	06	-0-	-0-	35	26	37								
10. Supportive (friends)	12	07	-12	09	-17	-05	16	53	40	48							
11. Intellectual	09	05	-16	10	-15	-01	12	37	45	68	64						
12. Involved	16	11	02	05	-0-	13	38	28	46	49	46	43					
13. Supportive (laity)	16	15	-0-	13	-09	07	27	49	50	30	67	43	69				
14. Intellectual	22	21	01	10	-04	11	23	38	56	37	56	55	72	71			
15. Involved	11	02	-02	-0-	-01	06	36	30	38	63	45	54	73	46	47		
16. Supportive (general)	15	13	-06	07	-17	-04	12	54	41	30	78	51	41	68	52	46	
17. Intellectual	14	15	-06	14	-12	-05	09	40	52	42	54	72	47	54	70	57	65
18. Involved																	

[1] Decimals have been omitted. Sample size is approximately 198; it varies due to missing data on some variables.

Intercorrelations of Criterion Measures for Specials[1]

	1	2	3	4	5	6	7	8	9	10	11	12	13	14	15	16	17
1. Use of skills and abilities																	
2. Work satisfaction	48																
3. Pay satisfaction	09	17															
4. Promotion satisfaction	35	39	14														
5. Supervision satisfaction	05	-27	-0-	03													
6. Co-worker satisfaction	09	23	-09	14	18												
7. Supportive (superior)	-03	08	-01	14	38	20											
8. Intellectual	-09	01	-07	18	17	14	76										
9. Involved	-13	03	09	18	17	32	75	64									
10. Supportive (friends)	06	22	03	-07	-04	13	69	60	48								
11. Intellectual	03	13	-05	23	-16	04	31	71	34	50							
12. Involved	-15	11	02	05	-25	04	32	59	44	65	74						
13. Supportive (laity)	10	17	-06	-14	-06	04	57	57	41	81	44	61					
14. Intellectual	23	24	-02	17	-24	12	29	57	42	40	68	56	59				
15. Involved	09	15	01	-09	-22	05	33	43	39	52	51	71	74	67			
16. Supportive (general)	15	34	03	07	-02	07	49	48	41	66	43	52	86	60	68		
17. Intellectual	21	39	-12	23	-10	30	32	62	44	36	68	51	49	77	52	62	
18. Involved	-04	26	10	05	-30	06	34	49	47	53	51	75	63	54	77	66	59

[1] Decimals have been omitted. Sample size is approximately 55 with some deviations due to missing data.

References

Alderfer, C. P. An empirical test of a new theory of human needs. *Organizational Behavior and Human Performance*, 1969, **4**, 142–175.

Alderfer, C. P. *Human needs in organizational settings*. New York: The Free Press of Glencoe, 1972.

Argyris, C. *Personality and organization*. New York: Harper, 1957.

Argyris, C. *Understanding organizational behavior*. Homewood, Ill.: Dorsey, 1960.

Argyris, C. *Integrating the individual and the organization*. New York: Wiley, 1964.

Argyris, C. *Organization and innovation*. Homewood, Ill.: Irwin-Dorsey, 1965.

Argyris, C. *Intervention theory and method*. Reading, Mass.: Addison-Wesley, 1970.

Atkinson, J. W. (Ed.) *Motives in fantasy, action and society*. Princeton, N.J.: Van Nostrand, 1958.

Bakke, W. E. *Bonds of organization*. New York: Harper, 1950.

Becker, H. S. *Outsiders: Studies in the sociology of deviance*. Glencoe, Ill.: The Free Press, 1963.

Becker, H. S., & Carper, J. The elements of identification with an occupation. *American Sociological Review*. 1956, **21**, 341–347.

Becker, H., Geer, B., Hughes, E., & Strauss, A. *Boys in white*. Chicago: University of Chicago Press, 1961.

Bennis, W. G. Organizational developments and the fate of bureaucracy. In L. L. Cummings and W. E. Scott (Eds.), *Readings in organizational behavior and human performance*. Homewood, Ill.: Irwin, 1969.

Bennis, W. G., Schein, E. H., Steele, F. I., & Berlew, D. E. (Eds.) *Interpersonal dynamics*. (2nd ed.) Homewood, Ill.: Dorsey, 1968.

Berlew, D. E., & Hall, D. T. The management of tension in organizations. *Industrial Management Review*, 1964, **6**, 31–40.

Berlew, D. E., & Hall, D. T. The socialization of managers: Effects of expectations on performance. *Administrative Science Quarterly,* 1966, **11**, 207–223.

Bettelheim, B. Individual and mass behavior in extreme situations. In E. Maccoby, T. Newcomb, and E. Hartley (Eds.), *Readings in social psychology.* (3rd ed.) New York: Holt, Rinehart and Winston, 1958.

Bier, W. C. A comparative study of a seminary group and four other groups on the MMPI. *Studies in psychology and psychiatry, Catholic University of America.* Vol. 7, No. 11, 1948.

Bier, W. C. Practical requirements of a program for the psychological screening of applicants. *Review for Religions,* 1954, **13**, 13–27.

Bier, W. C. Basic rationale of screening for religious vocations. In W. C. Bier and A. A. Schneiders (Eds.) *Three joint symposia from the ACPA-APA meetings of 1957, 1958, 1959.* New York: American Catholic Psychological Association, 1960.

Blake, R. R., & Mouton, S. S. *The managerial grid.* Houston: Gulf, 1964.

Blalock, H. M. *Causal inferences in non-experimental research.* Chapel Hill, N.C.: University of North Carolina Press. 1964.

Blalock, H. M. *Theory construction: From verbal to mathematical formulations.* Englewood Cliffs, N.J.: Prentice-Hall, 1969.

Blau, P., & Scott, W. R. *Formal organizations.* San Francisco: Chandler, 1962.

Blizzard, S. W. The minister's dilemma. *Christian Century,* 1956, **73**, 508–509.

Bowlby, J. *Maternal care and mental health.* Geneva: World Health Organization, 1951.

Brayfield, A. H., & Crockett, W. H. Employee attitudes and employee performance. *Psychological Bulletin,* 1955, **52**, 396–424.

Buehler, C. *Der menschliche lebenslauf als psychologisches problem.* Leipzig: Hirgel, 1933.

Cain, L. D., Jr. Life course and social structure. In R. Farris (Ed.) *Handbook of modern sociology.* Chicago: Rand-McNally, 1964.

Campbell, D. T., & Fiske, D. W. Convergent and discriminant validation by the multitrait-multimethod matrix. *Psychological Bulletin,* 1959, **56**, 81–105.

Campbell, J. P., Dunnette, M. D., Lawler, E. E., & Weick, K. E. *Managerial behavior, performance, and effectiveness.* New York: McGraw-Hill, 1970.

Campbell R. J. The young business manager: Developmental change and career choice. In J. R. Hackman (Chm.) Longitudinal approaches to career development. Symposium presented at the American Psychological Association Annual Convention, 1968.

Caplow, T. *The sociology of work.* Minneapolis, Minn.: The University of Minnesota Press, 1954.

Caplow, T., & McGee, R. *The academic market place.* Garden City, N.Y.: Anchor Books, 1958.

Carr-Saunders, A. M., & Wilson, P. A. *The professions.* New York: Oxford University Press, 1933.

Carter, L. F. Recording and evaluating the performance of indivduals as members of small groups. *Personnel Psychology,* 1954, **7**, 477–484.

Catholic Transcript. Report on national survey of priests. April 23, 1971, p. 1.

Cooley, C. H. *Human nature and the social order.* Glencoe, Ill.: The Free Press, 1956.

Coville, W. J., D'arcy, P. F., McCarthy, T. N., & Rooney, J. J. (Eds.) *Assessment of candidates for the religious life.* Washington, D.C.: Center for Applied Research in the Apostolate, 1968.

D'arcy, P. F. Bibliography of psychological, sociological and related studies on the catholic priesthood and religious life. In W. J. Coville, P. F. D'arcy, T. N. McCarthy, and J. J. Rooney (Eds.) *Assessment of candidates for the religious life.* Washington, D.C.: Center for Applied Research in the Apostolate. 1968.

Davis, F. The cabdriver and his fare: Facets of a fleeting relationship. *American Journal of Sociology,* 1959, **65**, 158–165.

Deutsch, K. W. *The nerves of government.* New York: The Free Press of Glencoe, 1963.

Dubin, R. Attachment to work. In L. W. Porter (Chm.) Attachment to work and identification with organizations. Symposium presented at American Psychological Association Annual Convention, 1970.

Dunn, R. F. Personality patterns among religious personnel: A review. *Catholic Psychological Record,* 1965, **3,** 125–137.

Dunnette, M. D. *Personnel selection and placement.* Belmont, Calif.: Wadsworth, 1966.

Erikson, E. H. *Childhood and society.* (2nd ed.) New York: W. W. Norton, 1963.

Evan, W. M. Peer-group interaction and organizational socialization. *American Sociological Review,* 1963, **28,** 436–440.

Ferguson, G. A. *Statistical analysis in psychology and education.* New York: McGraw-Hill, 1966.

Fichter, J. H. *Religion as an occupation.* Notre Dame, Ind.: University of Notre Dame Press, 1961.

Fichter, J. H *America's forgotten priests.* New York: Harper, 1968.

Fiedler, F. E. *A theory of leadership effectiveness.* New York: McGraw–Hill, 1967.

Flanagan, J. C. The critical incident technique. *Psychological Bulletin,* 1954, **51,** 327–358.

Flavell, J. H. *The developmental psychology of Jean Piaget.* Princeton, N.J.: Van Nostrand, 1963.

Fleishman, E. A, Harris, F.F., & Burtt, H. E. *Leadership and supervision in industry: An evaluation of a supervisory training program.* Columbus, Ohio: Ohio State University, Bureau of Educational Research, 1955.

Fox, R. Training for uncertainty. In R. Merton, G. Reader, P. Kendall (Eds.) *The student physician.* Cambridge, Mass.: Harvard University Press, 1957.

Ghiselli, E. E. *Theory of psychological measurement.* New York: McGraw-Hill, 1964.

Ginzberg, E. Toward a theory of occupational choice. *Occupations,* 1952, **30,** 491–494.

Ginzberg, E., Ginzberg, S., Axelrod, S., & Herma, J. *Occupational choice: An approach to a general theory.* New York: Columbia University Press, 1951.

Glaser, B. *Organizational scientists: Their professional careers.* New York: Bobbs-Merrill, 1964.

Glaser, B. (Ed.) *Organizational careers.* Chicago, Ill.: Aldine, 1968.

Glasse, J. D. *Profession: Minister.* Nashville, N.Y.: Abingdon Press, 1968.

Goffman, E. *Asylums.* Garden City, N.Y.: Anchor Books, 1961.

Gouldner, A. Cosmopolitans and locals: Toward an analysis of latent social roles I. *Administrative Science Quarterly,* 1958, **2,** 281–306. (a)

Gouldner, A. Cosmopolitans and locals: Toward an analysis of latent social roles II. *Administrative Science Quarterly,* 1958, **2,** 444–480. (b)

Greeley, A. M. *The Catholic experience.* Garden City, N.Y.: Doubleday, 1967.

Hall, D. T. Identity changes during an academic role transition. *School Review,* 1968, **76,** 445–469.

Hall, D. T. A theoretical model of career subidentity development in organizational settings. *Organizational Behavior and Human Performance,* 1971, **6,** 50–76.

Hall, O. The stages in a medical career. *American Journal of Sociology,* 1948, **53,** 327–336.

Hall, D. T., & Lawler, E. E. Job characteristics and pressures and the organizational integration of professionals. *Administrative Science Quarterly,* 1970, **15,** 271–281.

Hall, D. T., & Nougaim, K. E. An examination of Maslow's need hierarchy in an organizational setting. *Organizational Behavior and Human Performance,* 1968, **3,** 12–35.

Hall, D. T., & Schneider, B. Work assignment characteristics and career development in the priesthood. In L. W. Porter (Chm.) Traditional bureaucratic organizations in a changing society. Symposium presented at American Psychological Association Annual Convention, 1969.

Hall, D. T., Schneider, B., & Nygren, H. T. Personal factors in organizational identification. *Administrative Science Quarterly,* 1970, **15,** 176–190.

Hathaway, S. R., & McKinley, J. C. *Minnesota multiphasic personality inventory: Manual.* New York: The Psychological Corporation, 1951.

Herzberg, F. *Work and the nature of man.* Cleveland, Ohio: World, 1966.

Herzberg, F., Mausner, B., & Snyderman, B. *The motivation to work,* (2nd ed.) New York: Wiley, 1959.

Hess, E. H. Ethology: An approach toward the complete analysis of behavior. In R. Brown, E. Galanter, E. H. Hess, and G. Mandler, *New directions in psychology.* New York: Holt, Rinehart and Winston, 1962.

Hinrichs, J. R. The attitudes of research chemists. *Journal of Applied Psychology,* 1964, **48**, 287–293.

Holland, J. L. *The psychology of vocational choice.* Waltham, Mass.: Blaisdell, 1966.

Hovland, C. I. Studies in persuasion. In H. J. Leavitt and L. R. Pondy (Eds.) *Readings in managerial psychology.* Chicago: The University of Chicago Press, 1964.

Hulin, C. L., & Blood, M. I. Job enlargement, individual differences, and worker responses. *Psychological Bulletin,* 1968, **69**, 41–45.

Huntington, M. J. The development of a professional self-image. In R. Merton, G. Reader, and P. Kendall (Eds.) *The student-physician.* Cambridge, Mass.: Harvard University Press, 1957.

Janis, I. L., & King, B. T. The influence of role playing on opinion change. *Journal of Abnormal and Social Psychology,* 1954, **49**, 211–218.

Jud, G. J., Mills, E. W., Jr., & Burch, G. *Ex-pastors.* Boston, Mass.: Pilgrim Press, 1970.

Kaiser, H. R. The varimax criterion for analytic rotation in factor analyses. *Psychometrika,* 1958, **23**, 187–200.

Kaplan, A. *The conduct of inquiry.* San Francisco, Calif.: Chandler, 1964.

Kaufman, H. *The forest ranger.* Baltimore, Md.: Johns Hopkins Press, 1960.

Korman, A. K. Consideration, initiating structure, and organizational criteria—a review. *Personnel Psychology,* 1966, **19**, 349–362.

Korman, A. K. Self-esteem as a moderator of the relationship between self-perceived abilities and vocational choice. *Journal of Applied Psychology,* 1967, **51**, 65–67.

Koval, J. P. The priesthood as career: Yesterday and today. In W. E. Bartlett (Ed.) *Evolving religious careers.* Washington, D.C.: Center for Applied Research in the Apostolate, 1970.

Lawler, E. E., & Hall, D. T. Relationship of job characteristics to job involvement, satisfaction, and intrinsic motivation. *Journal of Applied Psychology,* 1970, **54**, 305–312.

Levinson, D. J. *A psychological study of the male mid-life decade.* Unpublished research proposal, Department of Psychiatry, Yale University, 1968.

Levinson, H. On being a middle-aged manager. *Harvard Business Review,* 1969, **47**, 51–60.

Levinson, H., Price, C., Munden, K., Mandel, H., & Solley, C. *Men, management and mental health.* Cambridge, Mass.: Harvard University Press, 1962.

Lewin, K. The psychology of success and failure. *Occupations,* 1936, **14**, 926–930.

Lewin, K. *Field theory in social science.* (D. Cartwright, Ed.) New York: Harper, 1951.

Lewin, K., Dembo, T., Festinger, L., & Sears, P. Level of aspiration. In J. Mc V. Hunt (Ed.) *Personality and behavior disorders.* New York: Ronald Press, 1944.

Lieberman, S. The effects of changes in roles on the attitudes of role occupants. *Human Relations,* 1956, **9**, 385–402.

Likert, R. *The human organization.* New York: McGraw-Hill, 1967.

Litwin, G. H. Achievement motivation, expectancy of success and risk-taking behavior. In J W. Atkinson and N. T. Feather (Eds.) *A theory of achievement motivation.* New York: Wiley, 1966.

Litwin, G. H., & Stringer, R. A., Jr. *Motivation and organizational climate.* Boston, Mass.: Division of Research, Harvard Business School, 1968.

Livingston, J. S. Pygmalion in management. *Harvard Business Review,* 1969, **47**, 81–89.

Locke, E. A. Toward a theory of task motivation and incentives. *Organizational Behavior and Human Performance,* 1968, **3**, 157–189.

Locke, E. A. Job satisfaction and job performance: A theoretical analysis. *Organizational Behavior and Human Performance,* 1970, **5**, 484–500.

Lodahl, T. M., & Kejner, M. The definition and measurement of job involvement. *Journal of Applied Psychology,* 1965, **49**, 24–33.

Lortie, D. C. Layman to lawman: Law school, careers, and professional socialization. *Harvard Educational Review,* 1959, **29**, 363–367.

MacCorquodale, K., & Meehl, P. E. On a distinction between hypothetical constructs and intervening variables. *Psychological Review,* 1948, **55**, 95–107.

Mansfield, R. The initiation of graduates in industry: Satisfaction in the early months at work. London: London School of Business, Mimeo., 1970.

March, J., & Simon, H. *Organizations.* New York: Wiley, 1958.

Maslow, A. H. A theory of human motivation. *Psychological Review,* 1943, **50**, 390–396.

Maslow, A. H. *Motivation and personality.* New York: Harper, 1954.

Maslow, A. H. Deficiency motivation and growth motivation. In M. R. Jones (Ed.) *Nebraska symposium on motivation.* Lincoln, Neb.: University of Nebraska Press, 1955.

Maslow, A. H. A theory of metamotivation: The biological rooting of the value-life. *Psychology Today,* July, 1968.

Mayo, E. *The social problems of an industrial civilization.* Cambridge, Mass.: Harvard University Press, 1945.

McCarthy, T. N. Evaluation of the present scientific status of screening for religious vocation. In W. C. Bier and A. A. Schneiders (Eds.) *Selected papers from the APA meetings of 1957, 1958, 1959.* New York: Fordham University, 1960.

McCarthy, T. N., & Dondero, E. A. Predictor variables and criteria of success in religious life: Needed research. *The Catholic Psychological Record,* 1963, **1**, 71–80.

McClelland, D. C. *The achieving society.* Princeton, N.J.: Van Nostrand, 1961.

McCormick, E. J. Job dimensions: Their nature and possible uses. Paper read at American Psychological Association, Annual Convention, 1965.

McGregor, D. M. *The human side of enterprise.* New York: McGraw-Hill, 1960.

McGregor, D. M. *The professional manager.* New York: McGraw-Hill, 1967.

McKelvey, W. Expectational noncomplementarity and style of interaction between professional and organization. *Administrative Science Quarterly,* 1969, **14**, 21–32.

Mecham, R. C., & McCormick, E. J. *The rated attribute requirements of job elements in the position analysis questionnaire.* Lafayette, Ind.: Occupational Research Center, Purdue University, 1969.

Menges, R. J., & Dittes, J. E. *Psychological studies of clergymen: Abstracts of research.* New York: Thomas Nelson & Sons, 1965.

Menzies, I. A case study in the functioning of social systems as a defense against anxiety. *Human Relations,* 1960, **13**, 95–121.

Merton, R. K. *Social theory and social structure.* (2nd ed.) Glencoe, Ill.: The Free Press, 1957.

Merton, R. K., Reader, G., & Kendall, P. (Eds.) *The student physician.* Cambridge, Mass.: Harvard University Press, 1957.

Mills, E. A study of clergy careers at mid-life. In W. E. Bartlett (Ed.) *Evolving religious careers.* Washington, D.C.: Center for Applied Research In the Apostolate, 1970.

Mills, T. *The sociology of small groups.* Englewood Cliffs, N.J.: Prentice-Hall, 1967.

Miner, F. Conformity among university professors and business executives. *Administrative Science Quarterly,* 1962, **7**, 96–109.

Mitchell, K. R. *Psychological and theological relationships in the multiple staff ministry.* Philadelphia, Penn.: The Westminster Press, 1966.

Moore, T. V. Insanity in priests and religious. Part I. The rate of insanity in priests and religious. *American Ecclesiastical Review,* 1936, **95**, 485–498. (a)

Moore, T. V. Insanity in priests and religious. Part II. The detection of pre-psychotics who apply for admission to the priesthood or religious communities. *American Ecclesiastical Review,* 1936, **95**, 601–613. (b)

Moos, R. H. The differential effects of ward settings on psychiatric patients. *Journal of Nervous and Mental Disease,* 1967, **145**, 272–283.

Moos, R. H., & Houts, P. S. Assessment of the social atmosphere of psychiatric wards. *Journal of Abnormal Psychology,* 1968, **73**, 595–604.

Murray, J. B. Training for the priesthood and personality and interest test manifestations. Unpublished doctoral dissertation, Fordham University, 1957.

Murray, J. B., & Connolly, F. Follow up personality scores of seminarians: Seven years later. *The Catholic Psychological Record,* 1966, **4**, 10–19.

Neal, M. A. *Values and interests in social change.* Englewood Cliffs, N.J.: Prentice-Hall, 1965.

Nunnally, J. C. *Psychometric theory.* New York: McGraw-Hill, 1967.

Olesen, V. L., & Whittaker, E. W. *The silent dialogue.* San Francisco, Calif.: Jossey-Bass, 1968.

Osgood, C. E., Suci, G., & Tannenbaum, P. *The measurement of meaning.* Urbana, Ill.: University of Illinois Press, 1957.

Osipow, S. *Theories of career development.* New York: Appleton-Century, 1968.

Pace, C. R. The measurement of college environments. In R. Taguiri and G. H. Litwin (Eds.) *Organizational climate: Explorations of a concept.* Boston, Mass.: Division of Research, Harvard Business School, 1968.

Parsons, T. *Structure and process in modern societies.* Glencoe, Ill.: The Free Press, 1960.

Pelz, D. C., & Andrews, F. M. *Scientists in organizations.* New York: Wiley, 1966.

Peres, S. H. *Factors which influence careers in General Electric.* Crotonville, N.Y.: Management Development and Employee Relations Services, General Electric Co., 1966.

Personnel Board. *Final report of the preliminary personnel board Archdiocese of Hartford.* Hartford, Conn.: Hartford Archdiocese, Sept. 30, 1969.

Pervin, L. A. Performance and satisfaction as a function of individual-environment fit. *Psychological Bulletin,* 1968, **69**, 56–68.

Porter, L. W. A study of perceived need satisfaction in bottom and middle management jobs. *Journal of Applied Psychology,* 1961, **45**, 1–10.

Porter, L. W., & Lawler, E. E. *Managerial attitudes and performance.* Homewood, Ill.: Irwin-Dorsey, 1968.

Potvin, R. H., & Suziedelis, A. *Seminarians of the sixties.* Washington, D.C.: Center for Applied Research in the Apostolate, 1969.

Primoff, E. S. The J-coefficient approach to jobs and tests. *Personnel Administration,* 1957, **20**, 34–40.

Rodenmayer, R. N. The parish clergyman: A profile. *The Episcopalian,* 1970, **33**, 8–10.

Roe, A. A psychological study of eminent psychologists and anthropologists and a comparison with biologial and physical scientists. *Psychological Monographs,* 1953, **67** (whole No. 352).

Rubin, I., Stedry, A., & Willits, R. Influences related to time allocation of R & D supervisors. *IEEE Transactions in Engineering Management,* 1965, **12**, 70–78.

Ryan, T. A. *Intentional behavior: An approach to human motivation.* New York: Ronald Press, 1970.

Schachter, S. *The psychology of affiliation.* Stanford, Calif.: Stanford University Press, 1959.

Schaie, K. W. A general model for the study of development problems. *Psychological Bulletin,* 1965, **64**, 92–107.

Schein, E. H. *Organizational psychology.* Englewood Cliffs, N.J.: Prentice-Hall, 1965.

Schein, E. H. The first-job dilemma. *Psychology Today,* 1968, **1**. 26–37.

Schein, E. H., & Hall, D. T. The student image of the teacher. *Journal of Applied Behavioral Science,* 1967, **3**, 305–337.

Schein, E. H., Schneider, I., & Barker, C. *Coercive persuasion.* New York: Norton, 1961.

Schneider, B. A theoretical model for the collection and interpretation of career development data: Piaget. In J. R. Hackman (Chm.) Longitudinal approaches to career development. Symposium presented at the American Psychological Association Annual Convention, 1968.

Schneider, B. The role of personal and job characteristics in predicting changing organizational identification. In L. W. Porter (Chm.) Attachment to work and identification with organizations. Symposium presented at American Psychological Association Annual Convention, 1970.

Schneider, B. The perception of organizational climate: The customer's view. *Journal of Applied Psychology*, 1973, in press.

Schneider, B., & Bartlett, C. J. Individual differences and organizational climate I: The research plan and questionnaire development. *Personnel Psychology*, 1968, **21**, 323–333.

Schneider, B., & Bartlett, C. J. Individual differences and organizational climate. *The Industrial Psychologist*, 1969, **7**, 27–33.

Schneider, B., & Bartlett, C. J. Individual differences and organizational climate II: Measurement of organizational climate by the multitrait-multirater matrix. *Personnel Psychology*, 1970, **23**, 493–512.

Schneider, B., & Hall, D. T. The role of assignment characteristics in the career experiences of diocesan priests. In W. E. Bartlett (Ed.) *Evolving religious careers*. Washington, D.C.: Center for Applied Research in the Apostolate, 1970.

Schneider, B., & Hall, D. T. Toward specifying the concept of work climate: A study of Roman Catholic diocesan Priests. *Journal of Applied Psychology*, 1972, in press.

Schneider, B., Hall, D. T., & Nygren, H. T., Jr. Self-image and job characteristics as correlates of changing organizational identification. *Human Relations*, 1971, **24**, 397–416.

Scott, W. A., & Wertheimer, M. *Introduction to psychological research*. New York: Wiley, 1962.

Simon, H. A. *Administrative behavior*. (2nd ed.) New York: Macmillan, 1957.

Smith, M. B., Bruner, J. S., & White, R. W. *Opinions and personality*. New York: Wiley, 1960.

Smith, P. C., Kendall, P., & Hulin, L. M. *The measurement of satisfaction in work and retirement: A strategy for the study of attitudes*. Chicago, Ill.: Rand-McNally, 1969.

Steiner, G. A. (Ed.) *The creative organization*. Chicago, Ill.:University of Chicago Press, 1965.

Stern, G. C. *People in Context*. New York: Wiley, 1970.

Strauss, A. *Mirrors and masks: The search for identity*. New York: Norton, 1959.

Strauss, A. Some neglected properties of status passage. In H. Becker, B. Geer, D. Riesman, & R. Weiss (Eds.) *Institutions and the person*. Chicago, Ill.: Aldine, 1968.

Super, D. *The psychology of careers*. New York: Harper & Brothers. 1957.

Taguiri, R. Value orientations and the relationships of managers and scientists. *Administrative Science Quarterly*, 1965, **10**, 39–51.

Taylor, F. W. *The principles of scientific management*. New York: Harper, 1911.

Thornton, G. C. The dimensions of organizational climate of office situations. *Experimental Publication System*, 1969, **2**, Ms. No. 057.

Tiedeman, D. V. Comprehension of epigenesis in decision-making. In W. E. Bartlett (Ed.) *Evolving religious careers*. Washington, D.C.: Center for Applied Research in the Apostolate, 1970.

Tiedeman, D. V., & O'Hara, R. *Career development: Choice and adjustment*. New York: College Entrance Examination Board, 1963.

Tolman, E. C. Identification and the post-war world. *Journal of Abnormal and Social Psychology*, 1943, **38**, 141–148.

Tyler, L. E. *The psychology of human differences*. (3rd ed.) New York: Appleton-Century, 1965.

Vroom, V. H. *Some personality determinants of the effects of participation.* Englewood Cliffs, N.J.: Prentice-Hall, 1960.

Vroom, V. H. *Work and motivation.* New York: Wiley, 1964.

Vroom, V. H. Organizational choice: A study of pre and post decision process. *Organizational Behavior and Human Performance,* 1966, **1,** 212–225.

Walberg, H. J. Professional role discontinuities in educational careers. In J. R. Hackman (Chm.) Longitudinal approaches to career development. Symposium presented at American Psychological Association Annual Convention, 1968.

Walberg, H. J. Professional role discontinuities in educational careers. In J. R. Hackman approaches to career development. Symposium presented at American Psychological Association Annual Convention, 1968.

Wauck, L. A. Organization and administration of a screening program for religious vocations. In W. C. Bier and A. A. Schneiders (Eds.) *Three joint symposia from the ACPA-APA meetings of 1957, 1958, 1959.* New York: American Catholic Psychological Association, 1960.

Webb, E. J., Cambell, D. T., Schwartz, R. D., & Sechrest, L. *Unobtrusive measures: Nonreactive research in the social sciences.* Chicago: Rand-McNally, 1966.

Weber, M. *The theory of social and economic organization.* New York: Oxford, 1947.

White, R. Motivation reconsidered: The concept of competence. *Psychological Review,* ·1959, **66,** 297–323.

Wright, B., & Tuska, S. Career dreams of teachers. *Trans-action,* 1968, 43–47.

Wylie, R. *The self-concept.* Lincoln, Neb.: The University of Nebraska Press, 1961.

Author Index

Numbers in *italics* refer to the pages on which the complete references are listed.